REFLECTIONS OF A
FOOTBALL DINOSAUR

BY JOHN LIGHTFOOT

In memory of my parents, and for Jennifer, Martin & Daniel, as well as all of my family ; you all contributed just by being there.

CONTENTS

CHAPTER 1
INTRODUCTION

What prompted me to write this?

I had been thinking about it for a long time but that's all I did - just think about it. When I managed an early retirement from work and settled back to a life of doing nothing, I was bored rigid after only three months and so got myself a part time job in a retail store, ASDA.

A young work colleague and fellow football fan, Michael Oates, and I talked for hours about the game. Anything and everything linked with football. Countless books were exchanged plus discussions on great footballers present and past, some way past. Matches and incidents were covered going back to the 1960s.

"You could write a book about the stuff you've told me", said Michael. He was right, and so here it is. It's my reflections, observations and memories of football as a fan, very personal to me and maybe some of it might be to you too. Where I came from influenced who I'd end up supporting for the rest of my life, Sunderland, and there are many references to them in here. It's been a struggle at times but I'm still here to tell the tale. My adventures following them down the years might even bring back similar memories for you. We all have them and they never leave us.

It's a bit irreverent, both sad and funny, very much tongue in cheek and it shouldn't be taken too seriously. It's written from the heart after watching, listening, talking, reading and observing people and places. It's built around a lifetime of going to matches, the people and surroundings I grew up in, mixing with fans of all ages from all over the country, and all having the same dream.

Some fans were quite realistic about what they dreamt for their clubs. All had the same ambition and, in most cases, blind faith in their team. And if you think love is blind then so, too, is faith after what I've seen down the years. It's for all those fans convinced that their club is on the verge of something big and that their day in the sunshine is just round the corner. The likes of Barnsley, Bradford, Hull and Swindon who down the years dreamt about playing in the Premier League and got their wish even whilst they were traipsing round Darlington, Crewe and Rochdale on the way there. And even if it didn't last long, they did it once and who's to say one day they might not do it again?

And it's focussed on the game itself, past, present and future. But mostly the past because, apart from today, that's where we've all grown up in. It's also a story about me, an ordinary fan, and it's dedicated to an extraordinary man, my father. He was the one who took this little boy, circa 1961, not to his first match but many others after that.

I remember it like it was yesterday.

CHAPTER 2
FOOTBALL'S BEGINNINGS

How's your history? Contrary to many of the modern breed of football fan who thinks that the be all and end all of the game we have today began in 1993 with the birth of the Premier League, the real game evolved way, way before then. All around the world today nothing else seems to matter about the game, whether you are in a bar in Cairo or Madrid. Personally, I think that's all cobblers (or Northampton Town to the uninitiated.)

The real fun and games, the real joy, spirit and meaning of the game is now long forgotten, and some would say conveniently so. It needs to be revered, revived and be something to cherish, not just as a pointer to the past but maybe also the future. Just as in life, what goes around comes around, what happens in the past not only affects the present but also the future if you choose to ignore it through apathy, ignorance or even because you no longer consider it relevant. Ignore it and all it stands for, and you'll just grind to a halt and we'll all end up with the same situation happening today, right here and right now in loads of schools round the country. As a pointer to what I'm getting at, today, for example there are kids who think that the Battle of Hastings happened in 1966. Some don't even know who Winston Churchill was. Do you find that modern grasp of our history funny or appalling, or maybe it's irrelevant in today's society. If you think it's funny then that's fine, but God help us all if you do. Because if you do and all this goes unchecked, then just be prepared for future boffins thinking that Sir Alf Ramsey lost an eye when he was defeated by William The Conqueror at Wembley or Sir Winston Churchill driving the Romans out of Britain on the same chariot driven by Henry VIII.

Our football heritage was mapped out long, long ago and is just as important now as then. I am a bit dazed and sometimes shocked when I talk to opposing footy fans, some of whom have never heard, or are remotely bothered about their own past icons. The trendy young Arsenal fan who has never heard of or even been interested in who Herbert Chapman was or the Sheffield United fan who didn't even know who William "Fatty" Foulke was. That classic football song "Who ate all the pies?" may well have stemmed from good old Fatty and his voracious appetite. If you don't know either, then get to the back of the class. That's the end opposite the front of the class, by the way.

We need to go way back before the 1960s, where even my earliest memories came in. That was only yesterday as we delve back to around the birth of my great grandfather, two centuries ago. At the beginning of the 19th Century we were just starting to prepare to say farewell to stagecoaches, Dick Turpin impersonators and ushering in the brave new world of the railway. "It'll never last" said pessimists as they stockpiled horses and carriages in livery stables, waiting for the inevitable crash and the return of the good old days. Those sceptics probably said the same thing about the birth of The Football League, with the emphasis on the word "the". The Football League because it was the first of its kind in the world.

And here's where I think the difference comes in between a modern footy fan (who thinks 20 years ago is ancient history and therefore irrelevant) and a real die-hard fan who is fascinated at where it all evolved. I would love to go back to a game circa1880, and I'm not the only one, with a chance to see how it was played then, what kind of atmosphere there was, and also to just look at something totally original, fresh and brand new based around the culture of the time. It would come as a surprise to many but all cultures would be strange to those outside its immediate surroundings or time frame. Just imagine, for example, anyone from our future coming back today and spending a few hours walking around a local Town Centre. By the time they'd taken in the fashions, music and listened to the patter of the locals they'd think they were in a mad house and would be screaming to be back in 2133. The same applies to what you'd have seen in the 1880s. You'd have to be pretty stupid to laugh because, if you did, you'd be laughing at yourself and your own ignorance. Again, imagine a time traveller from our future taking in a Premier League game now and what he'd have to say (apart from "Why are all these seats empty?"). A wise man would observe and learn from it for future reference. A fool would simply laugh and learn nothing from the experience. And if you'd really looked hard enough back then, you'd see people whose views and knowledge of the modern game as it was then, were exactly the same as our own today. Intelligent supporters and footballers, whose ideas about how the game should be played and ruled over, would be just as apt and meaningful today. After all, their ideas shaped and changed the game as we know it today, so why insult them by burying and deriding them as irrelevant because it happened so long ago? Even though they're all long gone, we can, and should, still listen to them.

I've read and researched many football books and autobiographies about all eras of football. It is habit forming and I'm not alone. Others are jumping on the band wagon. If you delved back into the archives, and it's fairly easy now with the advent of the internet, you would be stunned at the sheer scale and number of superstars, characters funny and sad, hard men, speed merchants, football geniuses and genuine personalities they had even way back then. You'd be a fool not to want to find out more about them.

There were plenty around and I could write another book just by listing fifty of them (now there's an idea!). My favourite of them all would have to be Steve Bloomer, a 19th Century version of David Beckham. A genuine Victorian Superstar, with white boots, sullen looks and all. Ask any real Derby County fan about him. Steve's heyday was well over 110 years ago. A man who was so influential in Derby's history, that they still sing songs about him to this day. I've read about this humble man's life and I would have paid top dollar to have seen him in his prime, or, even better, seeing a film about his life story. Nicknamed "Paleface," had he been around today he would have had a world brand name and probably a miserable wife to match.

Perhaps if Hollywood ever did decide on a movie there might be a perfect cameo role for Mr Beckham (they do have a strange sullen resemblance to each other). And as an added bonus for us, it would probably be silent. If Denis Waterman can play the part of a West Auckland player when they won the Thomas Lipton (World Cup) Trophy back in 1909, then why not our David? His accent couldn't be any worse than Denis's impersonation of a Durham Collier. And before you say you've never heard of it, it's true, just look it up- "A Captain's Tale". And just think, also, if they'd actually invited the right team along at the time - Woolwich Arsenal FC, not West Auckland FC - then you'd never have been reading about this, anyway. Personally, I think David Beckham would make a great Steve Bloomer. There might even be a small role or walk on part for his missus Posh Spice wearing a hair net and very fashionable retro clogs. The mind boggles. And because they never smiled much in those days it would be even more perfect for her.

If you go back to where it all began, it will give you a whole new insight into the game as it's shaped today. It'll also probably leave you pleasantly surprised, just like I was when I first discovered things about football that I thought were brand new ideas today. There really is nothing new under the sun. Even if you are in your eighties or nineties, it'll still make you feel like a young whippersnapper, especially when you consider that you weren't even an apple in your granddad's eye (never mind your dad's) as we begin our travels.

Notts County, the original Magpies, evolved in 1863 but the whole structure of the league then meant that both they and a lot of others, including every football romantic's favourite, Accrington Stanley, could then begin to play competitively for the first time ever and judge how good - or bad - they were against opposition from all over the country. Before that it was little more than parks football, where you would have a series of local games that were basically just kicking matches, both the man and the ball, and they usually ended in punch ups. You can only imagine what sort of fights they'd have had back then if they'd also had a Sunday League set up, with lager fuelled blokes taking the field the morning after the night before. Just think, "The Flat Cap and Billy Goat" from Barnsley might have become just as famous as Woolwich Arsenal.

Any footy fan worth his salt will tell you that the father of football was a man called William McGregor, a Scotsman with a huge vision and a beard to match. Today he'd pass for lead guitar with ZZ Top. And just to put the boot in to all us Sassenachs, it really was someone from North of the Border to thank for our league in England. Golf and football; those Scots were no mugs, were they? And most of the early footballers entering into our game came from Scotland as well.

McGregor was football's equivalent of Robert Johnson. Any true music fan will tell you that if it wasn't for some black guitarist called Robert Johnson selling his soul to the Devil, then that wouldn't have led to the birth of the Blues, followed by Rock & Roll and then all forms of music after that. William McGregor didn't play the guitar and didn't have to sell his soul to the Devil, but his influence was there for all to see. He was handily placed, too, living just round the corner next to The Chip Shop and over the road from Villa Park, Birmingham. Maybe he was eating a fish and sixpenny worth of chips at the time, when the idea came to him like a bolt out of the blue. If you ever wonder why Aston Villa is famous the world over (even Tom Hanks supports them) and is so richly steeped in tradition, then look no further than this man.

Don't get the idea that somebody waved a magic wand and all of a sudden there it all was, as it would be today X Factor style. All neatly packaged, labelled, branded and ready for immediate delivery to cash in on the paying punter. People back then had more sense than that. They would need some very persuasive arguments and coaxing before they parted with their hard earned brass. Besides, there was already football being played everywhere but it was all in a hellish mess. At least, though, they were spared the Victorian version of Simon Cowell to lend his influence. Otherwise real football would have been strangled at birth.

There was no organisation or planning and matches were called off regularly, with no regard to either opponents or even anyone turning up to watch. There would have been a few going home gutted in those early days after finding out the away team hadn't bothered to show up. In some cases, there were no crowds as nobody actually knew there was a game on (apart from maybe the legendary one man and his dog). "Oh, that was last week" would have been the limp excuse as teams turned up on the wrong day, and in the wrong town. It was absolute chaos.

And so the Football League was born in March 1888. Clubs with familiar names even now were already in existence back then but very much in name only. They had no clout or status for any wide eyed 12 year old, who might well have been keen to put posters on his bedroom wall had they been around at the time. All these teams were just starting out on the beginning of a long, long journey. They had no street cred back then. Just imagine, say, Wolves and Stoke City playing each other on a neutral ground. Nobody knew who they actually were, what time the kick off was, or where the ground was. Teams had to build up their own history from scratch and for every Liverpool there'd be five sides like Gainsborough Trinity. Like salmon swimming upstream, not all of them made it.

There were no cups or competitions to play in and, frankly, nobody outside the immediate local area gave a damn anyway. It was all very parochial and all very dull. And besides, what was the point of being the best team in your own backyard if nobody even 50 miles away knew about you or, indeed, cared? In short, it were a reet waste of bloody time as many Yorkshire cynics of the day would have said.

Just as there will only ever be one Elvis so there will only ever be one Football League. Other countries have their own versions but they're all green with envy at ours. As proof, even today the rest of Europe have been trying to shaft us no matter which way we turn, both on and off the field. Twelve teams, all from the North, started it all. If ever a game came along that offered an escape route from drudgery for the ordinary hard working man, even for a few fleeting hours, then football was it. It was inevitable that it would also be a huge success as it gave thousands of poorly paid industrial workers a chance to escape from their mundane lives and let off steam. Football in the South of England didn't even exist as such, but it wouldn't take them long to realise what they were missing. Football was the Victorian equivalent of rock & roll and there was no way those Northern hillbillies were going to corner the market.

For some obscure reason, professionalism was a dirty word in the South of England and was regarded as crass, vulgar and not very British. "Grown men being paid to kick a piece of leather about?" How ghastly. It could even have spelled the end of the Empire. It was a time of real social change and some people were still aghast at having to buy chimney brushes when they had pleasant memories of the good old days when an eight year old boy was a much more effective and cheaper method of obtaining a clean sweep. The peasants were revolting, in the correct sense of the word, and those at the top didn't like it.

It wouldn't be long, however, before money talked down South too (no change there then, eh?) as this new phenomenon took a quick hold. Spurred on no doubt by the public's imagination, plus intense local pride and honour, and the desire to spend coppers watching their town or city take on and beat (no, humiliate) another town in another part of the country, it quickly become as territorial then as it is today. If you lived in the North there was no finer feeling than whipping some side from down South 5-0. The dominance of Northern sides would take a while to shake off but then, as now, money changed all that. The rich South had a massive advantage in catching up on their Northern Cousins with money no object and the necessary infrastructure and stadiums were quickly put in place to bridge that gap.

Familiar names quickly emerged and dominated in the first five seasons of the league with Preston and Sunderland leading the way. And back in 1888-89 there was a certain Accrington who more than held its own in those early years. Once a very jealous Stanley caught wind of Accrington's success, they very quickly insisted on a double act that has survived (just) to this day. Even today in some far flung corner of the world there is some poor little lad having to wear an Accrington Stanley replica kit. Everyone's wearing Chelsea so dare to be different, I say.

Because of the massive size and scale of this monster that had been created (remember the scene from "Jaws" when they decided they'd need a bigger boat?) there then followed the quick creation of a Second Division in 1892-93. This added to the fun and frolics and also gave sides the chance of promotion to the top tier. Can you even begin to imagine something so radical and contemporary being done so quickly today in such a short time frame by the powers that be? No, me neither. They'd probably set up a steering committee with monthly meetings held all over Europe spending about £20 million of public monies before producing a comprehensive ten volume report basically saying "No". Back then everyone just got on with it, sorted matters out quickly, and usually used two words so sadly lacking amongst today's movers and shakers - common sense.

No doubt, even then, the elite First Division sides might well have decided the concept of relegation was a bad idea because what would happen - perish the thought - if they were to fall through the former safety net and were relegated? Happily, sanity and fan power must have won through, and I'm sure many fans then whose teams went down must have thought they'd quickly bounce back, even though as it later transpired, the return trip would take them 20 or 30 years. Some sides are still waiting.

There were some glamorous and strange names breaking through then, no doubt thinking they would dominate the game for years to come and well into the new century. And so Darwen, Newton Heath, Small Heath, Ardwick, Burton Swifts, Northwich Victoria, Bootle, Burslem Port Vale, Walsall Town Swifts, Woolwich Arsenal (I wonder what became of them?), Middlesbrough Ironopolis, Rotherham Town, Leicester Fosse, Burton Wanderers, Loughborough, Gainsborough, Glossop North End and New Brighton all set out on what they thought would be their place in history. Some bit the dust quicker than some of those cowboys in John Wayne films but others, as we now know, carried on, or came back stronger and wiser. Some had their five minutes of fame and then fell by the wayside but must have been enriched by the experience. As you ride through some of these towns today, you'll probably think to yourself: "How the hell could they have even imagined they would even survive or get up and running in the first place?" But they did. They had a dream and even if it was unfulfilled, short lived and doomed to failure from the off, they are still remembered today, even if it is only by a few.

Just as people now think that football is no longer a sport and is some vast business empire growing ever bigger and more unmanageable, then so it also was a hundred years ago at the beginning of the 1900s. There were vast improvements in the game during the relatively short life of the league. It was probably much more radical and changing than at any other time in its history. Picture those old Wild West towns in the States and how they were transformed so rapidly and dramatically with the advent of the railway and then substitute the word "railway" for Football league, That would have been the effect having a league team had on your town. With apologies to Tony Blair but it really was "the people's game". It was relatively cheap to get in, there were huge crowds everywhere at all levels, and nearly all or most clubs adopted the very liberal "pack them in at all costs" policy. By then, most club directors, recognising the willing cash cow, took full advantage. They were just as greedy as they are now in some cases, but the difference then was there were no constraints on crowd safety. I often wonder if that's where the old saying "getting a quart into a pint pot" came from.

Newcastle United was very much the team of the 1900s. They won the league three times and reached five cup finals. There was also the familiar name of Manchester United winning the League in 1908 and not a prawn sandwich in sight. There wasn't much call for them back then. There was even a football scandal which shook the game to its core and was raised in the House of Commons. Some saw it as the fall of the Empire and angry letters from retired Colonels found their way to The Times at the lunacy that had gripped the game. In 1904 Alf Common made his way from Sunderland, a short trip by horse and cart down the road to Middlesbrough, for a scandalous £1,000 fee. Money well spent as it happened as he kept the Boro up, but the furore from this seemed to drag on for ever. It was true professionalism as clubs realised that money could not only buy you success it could also keep you from the dreaded drop into football anonymity. People from all walks of life complained vigorously that it could lead to teams buying success at any cost and wondered where it would end. It still hasn't, of course, 107 years later and that's the beauty of the game. It goes to also prove that old saying "the more things change, the more they stay the same". As we laugh now at this story, then just picture the scene in season 2245/46 when Team Brand Manchester Universal PLC Inc. pay £5,000 million for Safe Hands O'Rafferty, the Irish international keeper from Tottering Hotspurs. "When will it ever end?" they'll all scream in disgust as angry letters are sent to The Times from concerned citizens and retired space galaxy veterans everywhere.

Sheffield Wednesday also won the league twice in this decade although way back then, they were just plain old Wednesday - no Sheffield in their title. Handy, I suppose if you were a fan of the club and you could conveniently disassociate yourself from both your town and your team after you'd just been battered by five or six, especially if it was a local derby against United. On the other hand, if you won by the same score, then you'd want to shout it from the rooftops that your team, Sheffield Wednesday, had just mauled someone. Such is the fickle finger of football. You can never have it both ways

The old saying that football really is just a game was never truer during this time and certainly the decade that was to follow. World War 1 was looming, although many people must have wondered then, even as they do today with all modern wars, "What's it got to do with us?" The First World War was expected to be all over in months and those young lads who signed up could, surely, never have dreamed of the horror that awaited them. It was so shocking for so many that its impact still reverberates to this day, and will for many years to come. Many footballers fought and lost their lives for no real gain. No village, town or city in the country escaped its reach. I remember when I was only very little, maybe nine, talking to an old soldier who would then have only been in his early sixties. He told me he'd lost his leg after just one week in France. The luckiest day of his life, he said, and it was only when I'd grown up I knew exactly what he'd meant. He'd escaped the real horror of it all, even if it meant losing his leg. Nearly all his friends he went with never came home.

In the five years leading up to the suspension of football, Blackburn Rovers won their first championship and they would have to wait until they were in the Premier League before it happened again. Some of their fans at Anfield, over 80 years later where they clinched it, poignantly wore Tommy uniforms circa 1914. It'll be at least another 80 years before they do the same again. Who knows what commemorative uniform they'll have on then to celebrate? Perhaps it will be a nice little off the shoulder Robbie Williams number or something? Both Aston Villa and Sunderland also nearly did the double but, as bad luck would have it for both of them, it was in the same year, 1913. Something had to give. Villa beat the Rokermen in the cup final at Crystal Palace in front of a then world record crowd of 120,000 with Sunderland taking their revenge by pipping Villa for the championship the following week. Not a bad consolation, although the cup then was considered to be the real Holy Grail of football. Nearly 100 years later the FA Cup is still regarded as such in other parts of the world, but sadly not here. The Holy Grail is now the Premiership and everything else on the domestic front is just secondary.

During this era Manchester United moved to Old Trafford at a total cost of £60,000. Women swooned and grown men threw themselves under horses' hooves at the outrage of it all. Today you couldn't buy a good non-league player for that much, or maybe a 10 year season ticket at Arsenal. 100 years ago it bought you a state of the art stadium that even then other clubs could only drool over and wonder how United could have afforded it. Pretty much the same reaction you'd get today from some clubs when Arsenal moved to the Emirates.

Speaking of reaction, then on the lighter side of it all, if you ever get the chance go to your local library, or on the net, look at old footballers from round about 1908. You'll be astonished to see how very 1960s they all looked. Ever so tight,

tight shorts that leave very little to the imagination and would have you struggling in a "Guess the Year" competition. And also struggling even more would be the player trying to get into a pair of them. You'd even imagine the likes of George Best pitting his wits against some of these players but you'd have been out by an incredible 60 years. Today's baggy type shorts, too, seem to be a direct throwback to the 50s whereas the 1980s/1990s shorts look very 1900s. Confusing or what? Nothing new there and, again, just going to show how fashions, and in some cases styles of football keep coming and going. The 1920s hairstyles also look trendier now than the 1980s mullets did. And as for Kevin Keegan and Bryan Robson's curly perms don't get me started. Although I'll give you this, I thought they both looked absolutely gorgeous.

It also demonstrates perfectly how we should never misjudge or scorn anything from another era. It'll only come back to bite you on the bum and, besides, you could be drooling over it 30 years from now when it's back in style once again. And in case you think that's fanciful, then if people today still yearn nostalgically for The Pet Shop Boys - who are to pop music what John Inman was to Rugby League - then anything is possible.

After the horrors of 1914-1918, football returned to the masses with a vengeance as fans chomped at the bit to get back to some semblance of normality, if such a thing were possible. It came as a shock to many, though, who quickly realised that nothing would ever be quite the same again. Not only were teams 4-6 years older and playing with new, vastly inexperienced, replacements, tragically many players never came back at all. How can anybody of today's generation even begin to understand the horrors of what both spectators and players alike went through in the first season or two after all that carnage or, indeed, how they could ever recover from it. And more shockingly, to now dismiss it all as an irrelevance because it happened so long ago. That link or bond between both team and fans then must never have been so strong, and certainly far stronger than the fickleness that seems so prevalent today. Is it any wonder that after enduring all that and drawing strength from it, their descendants today feel so remote and isolated from the modern breed of players and their often aloof and arrogant attitude? How could anyone describe the effect of what it must have been like dealing with, and learning to live with afterwards, such a catastrophic event?

As an attraction after The Great War, there was the added bonus, or consolation maybe, of two additional divisions. There was the very originally named Division Three (North) for Northern teams and Division Three (South) for... you can guess the rest. If that wasn't enough to get fans of these new Football League teams salivating, there was soon to be the building of the brand new Empire

Stadium to herald the arrival of the roaring 20s. It was just the tonic the general public wanted, and the allure and magic then of the new Wembley Stadium, and its charisma, still exists today 90 years on, not just in Britain but all over the world. Ask any football-daft schoolboy anywhere in the world where they would love to play and I bet 8 out of 10 of them would say "Wembley". Even the new stadium, too, would probably be well up there, but the real magic of Wembley itself was lost when the old stadium, and all that it represented, was demolished completely. I think they missed a real opportunity by doing this. It was as if the thought of retaining any aspect of its old grandeur would have been considered uncool and maybe embarrassing to the new order.

And here's a link between old Wembley and my youth. As a young man of 23, spreading my wings and living it up away from the beady eyes of my mother and father in a grotty downstairs flat in Acton, West London with three other mates, we built up a real friendship with a lovely old man in the flat upstairs. He was 85 years young and his name was Arthur Ashe (the same name as the tennis player who won Wimbledon round about that time). My other three flatmates, all Liverpool fanatics, and me were in his flat one Friday night on the cadge, after Arthur had made a massive pan of Irish Stew, a real treat towards the end of the month when the four of us were broke as usual. The talk turned to football and Arthur left us all under his spell as he recounted the only football match he'd ever been to in his life. It was the 1923 Cup Final between West Ham and Bolton. We'd all finished our stew by then, but any thoughts of leaving after the free food, went out of the window there and then. Arthur and his mate had been drinking all day in Hammersmith that particular Saturday 50 years before and he thought it would be a "jolly jape" (Arthur's words, not mine) to pop along and see the new stadium. He didn't have a ticket, didn't even like football and yet, incredibly, somehow he managed to end up inside the ground, swept along by a tidal wave of fans who smashed through gates and easily overpowered the flimsy police attempts to keep them out, carrying him on - and in - with them. Before kick off they were still pouring though the breach, ticket or no ticket. Arthur ended up on the touchline, only about 40 yards from Billy the White Horse, all thoughts of getting out of this hell hole long abandoned as some 250,000 others jostled behind, in front and around him to get a better view. There he was ringside, bursting for a pee, and wishing he'd never left the pub in Hammersmith. It took him two hours after the final whistle to get outside the ground. He never went back, there or any other football ground, for the rest of his life. I suppose it was understandable after all that.

I still think of Arthur whenever I see pictures of that 1923 final, and it dawns on me now that he would have been born in 1888 or 1889. Had he been a footy addict he'd have been watching virtually the birth of the game and would have been able to tell us some real hair raisers. One thing puzzles me to this day and I never did ask him the million dollar question. Did he ever manage to get to the toilet and if not, after all those pints he must have had, how did he hold it in? If it was anything like being in the middle of a packed terrace at a Glasgow derby, I've got a pretty good idea what the answer would have been.

It's strange how younger fans tend to avoid older ones (especially much older) as if they had nothing worthwhile in common with them or their views. It's as if coming from another generation means that they aren't of any possible relevance to them. My advice to them is that you really don't know what you're missing out on and the magic they have to offer. All of those stories, memories, wisdom, experience and all yours for nothing. That's how I managed to glean so much of my own experience and wisdom, and stories too. Whenever anybody asks me: "How do you know all these things?" I just say "I took the time to listen".

If any one man dominated the early years of football in this same era, without even kicking a ball, then I would say that it was manager Herbert Chapman of Arsenal, who died very young in 1934. I once read a book about this man fittingly entitled "Football Emperor" and was amazed at how he set the benchmark for so many others who tried to emulate him. If you ever get the chance, then read it, too. He was light years ahead of his time, over the hills and far away from his nearest competitors and he encountered real "stick in the muds" at every turn. Every one of them, in their ignorance, decreed him as a bit of a maverick and too clever for his own good. Why didn't they listen to him? I realised why. Had he been around today, outspoken, brash and self-opinionated, he would probably have got exactly the same treatment as he did then, and been booted into touch in much the same way as a certain bloke called Clough was years later. The names may be different but the regime and red tape remain the same. Chapman wasn't exactly a big man, but he was still a giant among pygmies and he rattled cages. And that's a dangerous thing to do in any era. In the 1920s, he took then unfashionable Huddersfield Town (hang on a minute, Huddersfield Town have always been unfashionable!) to three consecutive league titles and to prove it was no fluke, he did the same thing with Arsenal in the following decade. It was to be another 50 years before Liverpool repeated this feat. Chapman advocated the use of numbers on players' jerseys, better trained and fitter referees, floodlit football, winter breaks, and even the idea of European football. Not surprisingly he was shot down in flames by his contemporaries of the time, none of whom were fit to tie his bootlaces. Next time you are in London and away to the Gunners, when you get out at Arsenal station remember his name as you look at that Underground sign. He was the one who single-handedly persuaded London Transport to change the name from "Gillespie Road" to "Arsenal". Would anybody today have the clout to do that? All answers on a postcard to "Fat Chance".

As for key players from this era, then where do you start? Off the top of my head, I could quickly list maybe twenty but to do them all justice, plus the other great ones not even on the list, would require yet another book (now there's another idea). But I'll briefly name one that I would love to have seen. Step forward, Frank Barson of 1920s Aston Villa, Manchester United and calling at most other teams in the league. This man would have made Tommy Smith, Vinnie Jones, Billy Bremner and Johnny Giles all look like schoolboy cherubs. So mean was Barson that referees used to warn him before the match kicked off. A loose cannon, suspended for months, he didn't give a flying fig, usually saw the red mist even quicker than the red card, and in his last ever match of his long, hard-tackling, bruising, brawling career he went out in true Barson style. Sent off after yet another scything tackle. They don't make them like that anymore.

There were a number of massive key changes to the game taking place in the 1920s too. Another urban football myth exposed by today's footy experts is that the modern game is constantly about change. Yes, it is, but mainly it isn't. It's mostly about that other modern word "hype" that was invented to disguise mediocrity as genius, and elevate mere mortals to God like status. It's a buttered up word and one that tells all us uneducated morons that, whilst we are in reality watching dross, it's really world class because they say so and they know better. My own view is that if it looks like it, plays like it and acts like it, then it definitely is it. If today's lot wanted to see real and radical change they would have been left scratching their heads in amazement 80 odd years back not only by the amount of it, but also the pace of it all. There was the major change to the offside law which produced an avalanche of goals and much bigger crowds. Even then, as now, those in charge ignored the man on the terraces and decreed that these changes would be bad for the game and it wouldn't possibly improve the quality (does this ring a bell with you?). These experts ignored completely the mass hysteria from the men - and women - on the terraces who loved all the goals, thrills, spills, and cock ups as cumbersome defenders struggled to get to grips with the new rules. I can just visualise it now as a fictional Willie Eckerslike of Halifax Town puts his arm up to scream "Offside, ref!" and then a second later thinking "Bugger it, no he isn't". Then, as now, it was the minority telling the majority what was meant to be good for them. And look where that's got us all now, folks. I suppose it'll never change. Got to keep these overpaid wasters in work haven't we?

These changes brought about a whole new meaning and concept to the game, and how it should be played. Sides battled to cope and deal with the new laws and the science of it all. Some adapted much quicker than others, and went on to become bigger and better clubs. Others did not. And so, today, we have supporters now arguing, 80 years later, that their team still haven't quite got the hang of it. Certainly then, it helped considerably with Dixie Dean grabbing 60 goals in a season for Everton, just one in front of George Camsell of Middlesbrough. I'd just like to see my team manage that tally amongst the lot of them in one season.

The 1930s can perhaps be summed up in one word - Arsenal. The comparisons between then and now are very similar with a massive economic downturn, or the recession, and huge unemployment. The only real subtle difference then was that everybody North of Watford hated Arsenal and what they stood for. They represented the soft South seemingly much more illustrious and less hungry than their Northern counterparts. Absolute rubbish, of course, but ideal propaganda to give the masses someone to blame, and they've really been doing it ever since. Today you could quite easily substitute Chelsea for 1930s Arsenal, but for entirely different reasons. Arsenal were just Champagne Charlies as far as the North with its mass of unemployed and angry people were concerned. They took their anger and venom out on them big-style whenever Arsenal were in town and they also usually turned their team over, too, to ruin their weekend. The ignominy of actually being on the dole back then also hurt, too. It was a real dirty word and definitely not a fashionable comfortable lifestyle to fall back on. It was then the modern equivalent of bread and water, the whole point of which was to prop you up temporarily and get you back on your feet into work as soon as possible from a life of drudgery.

Arsenal way back then was the futuristic model of how the game was to become 50 or 60 years down the line thanks to Herbert Chapman. They were business-like, shrewd, calculated, professional, slick, and years ahead of their time. Just like their manager. They devoured all around them and so it was no wonder every bugger hated them. In the absence of telly, they probably thought they were aliens. To actually beat them guaranteed you hero status, no matter where you came from. There were probably statues erected in some provincial towns if they managed to turn them over. In music terms they would have been the South's equivalent of Take That; smooth, rich, slinky and slick compared to the industrial North's working class version of a cheap Heavy Rock Band tanked up on Brown Ale. This was the decade that saw them win the league five times, finish second and third and also win the cup twice. Not bad going, and easily eclipsing anything that had gone on before them, as they smashed forever the dominance of the North's previous stranglehold on the game.

This wasn't just in the age before telly but everything else, too. If Arsenal came to your town, you had to go and see them. No Sky or TV highlights. If you missed them that was it for another year, or maybe more if you got relegated. Arsenal were the Leeds United of the 1930s, only without the dirty tactics. They were smash and grab merchants who invariably came away with a 1-0 win after being under the cosh for 80 odd minutes. Just when you thought you would settle for a point against them, it was usually a case of "1-0 to The Arsenal". They got their nickname " Lucky Arsenal" back then because I imagine journalists couldn't very well write "Lucky Buggers" every week, could they? And it's stuck to this day. But there was no luck about it. It was all pre-planned and carried out with precise detail. Chapman, a canny, military-minded Yorkshireman, who left nothing to chance, saw to all that. What a pity he never lived to see the end of their golden decade but he set the seal on their continuing accomplishments even after death. Who knows what Arsenal – and the modern game - might have been like today had he lived even another ten years. Probably he would have met the same fate as the rest of the lions who tried to take on the donkeys in charge.

Other teams have good cause to remember the 30s too. Second Division West Bromwich did their own double in 1931, winning the cup and promotion. Today they'd have just concentrated on going up, and their reserve team would no doubt have gone out in round four of the cup away to Shrewsbury 3-1. More spectacularly, Everton, who pipped West Brom for the Second Division title, won the First Division the following season. Manchester City won their first ever league title in 1937, with Sunderland winning it the year before and also winning the cup in 1937.And if you are superstitious and your team play in stripes, then get them to change them. No team has ever won the top prize in football since Sunderland in 1936.

Sadly, another war was on the horizon, and the Second World War put paid to all football for six long years. It says a lot for the power and magic of the game that it survived after all that. You'd have thought that people would have had much more important things to get to grips with, but when football did return in 1946/7 it was like the opening of a dam across the country. Grounds were packed everywhere as people swept back into them. Newcastle United won promotion from the Second Division with average home crowds of over 56,000. They've always had fanatical support on Tyneside and you often wonder whether that's been a blessing or a curse down the years for them. A crafty board of directors wouldn't possibly take these loyal fans for granted, would they? Rumours once abounded on Tyneside that one of their directors, Lord Westwood, who wore an eye patch, used to often wear it over his good eye when the football was really dire. But still those Geordies rolled up like devoted lemmings.

After the end of the Second World War, the great teams and players of the late 1930s were now all a full seven years older and the football on offer was nowhere near the same standard as before. But when you've done without for so long, what difference did that make? A lot of things, not just football, had changed. Everyone had to start out all over again and a lot of them without even a roof over their head, on and off the field. All of that and the worst winter in over 100 years, in 1947, was a real test of your resolve.

Some teams took full advantage of this adversity. Dear old Portsmouth, inspired by Jimmy Dickinson, won the league twice in succession to draw the curtain on the 1940s.I remember seeing him in the twilight of his career at Roker Park in 1963, a shadow of the player he once was. Raich Carter, who won the Cup with Sunderland in 1937, did it again in 1946 with Derby County and went on to lift Hull City to new heights in later years.

With rationing still fashionable, Britain and football entered the 1950s.

The one event that dominated the whole decade was in 1958. Munich. To every real football fan, the name of Manchester United is synonymous with everything that is great, glorious and majestic about our game. How lucky we all are that Manchester United are an English side and belong to all of us. Didn't you cry, too, when Bobby Charlton lifted the trophy ten years later at Wembley? You didn't need to know or ask what was going on in his or Sir Matt Busby's mind at that moment either. Feelings of tremendous joy mixed equally with everlasting sadness. Just like everybody's life at some time or another.

The beginning of the 1950s onwards produced what many would regard as the birth of the modern game. It's also where I came in to the picture in 1951. It was the beginning of the start of a real revolution as the football playing peasants finally stirred and started their revolt against conditions and wages. It also signalled the beginning of the end for clubs like Blackpool, Preston and Bolton who would never again be able to realistically compete on a level playing field with the big city clubs. For those last few glorious seasons in the 1950s, they were able to just about hang on grimly to their bigger neighbours' shirt tails but the emergence of the end of the maximum wage structure heralding the start of the 1960s was to change all that forever. What happened to clubs like these, though, up to that period, enabled them to still become the stuff of legend and have fans clinging on to the hopes of better days. They are still waiting and the reason they still cling on in hope, is that this is all they have left. They are all of the same accord, though, and have the same dreams collectively. One day, they think, one day our time will come again.

Mention this era and many fans will automatically think of Wolverhampton Wanderers. They won the title three times in four seasons with their last great team. Some things never change, though, and Manchester United also did the same. The bright lights of European competition beckoned and Wolves initially grabbed the bull by the horns by competing in a series of friendlies against then crack European sides. This led to such excitement across Europe that it was only inevitable that an eventual European competition be introduced, imaginatively named The European Cup. Good job Sepp Blatter wasn't around at the time to influence the name. If he had, we'd no doubt be watching Barca and Inter playing today for the Sepp Bellend trophy (his middle name allegedly and, if it is, how very, very appropriate). Naturally this new competition was viewed with instant suspicion at the time by the collective wise monkeys that made up the Football League. Did this lot ever have their finger on the pulse of public opinion?

Dear old Chelsea, for so long a music hall joke, fluked through to win the league for the first time in their history in 1955, not bad for a bunch of comparative paupers compared to their modern counterparts, but Sod's law dictated that they didn't get to take part in any European venture. "Best not, lads" said the League and with a tug of the forelock Chelsea agreed. What could they possibly have had to lose if they stuck two fingers up and said "We're going!" Knowing Chelsea then, they'd probably have embarrassed themselves and the League by actually winning the thing. During the 1950s, if Chelsea and Fulham appeared in a Vaudeville show, you'd need to spin a coin to see who'd top the bill. The game was fun, if nothing else.

At the very beginning of that decade, Spurs won the title a season after doing the same thing in the Second Division. "It'll never happen again" said the experts of the day as they lectured the masses on who knows best. Obviously it wasn't them. In 1962 little Ipswich Town won the Football League the season after winning the Second Division. "It'll never happen again" said the experts of the day as they lectured the masses on who knows best. It never did happen again, not until 1978 anyway, when Nottingham Forest did it after finishing a lowly third in the Second Division the season before. Even then, some experts waited for Forest's collapse. Some collapse!

Stanley Matthews won a Cup medal in 1953, and floodlit football made its debut with the very first floodlit league match taking place at Fratton Park in 1956, over 20 years after some bloke called Herbert Chapman first muted the idea. That "slow burner" of an idea led to floodlit pylons going up like TV aerials all over the country, and the experts proffering their opinion on the future of floodlit football. There was mixed reviews when these same experts were asked if the experiment would be repeated. They quickly offered their pearls of wisdom: "It'll never happen again".

Some things never change though and England stirred the hearts of the nation in the 1950 World Cup by going down 1-0 to the USA. Worse, much worse was to follow in 1953 against Hungary, who proved that we were definitely not alone on the football planet by thrashing us 6-3 at Wembley. Just to prove it wasn't a fluke, they then spanked us 7-1 in Budapest. Thirteen years later, England's finest hour, and finest ever team, did us all proud and smashed the Germans 4-2. And, yes that ball was over the line. That Russian linesman had the same view, too, so how could he not say anything but "goal", only 21 years after the end of World War Two?

Forever after that victory, from 1970 onwards, and every four years on, T-shirt salesmen were kept in business with their shirts bearing the highly inventive logo "4 years of hurt, 8 years of hurt, 12 years of hurt" and so on. Today it's now 44 years of hurt and still counting. Both the years and the T-shirts.

CHAPTER 3

THE CHANGING FACE OF MATCH DAYS

Remember when you were very young, but still old enough to remember, waking up on a Saturday morning without a care in the world? Living at home with your mam and dad and the only thing that you'd ever have to worry about was whether you had the money to go to the match that afternoon. Not that you had money worries, of course. These were the sole domain of your parents who had magic pockets that never emptied, bills that they somehow always managed to pay and meals that were always on the table morning, noon and night.

Of course, there might well be the odd clip round the lug reserved just for you, just so that you knew your place in the order of things and didn't get too lippy. It was a small price to pay, though, for growing up safe and warm in the nearest thing this side to heaven. Long ago and far away in this place we all grew up in, hundreds of thousands of young footy fans all round the country used to get up on Saturdays and salivate about the game they were off to that afternoon. You might have the odd chore of a Saturday morning paper delivery round, or catching up on homework or earning your pocket money, but after that it was the countdown to three o'clock. That feeling was never to leave you, ever, even years later when the same ritual began again with your own children. Saturday was your day, belonged to you personally, and the only thing that could ruin it invariably happened at about quarter to five when the match was over. That's when you sulked off back home in the huff after getting beat 3-1.

It wouldn't matter if you were Stan from Stockport or Herbie from Huddersfield. The fact was when Saturday came the build up began from the moment you got out of your pit till kick off that afternoon. Not for the vast majority of those fans then a mammoth train journey or long bus or coach journey to the other end of the country to support the latest Nouveau Riche side as is the case today. No, it was just a short walk and a cold pork pie away to The Vetch, Ayresome Park, The Shay or Boundary Park. Come rain, hail or shine (and if you've ever been to Boundary Park, Oldham, it was usually a combination of all three over 90 minutes and even worse in the winter) you'd be there. It was a family affair handed down from grandfather to father to son. Brainwash them early and they'll be putty in your hands for life.

When you watched a match back then, nearly everybody kicked off at three and it was nearly always on a Saturday. That was just the way it was although you'd notice there'd be the odd side who always kicked off at 3.15. I used to think that they were being awkward buggers. Not so, when I later found out from my dad just by asking. This was a traditional thing going way back when sides like Millwall always kicked off 15 minutes later than the rest to allow for the thousands of dockers to get out of work, have a quick pint and then get along to The Den. If you were a football club, you'd be next to mad to kick off early and lose the support of thousands of these type of fans, so it was the clubs then bowing to fan pressure. Now, of course, it's the other way round. The tail wags the dog, so to speak, with clubs bluntly telling fans: "We're playing Sunday at 5.30pm". A more or less take it or leave it approach to supporters.
You'd have been ready for taking away by the men in white coats if you predicted 40 years down the line you'd be watching a match at high noon on a Sunday.

Yes, then in the past there was a strange but somehow common sense approach to playing every Saturday at 3 o'clock, not 5.30, or 8 o'clock on a Monday night. It was long before the days of Sky and the soft luxury of hot and cold running commentaries from the comfort of your own living room to any ground in Britain (calling in at Raith Rovers, Rochdale and Hereford United as a special treat). Back then the only way to find out the latest about your own club was to actually get off your backside and go along to where they played. Now everyone's an expert, even about your team, although they probably don't even know on the map where they even are. If you actually followed your side away then to other parts of the country, it was like going to the moon and back, such were the difficulties of circumnavigating your way from Torquay to say, Carlisle or Hartlepool. Rucksacks were packed, goodbye notes left to anguished family members just in case, as time zones were breached and language barriers overcome as you battled through the elements onward, ever onward, into the unknown. If you were a Southerner then you really were a long, long way from home setting out to somewhere like Barrow or Darlington.

I remember in the late 1960s hearing a tale of a bunch of Spurs fans stepping out at Sunderland Station, having obviously left King's Cross in the middle of a heat wave. They were dressed ever so smartly in Ben Sherman T shirts plus various other items of skimpy, expensive clothing, all obviously the latest gear in the heady heights of London. They must have thought they'd stepped out into downtown Moscow when they embarked at Sunderland, instantly being hit by a blizzard, police escort and barking dogs. Locals, who were wrapped up like Eskimos against the elements, gawped on in amazement and disbelief at these scantily clad fashion gurus. Trendy and chic they may have looked, but practical against the North East weather? Not a chance. They were then, ever so slowly, frogmarched on the long walk to Roker Park. They were cold, hungry, wet and miserable, and certainly wouldn't have been in any mood for aggro which was also fashionable back then. The more elderly witnesses must have had a feeling of déjà vu and may well have had flashbacks to the Jarrow Marchers as the frozen mob hobbled on by. Crossing the exposed River Wear must have been the equivalent, for many of them, of trying to set up base camp on Mount Everest as the wind, sleet and snow gained momentum, and the icy blast whistled and howled around them. Then, when they eventually reached Roker Park, there was the added ordeal of standing, soaked to the skin like drowned rats, in the open Roker End. All that would have been needed to complete the picture would have been a Japanese camera crew from that sadistic TV show "Endurance". We've all had days like this, but always check the local weather conditions at the other end before setting out on your expedition, just in case you end up like this poor lot.

Well over twenty years earlier than this, when Sunderland travelled all the way down to non-league Yeovil in the FA Cup in January 1949, my partner Jenny's father, Ronnie Holyoak, then a sprightly 21 year old and now an even sprightlier 82 years young, decided that he and some mates would go down there by train for the match. Then there really was no other way to get there. A car could do it, but not many had them then, and there wouldn't have been a car invented - other than a Rolls Royce - that could negotiate such a mammoth journey without breaking down. The train ride took thirteen hours each way, over a day's travel in total. After 90 minutes on the famous slope, the score was 1-1 and even though that would have been a disappointing score for a First Division side like Sunderland, Len Shackleton and all, Ronnie would have took it like a shot. He had a bad feeling with the extra half hour looming, the rules at the time. He was proved right as Yeovil snatched the winner and caused the biggest cup upset since Walsall beat the mighty Arsenal in 1933. I bet Arsenal fans were delighted that afternoon to get that particular monkey off their backs they'd been carrying around so long, and put it gratefully on to Sunderland's. You can only imagine what the conversation was like on the train journey back, but apparently Yeovil "looked a lovely place to live" even though their slope left a lot to be desired. "You couldn't see the corners coming in from the far end" according to Ron, "only the top of the head of the bloke who was taking them." Let's see "Match Of The Day" top that description. Last season, a friend of mine, who follows Hartlepool all over the place, went to Yeovil by car in just under five and a half hours, and they stopped to stretch their legs too.

1949 was last week compared to Ron's brother's record. Ron was the youngest of a large family of twelve, and his eldest brother Thomas, or "Tot" to family and friends, saw his first ever game at Roker Park when he was only 6 in 1913, a 6-0 win against Clapton Orient. It wasn't until 1919, after the First World War, that he saw his second game, against Burnley in the Cup. He was later on the books of Sunderland but left after only one year having failed to make the grade. He was manager Johnny Cochrane's first ever signing (you can't get them all right, can you?). Fate can be cruel, too, in any era. Tot turned down both Aston Villa, and the old enemy, Newcastle United to join his beloved Sunderland, and who knows what might have been at the time if he had gone down a different road. Not only did he see the real iconic players of the twenties and thirties, he actually rubbed shoulders with two who really stood out for him; Davey Halliday and the great Charlie Buchan (he of Football Monthly fame). Halliday joined Sunderland only because of Buchan, according to Tot, and was he angry when it turned out he'd been brought in to replace Charlie, not to play alongside him as he thought. Charlie was on his way to the Arsenal. What might have been with both of them in the same team. Both Ron and Tot's views on match days were identical, too. Work hard all week and Saturday afternoon for a few magical hours was when you had the chance to forget about everything and roar on the lads. From 1913 to today nothing has really changed, has it?

They say the past is a foreign country. Forty years or more back, as the above so aptly illustrates, it was more like another planet. According to today's modernists and those do it yourself politically correct junkies, it was round about the end of the Jurassic period and roughly some time between the Ice Age and when man first started walking on two legs. I'm also convinced that's how Columbus may well have discovered America. He'd set off, totally unprepared, on a short boat trip to Majorca trying to take in a Real Madrid away game, got hopelessly lost in the mist, and four months later discovered the New World.

My own little piece of Nirvana in my growing up years was 10 miles up the road at Sunderland. It was a time, in my own place in history, before motorways or mobile phones, the nanny state, obesity, KFC or the internet. A time when you had to actually think for yourself before the state did it all for you, and before the modern type of footy experts came along, extolling the virtues of how wonderful it is to follow one of the top four sides (the same people who also drool about Take That being the biggest band in the Universe - ever. Of course they are). I'm sure most of you have forgotten more about the game than this lot will ever know. Cocooned in their smug little worlds, and fawned over by flunkies carrying their latest coffee drink - chocca mocca frappocinnos with garnished egg white - they'll laugh at you, and me, for following the likes of Barnsley, Crewe and Hartlepool. These are real clubs with real fans who'll just go into a transport café and ask for a mug of coffee, white, with two sugars. Who would you rather sit with talking football?

Jeff Stelling has done his bit to make Hartlepool strangely trendy, though. They have now - horror of horrors - attracted a whole new set of fans apparently jumping straight onto the media bandwagon. Alright, I suppose, in terms of putting the town on the map, but surely it must irk all genuine Hartlepool fans out there who've followed them forever through thin and even thinner. Even Wigan Athletic, in the Premier League, is treated with snooty disdain by these connoisseurs of the game. Ditto for Stoke, Wolves and Blackburn who, according to the modernists, should all lie back and get steamrollered weekly by the aristocratic teams out there. They play the game far too rough, allegedly, and should be outlawed out of The Premier. How ghastly. I wonder where these chuckleheads were when Vinnie Jones and his Wimbledon mates were going through their little box of tricks?

Don't you get slightly irritated, feel the old heckles rising, when some ever so trendy, finger on the pulse, bright young thing (a probable New Model Army Chelsea fan of course) has the nerve to tell you that your team, and most of the others who make up the greatest league competition in the world, are basically crap? And that you are all just wasting your time trying to compete with their team of Superstars. They conveniently forget, of course, that long before some Russian bloke called Abramovich came on the scene to transform Chelsea's fortunes, they were also one of us, too. They didn't call them "The Pensioners" for nothing back in the 1950s, you know. According to this lot, how on earth did we ever survive watching our own particular favourites down the years? The answer is the same way we survive now, darlings.

I even wonder what the Premier League would have looked like now, if by some quirk of fate, a nine year old Abramovich had woken up one morning in Moscow reading a then modern equivalent of a Russian version of Charles Buchan's Football Monthly (ask your granddad) and thought to himself: " Hmmm, Plymouth Argyle and Crewe Alexandra? What lovely names. One day when I am rich and grown up, I am going to buy both of them".

I know I am going to come across as a right grumpy old git, but there's a very simple explanation for this. It's because I am. It comes with the territory that you'll all be entering into when you actually hit a certain age, and sometimes even earlier depending on your mood swings. It's not too great getting old but it's so much better than the alternative, don't you think? If you wait long enough, grasshopper, it's what will happen to you, too, along with that incredible moment when you become totally invisible to the younger generation. You'll find that they will have no further use for you once they've picked your brains, pockets, and then regurgitated your classic old songs into a more contemporary modern but bland style (without the guitar riffs of course). I believe it's what is called progress. If you don't believe me, read this book in forty, no thirty, years time and you'll see what I meant. And there's bugger all you can do about it. It's as inevitable as night following day, as inevitable as that banker home win letting you down on your fixed odds coupon. I bet you can't wait, can you?

I try to be tolerant and understanding, and think "It's not their fault, they haven't lived yet", but honestly it's a struggle. Have you restrained yourself, for example, from not putting your foot through the telly whenever one of these smug, sanctimonious prigs tell me, in the form of a patronising lecture, what's wrong with my team? What makes it even worse is that what they say isn't based on opinion, which I honestly wouldn't mind. No, as far as they are concerned, it's a guaranteed fact based on their perceived, self-obsessed, supposed superiority, and subtly ignoring the tradition and history of your club or even the town itself. They've never actually been to the place where you live and grew up in but they don't need to. Someone else may well have briefed them about it, or basically they just don't like your side because they don't play the game the same way as the elite do. Maybe your team don't roll over easily enough or get stuck in too fiercely to earn a point against all the odds. Maybe they're just shallow. They know absolutely nothing about my team, or yours, for that matter and know even less about the emotions built up by you, as you support your side down the years. They have never stood where you've stood on the terraces, or experienced the same joy, despair, misery and happiness of it all - sometimes in one afternoon. They weren't there with you when you've stood speechless after a 5-1 home defeat, lost six off the bounce, and just when you've said you were never ever going back, gone on a ten game unbeaten run that left you feeling ashamed of yourself for ever doubting your club. All that counts for nothing to them, an irritating irrelevance swept aside, as they court the viewers. Until they know all of those emotions about your team, then in the words of that old tried and trusted chant you often hear: "You're not fit to wear the shirt." Or, in their case, not fit to be on the air, coming out with such drivel. Instead, they are swept along by the media and hype, most of it self-created .They think big teams are those who can spend millions, stealing gems from lower division sides (the sides, of course, that they so readily denounce) or acquiring the services of cheap foreign mercenaries, here today and gone tomorrow, in so many cases. I bet they can't even remember the names of them in a couple of years, either.

But the best bit of all, and it nearly always happens, is that when some of these blowhards self-implode on their own garbage, they provide us fans with many moments of real enjoyment and hilarity. Sure as eggs are eggs, it always happens, too. It always blows up in their face. A bit like England and manager Fabio Capello in South Africa, Who would ever have guessed that England weren't going to win the World Cup? Who'd have actually believed we'd bomb like that? I did for one. I also had a few quid on Holland each way, so it can't be all bad, can it? Not as bad as Holland in the final, anyway.

I remember listening a while back to someone on the radio going on about Huddersfield Town, and asking what they had ever done. This moron obviously knew bugger all about football, otherwise he would have realised that they had won the First Division championship three years running back in the 1920s. A long time ago, granted, but still a record for any club, or any fan, not only to be proud of, but also something to cling on to. They can't take that away from them, even though, today, it's classed as irrelevant. In today's world of instant success, you see, it doesn't fit in with media pundits who dwell in the world of short term attitudes and revolving door managers. It's just so not in "the now", where we all smugly live and die on a week to week basis.

There are probably hundreds of thousands of fans who feel the same way as I do. They will have a sense of frustration and isolation that they are just a lone voice in the wilderness. But fear not, you aren't. There are still fans out there who dwell and earn in the realms of the ordinary, and might even see some of their own team's players slumming it in the in the local supermarket. Why, only a short while back, I saw Justin Hoyte of Middlesbrough in ASDA in Seaham, and what a lovely bloke to talk to. If you want to mix shoulders with the Gerrards and Rooneys of this world, though, then either buy their book (Wayne's even has free pencils in for you to colour all the pictures) or read about them both in The News of the World.

There are many more of us who don't fit into the modern football jigsaw puzzle because they think we are all dinosaurs. I've got bad news for all those who think that very soon we will all die out, and the game can then ascend to a new level of ultra modernism. It won't. The old ways will still persist. The plain fact is that there's a whole new generation of young fans coming along who don't buy into all this new wave thinking either. They, too, are rebelling and have all developed the same philosophies and beliefs as I have. We want our game back. It's just the same as if we don't hear classic rock or great pop songs on mainstream radio today, then it must mean that it's died out. Of course it hasn't. It's all still out there and still cherished. It's just been hidden for commercial reasons by people who will tell you it is all old hat. Be like me. Don't buy into any of the modern stuff, football or music, if you genuinely think it's rubbish. Don't put up with an alternative modern version in the mistaken belief that the old stuff no longer exists. It's just been hidden conveniently from view, that's all. Complain, make a protest, don't buy or make a big enough noise and they'll have to listen.

Here's my take on what you'd call a real fan, recently heard on the radio:
"Hello; Tommy from Crewe here."
"And which team do you support Tommy?"
"Erm ,Crewe Alexandra"
"Crewe Alexandra? Why?"

Don't answer that one Tommy. The man's obviously a bloody idiot. Or if you do answer, tell him it's because you live there and quickly hang up. Either way, he's not worth talking to.

The same goes for your modern type of fan (although more on that later). It seems now that to actually enjoy a match in the current climate, it is essential to claim maximum bragging rights, and by that I mean that it is absolutely necessary to follow those teams who are the latest fashion. That's the top four, regardless of the fact that you may have only climbed aboard that particular Premiership vessel when you were in your late teens. I'm surprised they didn't throw in a free poodle with your season ticket. I'd put in ten years hard graft watching Sunderland by the time I was 21, and didn't even get a free toffee apple, never mind a gold watch out of it.

Even worse than jumping on the football bandwagon, are those shysters who switch allegiance from one side to another, dependent on where they stand in the current latest popularity ratings. This, in particular, seems to be a common trait in London where Chelsea has procured a whole new army of fans in recent years. Many of them are either brand new or abandoning ship elsewhere. I wonder why? Ditto for Manchester, where some of their local fans have had to set out from Cornwall at six in the morning for home games.
It doesn't matter a jot that you know absolutely nothing about the history of your new celebrity club, the reason being that in your eyes, they'll be history anyway if they dare let you down by winning nothing over the next two years.

Otherwise, as far as you are concerned, you'll drift off to trendier pastures new. And why shouldn't you, you'll retort. After all, in taking on any new allegiance, there's a considerable outlay involved. It'll cost you at least eight hundred quid for a season ticket to watch them, and probably a fiver for a bag of French Fries (you only get chips at places like Darlington or Rochdale; it's far too vulgar a word for a top four side to use). Oh, yes, and it'll cost you extra, guvnor, if you want an atmosphere to go with the entertainment. I once sat through an Arsenal v Aston Villa game a few years back in the days of Highbury and, in all honesty, it was that quiet I was waiting for a priest to walk on followed by the coffin. I now hear that The Emirates, which boasts an extra 22,000 seats is even quieter. How is that possible? Are they gagging the fans on the way in, or are there "No shouting" notices being displayed? How can a 60,000 crowd be quiet? Is it a new trend in London, or what?

I'd honestly give up watching football at any level if they asked me to keep forking out those amounts of money every season. And I think that the worm has now slowly begun to turn as far as some fans are concerned. They are starting to protest. My season ticket currently costs me some £280 a year, and that price has been frozen for another season too. It's only common sense as many teams are finally starting to realise that people are tightening their belts and there's a recession going on. There's been one going on in several parts of the North East for years. The other factor is that some fans aren't getting value for money, and there are now lower league sides who might not have the same skills but they show a damned sight more effort and it's a lot cheaper too.

Some clubs in the lower leagues are even letting kids in for a couple of quid or less and if I wore a hat I'd take it off to them. I wondered why Bradford City in League Two were getting 12/13,000 crowds and that was the reason. If you take a five year old to his first ever match at lower league level in a crowd that size, he's not going to kick up a fuss about the level of football on offer. At that age he won't know the difference between Liverpool or Hartlepool (the pies are cheaper and bigger at Hartlepool, kids, and there's no Americans trying to ruin your club).

Not only are lower league clubs and others pointing the way forward in this respect, the Premier League should be looking at this trend and following their example, and rewarding and subsidising them, instead of finding new ways of screwing fans further. I've built up a lot of anger and frustration down the years watching the lunacy creeping into the game. It's not only the politicians who have gone barmy. Some of those running - or should that be ruining - our game aren't a kick in the backside behind them, both on and off the field. I got so sick of shouting and kicking the telly in frustration and thought I'd put it into words. My Dad predicted all this in the late 1980s.

I genuinely believe we've lost something from the game down the years. It has changed, but that's only understandable. Everything has to change. I don't believe, though, that it has changed for the better and I see far more cynicism, greed and hypocrisy in it than there ever was in the past. We should have built on the mistakes we made, and improved on the good things that were handed down. Instead, we conveniently choose to ignore both. No, I don't think the game has got better, certainly not at the top end of the scale.

The terraces have gone - inevitable I suppose - but what we are left with is sanitised stadiums and equally sanitised fans. It's now a competition at the top table to see who has the most expensive team, and highest wage earners. And don't we, the ordinary fans, just love it when these expensive flops fall flat on their backsides? I still see the magic of the game but worryingly this mainly applies in the Championship and below.

And why is it that the further down the pyramid you go, the more exciting games appear to be for the neutral? There certainly isn't the fear factor further down and I think, too, that most fans going to watch football in the Premier don't enjoy it as much as they did when it first appeared in 1993. Now, it's sometimes like a chore going to the game, and I've noticed that some fans even write certain games off before even a ball's been kicked. They've actually conceded in advance. At lower league level, there is still the sense of fun and genuine anticipation on match days that once used to embrace all the leagues. I believe we can still identify with that type of player, too, the further down the league we go. In some ways, they aren't that much different from us. Some are on the sort of wages that might even mean that they could live next door to us. The only way that you'd ever be living next to the Ashley Coles of the football world would be if you kipped in a cardboard box on the kerb outside his mansion one night. And it would be for one night only, before you were very quickly moved on.

The game now is so different from the one I grew up watching in the very early 60s. Whether you think it has changed for the better is no longer an age thing either. I know a few old and young fans who think the excitement and passion has gone from the game. Some young fans weren't around to even witness those days where their clubs had dilapidated stands that leaked in on rainy days and where some parts of the ground were exposed to the elements. It was brilliant on a lovely, sunny day in August, but in the middle of January?

The game is obviously a lot better in terms of the facilities now available but in terms of atmosphere, excitement and packed crowds swaying like corn in the field on a windy day, there really is no comparison. Even if you've just travelled all the way back from a two day weekend special hike from Sunderland to Yeovil, and been dumped out of the cup as a reward for it all.

CHAPTER 4
EARLY DOORS

I was born in July 1951 at Littlethorpe, near Easington in County Durham. The maternity hospital there, later to be the birthplace of my two sons Martin and Daniel, has now long gone, and so overgrown you'd never realise anything had been there at all. It has just been left to return to nature, like so many other former places in the area.

The North East I was born into then is now just a shadow of a bygone era. At the beginning of the 1950s, the whole of County Durham was a busy, industrial powerhouse with the area criss-crossed by local railway lines, stations and surrounded by mines and steelworks everywhere. My mother and father were on the verge of moving to a new home in a brand new town nearby, Peterlee, built specifically to accommodate the overspill from over populated collieries at Easington and other nearby pit villages. It was hard to imagine then but only 50 short years before my entrance on to the world stage, Easington Colliery didn't exist, and in its place was extensive farmland which rolled right down to the sea. The sinking of the first pit shaft and the abundant supplies of coal under the nearby North Sea was to change that landscape quickly.

My dad never worked in the mines and was a quarryman at nearby Hawthorn. My mam worked part time at the local hospital as a cleaner. Everybody worked then. It was deemed to be the norm, and if you didn't work you would quickly get talked about by the many miners, steelworkers and the shipyard workers living around you. It was a way of life and I can't honestly remember growing up seeing anybody who wasn't in some sort of employment. The only people who didn't work were the very old, retired or those really ill, badly injured from any of the two World Wars, or those with an industrial accident. You would have needed to be a real conman back then to pull the wool over the eyes of those in the benefits exchange, by even drawing the dole if there was work available or, even worse, if you were perfectly fit and didn't fancy doing it. What happened to change all that?

As I was the first grandchild I was spoiled rotten. My nan, granddad and large family lived at 4 Camp Street in Easington Colliery. My mother was the eldest of nine children, five brothers and four sisters, and all of them grew up in a three bedroom colliery terraced house with an outside toilet and no bathroom. By contrast, my dad was an only child brought up by his aunt at nearby Easington Village and never really knew his father. I think that was the reason my nan took an instant shine to him. Rationing was then still in place after the war, and many, including my dad made up for lost time when some restrictions were relaxed. He was that hungry he even used to eat Yorkshire pudding sandwiches, according to my mum.

I never knew that he had been a virtual orphan until a few years afterwards, and the loss of him having real parents in his youth was his own children's later gain. You couldn't have met a kinder, or more gentle, man than my dad, or a funnier one when he was in the mood, which was quite often. Some of the jokes he told us all then I still retell today, and these leave a whole new audience either rolling about laughing, or just rolling in agony. Just like football, you can't win them all. He was such a softy he left it to my mam to do all the telling off whenever we stepped out of line.

Living in a colliery at that time meant that there was always plenty of coal dust in the air, and on the washing that was hung out. There was no chance of keeping it clean for long.

Bath nights in a typical colliery house started with the tin bath being brought inside, hanging on the wall in the yard outside, and then put in front of a huge roaring coal fire in the living room to warm up. The adjacent front room was only ever used for special occasions, but nearly always got an airing on a Sunday. When someone was having a bath it really was like a military operation. The door would be locked to keep everybody out, and the curtains drawn. Sometimes there might be three for a bath, and so you'd get in one after the other in pecking order, littlest to biggest. If you did it the other way round then the littlest would come out as black as he went in.

When you think that the Ancient Romans, 2,000 years before, had more advanced methods of bathing, then that tells you all you need to know of what colliery owners not only felt about their employees at that time, but for years after as well. There was no boiler to heat up the water, and no central heating either. Other homes belonging to the more privileged members of society had these facilities in other parts of the country (even in nearby Peterlee) but not the miners. And so, you had to boil huge pans of water, and quickly, or the bath would get too cold. And you had to keep it topped up, as well. That coal fire would keep you lovely and warm, but the moment you stepped out of that bath it was only the front side of you that stayed warm. And when you did finish, after you'd tried hard not to lean back against the freezing cold tin sides, there was then the job of emptying it by hand.

The more luxurious the bath, and by luxurious I mean putting enough water in to actually call it a proper bath, the longer it took to empty. This was usually carried out to the yard by two of you and then emptied. It was always handy if it had been snowing outside, because at least that way, you'd be spared the job of clearing the snowy path with the still hot water doing the job for you. Next morning though, the chances are that you'd fall over on the thick ice caused by the melted snow from the bath water the night before. Then you'd get called all the names under the sun for being a lazy bugger and not doing the job properly.

In the very early 1950s right up to the mid to late 1960s, most miners and their families used to have to go through this primitive ritual practically every night, scrubbing down at home this way. The introduction of the pit baths meant that at least, for the miner, he could get cleaned at the pit. Some of them must have thought they'd died and gone to heaven. For the rest of his family, though, it was business as usual and they were still left to the tin bath method at home.

All collieries looked exactly the same, and they still do today, with row after row of terraced redbrick houses all very near the pit. This was very convenient for the owners who knew that there couldn't possibly be any excuses about not getting into work because of bad weather. All the streets were given visionary and imaginary names that just swept you off your feet. There was First Street, Second Street etc in most collieries. In Easington they must have been a bit more imaginative. They called one block of terraced houses the "A" Streets (Alnwick, Angus etc.), another "B"(Baldwin, Beattie etc.), and a third block "C"(Camp, Coxon, Charles etc.). Maybe this was all a ploy by owners to increase productivity, as they must have reckoned that miners would have thought: "Oh, well, at least it's better than living in somewhere called 1st, 3rd or 12th Street".

Coal for the miners and retired miners was delivered free, and dumped unceremoniously in the streets right outside the house. It was then shovelled into the coal house hatch situated next door to the outside toilets. Nearly always, when the National Coal Board wagons trundled round Easington dropping off these loads, they would be accompanied by hordes of youths who volunteered to put your coal in for you (I know, I was one of them). Some of the more experienced ones were pitch black, with the dust and muck from previous deliveries they'd been doing earlier in the day. If you can imagine a fishing boat surrounded by thousands of seagulls all eager for the odd scrap, it will give you an idea of what it was like.

The outside toilets were affectionately known as "netties" (from the French word "nettoire"). Did you know that word has now apparently finally caught on in London (where've they all been for the last fifty years?) and is regarded in some quarters as ultra cool and high chic. And yet they all recoiled in horror, and nearly fainted, when I first revealed what it meant to my London schoolmates in 1964. Watch out for Kate Moss coming out with the word, no doubt pretending she's invented it, next time she's on the red carpet somewhere.

There were cars around then in the North East but very few in Easington. I remember a relative who came up from Eastbourne – it must have been maybe 1959 - and the car he was driving was flash looking even then. Nearly every kid in the street was posing beside it. Hardly anybody around then, apart from maybe managers at the pit or the odd person outside the colliery, had a car. Nobody could afford them. Everybody went by buses or trains that ran regularly through Easington.

Washing day saw colliery women having to hang out loads of clothes and sheets to dry on a washing line between the backs of houses that faced each other. There were grass verges out the back, so that you could at least sit out on warm days. The washing was usually watched very carefully as smoky chimneys everywhere, and wind blowing in the wrong direction, could easily undo a whole day's hard work - and often did. Forget washing machines or tumble dryers, clothes were washed in a huge metal tub and then put through a mangle turned by hand.

At the very bottom of Camp Street was the pit wall about eight feet high where shunting engines and wagon loads of coal rolled back and forth all day long, up and down the coast, delivering their goods. Beyond those railway lines was the main East Coast rail line, farmers fields, allotments, the beach banks and then, lastly, the North Sea.

There was a real sense of community spirit everywhere then, and the streets were always busy with people bustling to and fro, backwards and forwards to work, to the shops, to other towns and villages, and, on the evening, to the various clubs and pubs. The Workingmen's Clubs were a cheap night out and were packed seven days a week. Miners were tough audiences to please and wouldn't put up with any old rubbish. Boy bands back then wouldn't have stood a chance. The local picture houses and various fish and chip shops were always busy, too, in the very early part of the 50s and right through the 60s. Easington used to have two main picture houses, the Hippodrome and the Rialto. Both would go on to struggle financially once the advent of the telly into people's homes took hold, and after that, they were finished off altogether. The Rialto still stands today as a carpet retailer's and you can still see internally that in its heyday it was a pretty impressive venue. The films they used to put on had already been on general release a good year or two before they hit the collieries. If you wanted to see them new then you had to go into the big towns.

The local shopping area consisted of one long row of shops on Seaside Lane that catered for everyone in the colliery. Nobody ever did their shopping elsewhere. All the collieries were very parochial, and people believed in putting their money into their own local shops. After all, if you didn't do that, then those shops could go under and maybe even close. And then where would you be? That simple and conscientious philosophy just doesn't come into the equation today in this competitive world we now live in. Now, it's survival of the fittest and people travelling miles to get a better deal.

Life was a lot easier then before the supermarkets came along. All you'd ever need was available in the colliery. The local butchers and greengrocers, hardware store, bakers, café, newsagent, banks, fish shops, solicitors, undertakers, even an Italian Ice Cream parlour called Equi's. Everything you bought from the shops came in eco-friendly, brown paper bags with butter, cheese and bacon and eggs all wrapped up. Little did we realise it then, but we were years ahead of our time as far as going green was concerned. We just didn't know it, that's all. Nobody bought in bulk. You used to eat fresh food daily, and get what you needed on a day to day basis.

For years I was told my grandfather had originally come from New York. He did, but not the one in America. This was the other one in Northumberland. He had moved south to work in the mines in Durham, and was also a big Newcastle fan (he kept that quiet as well). He was from a very big family - all families were big then - and lived very near to his sister, Norah, in Camp Street. He must have thought me and my brother Tommy were some kind of good luck omens for him, too, as Newcastle United won the Cup in 1951, 1952 and 1955. We were both born during this period.

The whole world seemed to be on our own little doorstep. To the south of Easington was Hartlepool and Teesside, and north was Sunderland and Newcastle, all linked by rail up and down the coast, and stopping at all stations. Nearby were two other coastal collieries, Horden and Blackhall, with Seaham, Dawdon and Vane Tempest just up the road and inland, Shotton, Murton, Hetton, Coxhoe, Kelloe and Houghton. Everywhere you went you'd be in a pit village, all of them belching smoke out morning noon and night. In 1951 there were over 250 working pits in Northumberland and Durham. All collieries, no matter where they were, had the same basic look. Row upon row of terraced houses and a huge pit heap always in close proximity. If you were really lucky (lucky?) the pit heaps would be like the ones at Easington, out at sea and washed out on a daily basis by the tide, with all the stones and shale distributed up and down the beach.

The mines themselves were still the major employer in the county and were dirty and dangerous places to make your living. My granddad and two of my uncles worked there, but several of my uncles, my dad and others, avoided like them the plague and preferred jobs above ground and with good reason. Only two months before I was born, there was a disaster at Easington Colliery and 81 men lost their lives in an underground explosion.

My earliest vague memory of growing up there was when I was just over two, and I had it in my mind to walk to my nan's from our new house in Peterlee, across the fields, less than two miles away. When you are two, and only have little legs, it seemed a lot further. The police were called out when my mam realised I'd gone AWOL and I got as far as halfway before I was rescued. Some really big strangers (they were kids about 11 years old) picked me up and carried me to their home whilst someone ran for help. All of this happened in the middle of a snowstorm so it was just as well I had my cowboy hat and jacket on to keep me warm.

I virtually lived down my nan's. I can still picture every detail of her home, and all the things she did to occupy her always busy day. There was a huge picture in the front room of her own father, a stern looking man called Macdonald, who looked down with authority on everyone. There was a collection of old magazines that I used to spend hours sifting through as well when I was really young. Even then, I was absorbed with history. They were called "The illustrated War News" and were a collection of weekly magazines that dated back to the First World War. All were originals with graphic details, stories and hand drawn pictures and events of the major battles and skirmishes covering 1914-1918. There must have been over two hundred of these individual magazines, all bound together in a huge leather folder. I don't know what happened to them but today they would be worth a fortune. Like so many things back then, they were probably discarded in later years as people got a bit more money in their pockets and didn't want old clutter in their homes. The fortunes and treasures they must have thrown away!

My nan even made all her own mats and carpets on a huge framed loom that she'd have set out in the front room, and when she had the time, which wasn't very often, she'd sit with various bags of wool clippings that she then hooked and threaded together on a huge patterned piece of threaded material. Some of the mats were real works of art. Today you'd pay a lot for these retro carpets and mats. I know that because I've seen the modern versions of them at Beamish Museum and not many of them could touch the ones my nan made. She always seemed to be forever polishing these huge brass ornaments that were actually cut down bits of bomb shells from the First World War (dud ones of course, or at least I hope they were). She'd make and bake bread rolls called "toughies" in the oven next to the fire place. You'd not be able to buy anything today that tasted that good. I used to get my "picture house money" off an uncle four streets away when I delivered them to him twice a week. Nan was always washing or boiling something on the open fire, too, and in between all this, there'd be constant visitors,

Her brothers Gerry and Petey ,from Sunderland, used to call in, usually whenever they were down on their luck (what's family for, eh?). Petey was a lovely and kindly man with a really good heart. His brother Gerry was more streetwise and looked a lot like Alex James, that legendary Arsenal footballer from the 1930s. Gerry was the life and soul of any party and used to play the piano. He could play anything and I once heard him belting out boogie woogie that would have put Jerry Lee Lewis to shame. He was very popular in the local bars in Sunderland and was probably the nearest thing you would get to a juke box. All it would have cost you was a free drink for Gerry and you'd get your two or three favourite songs. That probably explained also why he always had such a rosy complexion all the time.

Christmas was always a really special time when you were young but even more so when, in truth, we never really had that much in the way of material possessions. What we had was worth a lot more than money when you had a loving family around you, and I had a big family around me. On Christmas Eve we'd all go to midnight mass, trudging out late at night through the snow, when ordinarily I'd have been in bed, and then the excitement of getting back to see what we'd got for Christmas. My brother Tommy and I used to get so excited at just getting an apple, orange and nuts with a huge bar of chocolate in a red paper stocking. And that was for each of us as well. Maybe there were a few toys but nothing you'd call over the top, and that was it. Everything was easier, simpler and less complicated.

People really did go the extra mile then in so many different sorts of ways. Halloween parties in people's houses would be mammoth affairs, but no elaborate costumes or fortunes spent or anything like that. Each person there would have their own party trick. Neighbours would not only watch out for each other they would also take you in temporarily if they had to, and there'd always be help if you needed it in your hour of need. My nan's next door neighbours, Mr. and Mrs. Mills, were like an extended family to us and old Charlie Mills used to always invite us in regularly, once to show off a brood of chicks that had hatched out in his incubator in the back room. There were dozens of these chicks all scampering about, and the look of genuine pride in Charlie's eyes made you think he was the one who had laid the eggs. When they moved to Huddersfield so that they could be nearer their daughter and granddaughter, and Charlie could still get to work in a nearby pit, you'd have thought there had been a death in the family. Such evocative memories never really leave you. You store them away, thinking they're forgotten about, until a little incident like writing about your past has you remembering them all over again. It was sad when they left and shows what real friendship is all about and how it never ever really leaves you.

From maybe the age of eight onwards, in the summer months, we'd all go mushroom and blackberry picking, collecting rose hip syrups which we sold on to the local chemist for a penny a jar. We even got the jar back. That's something else that would be banned today under EEC Regulations. We played football and tennis in the back streets. For cricket, it was an old bin lid propped up by a brick that was moved quite regularly whenever the odd wagon or Brass's horse and cart, selling fruit and vegetables, trundled by. There was always a wild scramble for the horse muck by maybe two or three keen gardeners with buckets handy. They used to put it on their rhubarb, but we always had custard on ours. The cricket bat we used was just a makeshift sawn down bit of wood; none of us possessed the real thing. Football was a tennis ball that we used to have handy, and the goals were back gates into people's yards, at the top of two or three high pavement steps. After hours and hours of this, you had perfected your flick ups and volleying to a fine art, but you still had to be really skilful to not only dribble past your opponent, but also flick it up the steps and then beat the goalie guarding the gate. Hours of that made you an expert when you actually got hold of a real football. Are you listening Mister Capello?

We'd also, en masse, go up to the Welfare park for a kick about next to where Easington Colliery Welfare FC played. We once sneaked in the Welfare Ground one Saturday morning to see Easington play Horden in a Wearside League derby match which must have been in the very late 1950s. The reason for a Saturday morning kick off, although I didn't know this at the time, was because on the afternoons the collieries used to empty as fans made their way to watch Sunderland or Newcastle play. I don't think there were very many people who watched Middlesbrough in the collieries at that time, and there still isn't. There must have been 3,000 in there that morning.

There were huge crowds generally in the amateur game in the 1950s, and County Durham was a real stronghold. We had the famous Bishop Auckland, Crook Town and Willington sides on our doorstep, although, again, at the time we didn't know this and how near they were. They might as well have been on the moon for all we knew. For games of tennis, this usually saw us drawing imaginary nets with chalk against the gable end at the top of Camp Street where we'd all pretend we were Lew Hoad, the Australian who dominated Wimbledon in the late 1950s. The games always ended the same way when we were all usually chased off by neighbours. Shouts of " Play down your own end" or "Keep that ball out of my yard".

We even made our own entertainment which provided hours of fun. I'll give three examples but, as you often hear on TV, "please don't try this at home".

The first involved an old roller skate. Place on it an old hardboard book or small shovel. Sit on it and, hey presto, you have your very own 4 wheeled mini car/ skateboard capable of colossal speeds going downhill. Curl your two legs as tight as you can and keep them well clear of the ground. Warning: there are no brakes other than your two front feet. My cousin Steven ended up badly hurt and in hospital once when he went so fast down Camp Street that he ended up hurtling like an exocet missile out of control. Luckily his rapid speed was stopped when he hit the pit wall at the bottom of the street.

The next toy was a piece of bamboo stick about 24 inches long. Sharpen point at one end with a bit of weight attached near that end (sellotape wrapped round a couple of pebbles, or flat stones will do, or if you are a real professional, use a couple of tightly wrapped thick elastic bands. Arrow flights at the other end can be made from your dad's old cigarette packet. Make a notch in the bamboo about 3 inches from the sharpened point, then use a piece of fairly thick string to wrap round the notch loosely, and also wrap this string tightly round your index finger. Find loads of empty space - a beach or open field will do - and then run like the clappers, before hurling it into space. With string still tightly wrapped tightly round your finger, the string loosens on the bamboo and the arrow will go hurtling up, up and away. We used to have contests to see whose "flighty" went the furthest, and some of them cleared well over 100 yards easily. It was all about preparation - just like a footy team – as the good ones stood out and won all the medals, and the rubbish ones were quickly discarded. They would be absolutely banned today as they were definitely a lethal weapon, but we didn't think of the dangers then. To us it was just hours of cheap fun.

Lastly, the standard means of transport for any young blade about colliery, the go kart, or "bogies," as we called them. Take one old set of pram wheels, or any old set of wheels, a few bits of wood, a bolt, a length of rope and even a padded seat if you are really flash. I've seen these contraptions used many a time to pull some poor little kid home, flat out after the long day. Exhausted, he was transported in luxury all the way complete with his own chauffeur. Power supplied by two or three others dragging the bogie home.

Today, no self respecting eight year old would be seen within 100 yards of one of these things, unless it was disguised as a Ferrari. His street cred would go out the window big time. Then again we, in turn, would probably think he was a bore anyway, and would have wanted nothing to do with him. He'd probably have sat in at home on his own all day long, shunned for evermore, stuffing his face with junk food and probably inventing some futuristic computer game where you would never have to leave the house at all.

We were sometimes mischievous but not evil and we would never cheek our elders. That would get us an automatic clout not only from the old gent we'd insulted, but also one from your own dad too. Now both of them would be arrested but back then it was the law of commonsense; "Serves you right".

"Knocky nine doors" was an old favourite but for some reason these games didn't last long. It was the same game roughly as tying a thread to a door and retreating about 40 yards to a safe distance, and then pulling gently on the thread to rattle the door handle. Once the novelty had worn off, with some poor soul opening the door for the third time, you'd genuinely feel sorry for them and abandon the idea, Even more so when they'd yell out in the dark "I know who you are and I'll be round to see your father". We'd run off panicking and think "How did they recognise us in the pitch black?" Not once did we realise that they hadn't. They were just a lot smarter than we were. Game over, and then it was up to the pit baths for a spot of floodlit football where you could play for hours under gloomy lights until you got chased by the local one armed night watchman (no joking, it's true). One night he caught my cousin

Steven by the collar with his only arm. Then he uttered the immortal words I still laugh at to this day: "Stand still while I hit you".

We'd often see a few Teddy Boys in the colliery and we'd skit them, too, but obviously from a very safe, and long, distance away. You had to be careful with them as they had a fierce reputation. This was well before The Beatles were invented, and so these young elegant dandies, with their skin tight jeans, crepe soles and DA hairstyles, only had another three or four years to wait before they could exchange these outlandish outfits for the more trendy mop tops and winkle-pickers. Ah, the follies of youth.

We'd do messages for pocket money or take empty beer bottles down to the off licence at the Station Hotel, or "The Trust" as everybody called it, next to the Catholic Church and near the railway station. We'd get a penny a bottle and then we'd climb over into the pub yard, retrieve the empties and go back in for another penny until the landlord sussed out what we were up to.

We were often press ganged by my crafty Uncle Peter who had allotments and we used to spend hours up there helping him out, me and my cousins Steven and David Brown, Norah's sons. If Peter had hired manual labour, it would have cost him a small fortune even back then, but he tricked us by saying we'd have bodies like Charles Atlas if we did four hours digging each. The number of times we fell for it too.

For sheer thrills, spills and excitement, the beach was where we used to spend most of our summer days. A few of us went down there all day long. On the beach banks there were huge iron buckets that used to take discarded stones from the pit and dump them out into the North Sea. They would be dropped into the sea once they reached a tipping point, the bucket depositing its contents down onto a large mountain of stones below. Imagine row after row of buckets all heading on a conveyor belt system, day after day. By the time the stones and bucket reached the tipping point, they'd be well over 150 feet above sea- level and, once they had been emptied, they'd be back up to the pit to refill. If you ever see the film "Get Carter," made in 1971, you'll see something similar that was filmed on nearby Blackhall beach. I always liked the scene where Michael Caine chased this villain from Newcastle to Blackhall, a distance of some thirty odd miles, in just 20 seconds. Fast wasn't the word. No wonder he was out of breath when he caught him. Not many people know that, by the way.

I remember once seeing some idiot trying to be clever by hitching a free ride underneath one of these buckets on the beach banks as it lumbered slowly on its journey towards the cliff tops, over the edge of the cliff, and out to the waiting sea far below. Unfortunately he didn't realise the danger he was in as he hung on for that little bit too long, the ground beneath him sloping quickly away from him. We had to scream at him to jump some twenty feet to the ground before the bucket and him reached the cliff tops. He panicked and by this time the drop got to thirty feet before he realised he had to let go or be killed. He hurt himself badly when he did loosen his grip and dropped, but another ten seconds and he'd have been too far off the ground to jump. And another ten seconds after that, he would have still been clinging on to the bottom of that bucket as it went over the cliff edge, headed to the highest point on the beach and then tipped its load, and him, onto the mountain of stones and roaring seas way below. That would have took some explaining to his mam and dad.

Sometimes the beach was a dangerous place to be, especially in winter when we very rarely ventured down there. Once though, our brains must have deserted us when we decided to play a game of chicken, as giant waves came crashing, foaming and roaring up the beach towards us. "First one to run is a chicken". We were nearly swept away by a monster of a wave that we just didn't see, or even realise how big it was, until it was only a matter of fifty yards away and closing fast. We ran like the wind but it just engulfed us. We ended up choking and screaming, up to our waists in foaming water, trying desperately not to get carried out to sea. We struggled for what seemed an age, freezing cold, numb with fear but running high on adrenalin, until we got lucky. If the next wave had been anywhere near the same height then we'd all have drowned that day. It wasn't, and we managed to get out and ran for our lives as far up the beach as we could get. Even then we were still ankle deep in the returning foam. That was the last time we played that game as we flew back up the beach banks towards Camp Street, frozen when we got in. It was months before I even dared to tell any of my family what really happened.

The power of the North Sea came back only a month or so later when a lifeboat on a rescue mission in mountainous waves just outside nearby Seaham Harbour overturned and eight people, including a small boy, drowned. Those waves did their job in other ways, too, as they regularly washed away the many tons of stones at the bottom of the flight ready for the next lot to fall. Mixed in with them were bits of coal. Several people used to go down there picking this up in sacks, then making their way back up the beach banks, where they transported it home on old bikes. Even the late, great, Brian Clough, as he later revealed in his autobiography, did this, too. And if it was good enough for Cloughie, then it was good enough for us. Both old and young alike used to spend the whole day filling sacks in this way and would use it for either personal use or sell it. The sea coal wagons - the real professionals - also used to get down there and they'd really clean up, looking for the stuff. As for those pits inland that didn't have a lovely beach like ours to reclaim their waste for them, the stones there were dumped into an ever bigger heap from which there was no escape. There were no waves to wash them away. The pile just got higher and higher until it became like a small mountain. In the winter months, with snow on them, you could imagine it was the Swiss Alps. Some kids would sledge down there, and even in the summer without the snow.

With all those thousands of tons of loose unstable shale dumped, it was an accident waiting to happen and years later it did. In a little Welsh Mining Village called Aberfan, a pit heap collapsed and then engulfed a school with tragic results. All that lay long years in the future, though, and the dear old NCB turned a blind eye to it all until all the warnings and possibilities came to pass. For years they ignored the risk. After all, they were providing thousands of people with a valuable living.

Winters in Easington and the North East were hard and cold beyond belief. Snow storms could sweep in suddenly and were severe, especially from the cold North Sea. Front streets would be blocked quickly sometimes and this usually would mean buses and cars couldn't get up some of the steep banks. All colliery houses had no central heating. There were just the two coal fires roaring in the two rooms, front and back, keeping you warm. No heating up stairs and, of course, no indoor toilets. When there were really cold nights, there would be ice forming inside the windows and you'd end up with a huge old overcoat on the bed to keep you warm. Laughable now, I know, but that's how it was. We thought everybody at that time lived the same.

We didn't know that some houses, even then, had gas central heating and radiators up and down stairs that used to warm the whole house. They even had inside toilets and a bathroom. There was none of that softening life style in the colliery houses. The first one up on a morning had the job of lighting the fire. Sometimes if you were lucky, the fire would be banked up all night. Next morning all you'd have to do was rake out all the ashes that had built up and then top the fire up with coal again.

There was no more fantastic feeling than getting out of bed on a morning, absolutely freezing when you hit the cold air in the bedroom (you could see your breath on cold mornings), race downstairs and see a huge coal fire roaring away as you got to the bottom stair and turned into the room. There were no kitchens in the houses, just a pantry. As for fridge or freezers, forget it. You didn't really need them anyway.

Everything was fresh and bought on a day by day basis. You'd get rabbits from locals who went out catching them with their ferrets and sold them round the doors. Of course you would need to know how to clean and gut them yourself but that was where Uncle Peter was the expert. He'd be forever in the pantry plucking chickens, turkeys or cleaning out rabbits and hares. It was his forte. I remember him once cleaning out a really rank smelling old chicken that must have been at pension age. Peter was puffing away on an old pipe at the same time, trying to stop the smell hitting his nose. Peter couldn't have been more than eighteen at the time, probably the same age as that chicken. This was just a way of life to him and to all of us. It was our culture and we were totally oblivious to anything else. Today, some would probably think we were little better than barbarians. But, then again, we'd be just as equally horrified at modern society and their lax and liberal views on crime and how cheap a human life is today. "Swings and roundabouts", as they say in football.

The beach was also our playground but it was filthy, full of sludge, coal, dirt and dirty ponds with stagnant black water. Believe it or not, we'd end up going in those ponds up to our necks and washing off the muck in the sea. It was just a game to us. Today, you'd pay forty quid at some high class beauty parlour for the type of mud baths that we all got for nothing .We'd light giant fires down there to keep warm, and collect loads of winkles near the rocks. There was a sewer pipe that ran out into the sea and we'd often be round there crabbing. Looking back, it was a positive health risk and today it would be the nearest thing to a toxic waste dump that you'd get. It was a hell hole, but good enough for miners and their families. And yet, nearby to the south was beautiful Crimdon Dene, where beaches were a lot cleaner than either Easington, Horden and Blackhall .That was because the tides didn't carry the volume of coal and stones down that far. During the summer months, miners and their families used to take their holidays down at Crimdon, either weekends, days or for the week. There'd be sometimes 30,000 there over the weekend, and there'd be all kinds of attractions for them; fairgrounds, pavilion cafes and deckchairs all over the crowded beach and the dene. It was a favourite beauty spot for all living on the coast, and there would be bus queues about fifty yards long in both directions taking people there and back home again. There was even a Miss Crimdon Dene Beauty Queen annual event although that would be banned today.

We even had a dead whale once washed up on the beach at Easington, and it was there for days. No rescue missions or anything back then. It was a dead whale and it wasn't going anywhere. Besides, it was only Easington, so what was the problem? I think it just slowly disappeared as one or two of the more ghoulish bystanders cut bits of its skin away for souvenirs over the next few days. They probably flogged them round the doors as genuine leather doormats. The seagulls did the rest and must have really dined out big style for the next few weeks until eventually a high tide did the rest.

When we felt old enough to venture out of our own little universe, there was the local train station at Easington. This was closed in 1963, but before that we used to get the train up to Sunderland for the match or just go up that way to visit relatives. There were loads of these little railway stations dotted all over Durham. Today, they have all been converted into walkways and cycle ways. On boring Sunday afternoons we used to go down to the station and see the odd steam train come belting through or even better, stand over a bridge and get covered in that lovely smell of soot and steamed water that totally engulfed you. Today it would cost you a tenner at some outdoor railway fair to repeat that experience. The station was a lifeline to the colliery and others too. When I was a baby my nan and mam would often take me up to Sunderland in the pram, with a couple of sacks of coal tucked underneath for my great granddad who lived in Sunderland.

You never realise the sacrifices people make until years afterwards. My nan worked hard all her life and died only 62. As far as I can remember, she only ever had one real holiday away in her life. She had a week away in Great Yarmouth and I saw her off from Easington heading southwards. I thought it was the end of the world when she waved us goodbye. It was only a week, but I suppose a week then was an eternity, especially when each day was packed so full of living and things to do that even 24 hours seemed to last forever.

One of the reasons we never really saw much of our dads, and granddads for that matter, was because they were always out at work during the day - and for long hours too. So by the time they got home you were always flat out in bed. And then on a weekend when they maybe had the odd day that they weren't working, they'd be off relaxing somewhere. In my granddad's case it was down The Trust next to the railway. My granddad again - just like my nan - had a hard life, and all those years he worked seriously damaged his health. He died very young, aged 65, in 1969. He always looked much older than that to me. Seeing him, just before his funeral, made me think what a shame it all was and how his life had been cut short working in such a place. If the pits were all still open today would today's generation of 16 plus youths honestly want to work in them? They would have to drag them screaming down there.

I used to envy my dad when he told me stories about football in the fifties. Between my birth in 1951 and 1958 these were probably the last great years for Sunderland. I was around, of course, but way too young to either remember or be a part of it. Sunderland could have even won the First Division not long after I came into the world, but chucked it away right at the very end of the season losing to bottom of the league Manchester City. In 1955 there could have been the first ever North East FA Cup Final between Newcastle and Sunderland, but Sunderland lost again in the semis. And finally, when the Bank of England club did get it right by doing what they had to do on the last day of the season in 1958 to avoid relegation - win at Portsmouth - they did, but it was all to no avail. They were still relegated for the first time in their history. I never did get to see the great Sunderland players of that era Len Shackleton, Trevor Ford, Billy Elliott, Charlie Fleming, Don Revie and Billy Bingham. And because I missed them all, that was why I was so keen years later to make it my business to find out about the stars of the past, not only from Sunderland but other sides too. Why deny, forget or overlook the greatness of a player from another generation just because you never saw them play? It wasn't your fault you weren't there to see them, but to avoid finding out how good they were with just a little bit of research, then I think missing out on that is definitely your fault.

Whether, you've missed it by five years or fifty years doesn't matter. You owe it to yourself, and to their memory, to see what they were like. I do recall a special bit of my past, aged about five or six, and sitting at the top of Camp Street one Saturday night watching the world go by - my world, anyway. I saw the man who used to sell the local Football Echo at the far end of the street. I can still hear that loud shout of his over and over again: "Football Ech-eee-oooo!" and the queues he used to draw.

We didn't see too much of adults in our wild growing up days but they were never far away. Some days, down the beach banks, you'd see gangs of miners gambling. I didn't know this at the time but my granddad told me that they were often chased by the odd bobby. This outdoor gambling was illegal and there were big stakes involved then. My mam even told me he used to hide his winnings inside one of my old teddy bears, just for safe keeping. We often used to camp out over in the field opposite where he drank, at The Trust, and watch him slope off back up the bank to home.

Easington wasn't a very big colliery, maybe at the time an 8,000 population, but that pub used to be packed out every night of the week. It was the same for the working men's clubs, and you'd see queues of maybe 30 or 40 people, nightly, catching buses all over the colliery towards various watering holes. I imagine that this would have been the same in every pit village round about that time.

Weekends, during the summer, there were no distractions such as football, and that saw us all at the Saturday morning pictures where the poor manager must have been demented trying to control a packed house full of midgets. At the end, we'd all pour out with raincoats or coats over our heads, pretending to be Zorro or the Lone Ranger. The Annual Easington Carnival saw the streets packed from the bottom end of Easington all the way up Seaside Lane. There were loads and loads of girls' Jazz Bands then - now almost extinct - and parades that went on for what seemed one end of the colliery to the other. I can even recall one year my aunt Margaret, my mam's youngest sister, winning first prize as tennis player Maria Bueno. She got the lovely brown skin colour by coating herself with watered down coffee applied with a paint brush on her legs and arms. Stylish, or what?

There was also the Durham Miners Gala every July, when collieries all over County Durham emptied and made their way through to Durham City, complete with their individual Miner's Lodge banners. It's still going today but it's more like a remembrance service to commemorate the great days now gone, along with all of the pits.

Easington even had its own swimming pool in the very late 50s and early 60s. I vaguely remember going there with my Uncle Joe and one of his mates. It was an outdoor pool and the water was freezing. It relied on volunteers to stay open and, sadly, it didn't last long. If anything the water was warmer in the North Sea. Had Easington been in the South of France and we had their weather it might have been a runner and lasted longer. That sounds like an excuse that Ron Atkinson might have used once to describe a narrow 5-0 defeat for Sheffield Wednesday when he managed them.

There is so much going on in anybody's childhood up to the age of eleven that it becomes an impossible task to record every little detail of it. I even forgot our dog Sandy, who died on the beach banks at Easington, when he chased a seagull over the edge of the cliff tops. Or one miserable Christmas where my dad was not only laid off from his job, but was also fined £8 - a fortune then - for not having both his feet on the road whilst waiting in traffic on his 50cc motor cycle. He was spotted by some policeman on Christmas Eve, of all nights. He and my mam were absolutely devastated that anybody could be so petty when he was already on his way home to deliver the bad news about his job. Some things never change, do they? I bet that policeman was really proud of himself in his warm office afterwards.

Other events happened elsewhere that didn't register with me at the time, but made a lasting impression on me in later life when I read about them.

Roger Bannister's four minute mile in 1954, the World Cups of 1954 and 1958, Munich, the death of Buddy Holly in 1959, Spurs' double team of 1961 (and they won the league the year I was born, too). Telstar in 1961 and in the same year, Yuri Gagarin orbiting the earth - and I saw it from the playground of Acre Rigg School in Peterlee.

Although some collieries and surrounding areas to an outsider then might well have been the equivalent of Dante's Inferno, belching out their smoke, fire and soot, they weren't to me. To a young boy it was a magic place to grow up. We had everything we needed. Plenty of fresh air, the fields all around us, the railway line for easy escape north and south. We even had our own private cheap transport provided we could get four pram wheels, a bolt and some wood, We had the beach where we could cool off in the summers, the coal fires where we could get warm in the winters, the allotments where we could pick our own fruit and vegetables, and also help family members collect everything they needed for the Sunday dinner table (fresh chicken, plucked and cleaned by our own in-house gourmet Uncle Peter). If you liked seafood, there were boiled winkles, and even mackerel from the fishermen who had cabins and their boats kept down the beach.There were local denes and woods where you could lose yourself, nearby beaches such as Roker, Seaburn and Crimdon with golden sand on them, farms where you could escape to the country for the day, Saturday morning pictures where you could pretend to be John Wayne or Zorro, back streets where you could really hone up on your football skills and cricket and tennis skills too. From the top of the pit wall on a clear day you could see all the way as far as East Yorkshire, maybe 40 miles away. And on really red hot days, if you ignored the coal wagons, smoky chimneys and mucky beaches, you could thank your lucky stars you weren't one of those townies stuck in a clean, but soulless, unfriendly, overcrowded place where you had to pay a fortune for what we all had for nothing.

How I would miss it all when my father decided to make a better life for the family and move to a place called Southall in West London.

CHAPTER 5
SUPPORT YOUR LOCAL TEAM

At the end of 1962 I was still enjoying growing up in Easington Colliery, in between flitting back to my real home with my parents, in Peterlee which looked out over green fields stretching for miles, and a lane that led all the way up to Shotton Colliery in the distance. You can still see it today, if it wasn't for the houses, factories and flyover in between.

I was frantically swatting like mad for the forthcoming eleven plus exams, an education system mapping out an entire life for a youngster after they left junior school. Recalling it now, it was a form of child cruelty disguised as part of the Government's Education Bill. The stakes were high. Pass the exam and you'd automatically be selected for a new fangled Grammar School system that was then all the rage. Fail and you ended up in a Secondary School. I would have caused ructions if I'd been a parent back then. To put so much pressure on an eleven year old was unfair. Basically it was a case of a doting parent saying to their offspring as they set off for this test: "Screw this up and it could ruin the rest of your life - see you tonight." Anyway, I passed. I spent many hours and long weekends studying and looking through a 12 volume set of Encyclopaedia Britannica my dad bought from one of those door to door salesmen. The bloke flogging them must have waited till my mam was out when he knocked at the door. My dad was such a lovely bloke he couldn't say no to anybody. It cost us exactly £38 for the twelve volume set and I remember my mother went crackers when she found out. That was the best £38 my dad ever spent even though I must have been about 20 before he'd paid off the last instalment on them. Those books were a godsend and took me right round the world in exploring history, geography, science, inventions and sport - all without leaving the kitchen table.

I still remember going along to take this 11 plus. An old bus picked us all up on a freezing cold morning. I wasn't sure whether I was trembling with the cold or the uncertainty that lay ahead. When we got there, there must have been over a hundred of us, all nervous and sitting in a huge cold hall. And then the exams began. We were there all day because I vaguely recall having to neck down this awful tapioca pudding, and then it was back into the main hall and a case of "seconds out, round two". Meanwhile, a strict looking teacher walked up and down the line, scrutinising your every move. It was like one of those films where the chain gang's working flat out in the midday sun, while the warden with dark glasses on, surveys all the convicts at the same time, his trigger finger just itching to draw. You'd only have had to look up in that hall and yell: "I'm working, boss, I'm working" to complete the picture. And then it was over and everyone back on the bus. After that it was the waiting game and the letter on the mat with the results - and the feeling of immense pride my mam and dad had when they read I'd got through. Dad must have felt vindicated that day that the first three of the 120 instalments paid on the Encyclopaedias was already paying dividends.

The nearest Grammar School to us at the time was in Hartlepool, a Catholic school run by monks. I thought that Hartlepool was the end of the world; some footballers today still think it is. It might as well have been the other end of the planet as far as I was concerned. Nine miles to be precise, but at a time when everything was on the doorstep and within walking distance, it was a fair old hike all the same. Today it would be a doddle with mammy or daddy taking you there in the Land Rover, dropping you off with your packed lunch, complete with your easy to read guide in fifteen different languages on how to eat five pieces of fresh fruit per day. No such luck back then. On the winter mornings, or any cold morning really, it was an ordeal which involved two bus rides. I was still in short trousers at the time, everybody was when they were ten or eleven, and it was freezing having to walk the near half mile from our house to the nearest bus stop. From there, you got off at the Bus Station in Hartlepool where you then completed the expedition by catching another bus all the way to the top end of the town. The bus pass was free but it would have added insult to injury if I'd had to pay to get there as well. There were about five of us from the outlying districts making that journey every day, so it wasn't that bad. I always think that misery is so much easier to bear when it's shared as a group. At first I thought it strange being taught by men of the cloth, and I quickly realised that these feelings would pass. Sure enough they did. After three short months I no longer thought it was strange being taught by these hooded teachers. I knew with absolute certainty it was.

There are others out there right now (I still pass by one or two of them today with that shell-shocked look in their eyes) who will testify that some of these Monks were religious zealots with a mean streak. They were the Catholic version of a cross between the Spanish Inquisition and the Taliban. At times, some of the lessons were like psychological warfare as they had their own certain way of getting their point across. The school did have, though, a pretty nifty reputation for sports and round that time I was developing into quite a useful footballer, even though I do say so myself. I was only about six stone wet through then and having to eat loads of Virol - then all the rage for most kids who were still suffering from post war rationing - to try and fatten me up. It didn't work. You'd have seen more fat on a greasy chip.

Whenever I saw football matches at the local playing fields or on the telly (although football on TV was still very limited) I always liked the way that the wingers played. They were the ones in my mind who made it all happen. I didn't go in for all of this midfield dynamo nonsense, with all the closing down, creative pushing up, or running off the ball, and all that tosh. No, keep it simple. Give the ball out wide to either wing, right or left, down to the bye line and then whip it in for some big meat head to bang it home. It's still the most effective method even today and the most exciting. I have to laugh when these creative deep thinking teams and their managers who profess to play it the right way are 1-0 down with three minutes to go and what do they do? That's right, they hoof it into the box, and you get three minutes of marvellous mayhem as they search for the equaliser. Great stuff, but why wait till it's too late to try that tactic?

Playing out wide was for me alright and I liked the idea of plenty of space. I even managed to break into one of the Colts sides. You would describe me as an old fashioned right winger. I was so fast that I could catch pigeons, and used to head for the line and whip that ball in without thinking time after time. I used to practice for hours just crossing a ball against the Colliery houses gable ends so that it would hit the same spot time after time, and the ball would always come back to me, just daring me to do it again. I'd do this until I was usually chased by the people who lived in whatever gable end the ball was thumping against. I would have been worth a fortune today if all the others who did actually make it big didn't all grow up to be much better than I ever was.

We were doing well quite well in our league and were third only two points off top spot (two points then for a win). We all thought we were even going to win the league, especially as our last two fixtures were both against sides in the bottom three of the table. You know what thought does, don't you? That

Wednesday afternoon, we bombarded the first of our pushover opponents from the very start. If it had been a boxing match they would have thrown the white towel on after ten minutes. The big lump we had playing up front for us missed two sitters in the first five minutes that were put on a plate for him. The first landed at his feet only three yards out. With the whole goal to aim at, he nearly took the keeper's head off trying to blast the ball in. Jimmy Greaves would have had palpitations watching. A gentle tap in and we'd have been 1-0 up. The second was even worse. This time he missed the goal by a mile, but as a consolation, would at least have scored three points on the rugby field next door. Our opponents, and I can't even remember their name, must have come for the point. We didn't really need a goalkeeper. They had two shots all game, the first a penalty that never was. I think the ref felt so sorry for them that he thought he'd let them have a free shot at our goal. Even then, this little lad who took it - he was even smaller than I was - feebly shot straight at our keeper who tried to be flash and thought he could kick the ball away. He somehow contrived to smash it straight off the post and in. The second goal was going wide until it hit someone's backside and crawled in, completely sending our keeper the wrong way. We scored about a minute off the end and, even then, nearly got a draw. And how many times have you heard this one, but if that goal had come five minutes earlier we would have beaten them. And so we lost.

I've seen loads of games like that down the years in all four divisions of the league, and even non league too. And the thing is, whether you are playing or supporting, there's nothing you can do about it. Where do you think all these cup giant-killers came from down the years? We blamed the ref, couldn't blame the linesmen because there weren't any, we even blamed their good luck, but we should have blamed ourselves. Even at eleven years old it was a valuable lesson in what happens when you don't do a job properly. Also, how football is a lot about luck as well. Well, so much for the title, but little did we all know it as we crawled off that all of us hadn't heard the end of this. We'd committed the unforgivable sin of losing 2-1 to the bottom of the league side. I'm sure our manager on the touchline thought we'd done it on purpose. Although he was in a habit, he wasn't in the habit of losing to such a weak side. There was no brotherly love that afternoon. We thought no more about it until we were all publicly humiliated at assembly the next morning. And worse was to follow.

Our PE Teacher, who was also our football manager/coach, devised a particularly fiendish way of improving our self discipline. Hands outstretched, we had to exercise our wrists by flexing them back and forth, back and forth in a circular motion that lasted all of five minutes .After this amount of time, our arms were aching, and our wrists were fast losing the will to live. Try it yourself and relive that golden experience of a 1960s Grammar School fitness programme. One or two of the lads must have gone home unable to eat their dinner that night - there was no sensation in either hand for a long while - and they wouldn't have been able to hold on to their fork at teatime. I remember one angry father coming up to the school to remonstrate with this sadist hoodie. There was also another monk (what am I saying? They were all monks) who had a penchant for throwing chalk at you if you pronounced your French words wrongly. We all became quite adept at dodging this dusty flying missile, but I thought it would only be a matter of time before his aim improved as our pronunciations got worse, and he'd eventually hit one of us. I mentioned it casually one night to my mam and dad. My mother was down there like greased lightning and blasted both him and the head monk, Rasputin.

Things calmed down for a while after that, but never really changed. It must have been in their blood, or maybe there was something in the water. These whirling dervishers were forever thrashing some poor little victim within an inch of ecstasy. The psychological damage it must have done to some of them was nobody's business. I bet half of those kids ended up as MPs in later life, or Senior Civil Servants. One lad was even dragged in front of the Ayatollah because a member of the public on a bus ride home one night heard him slagging off one of the monks. Luckily for me, my stay at the school was very short as we were on the move down South. I will say one thing for that school though. They instilled within you a sense of self discipline and self determination. "You can fool anybody, but you can't fool yourself" would probably have been their motto, no doubt on a background of two flashing canes and an outstretched hand. I did learn a great deal when I was there too. My Latin ten times table for starters. But I can't help wondering whether those monks had missed a trick. Had they used a lot more carrot and a lot less stick, they would have had a lot more happier disciples on their hands.

We often had swimming lessons down at Seaton Carew on the seafront, very near the spot today where that bloke went sailing his canoe, got lost when he forgot to turn right at Germany, and ended up in Panama. There used to be a public swimming baths down there, the only one in the area, right next to the beach. They always put far too much chlorine in the water, and your eyes would be red raw and stinging for hours when you came out .There were no leisure centres or anything like that in those days. I suppose they thought as we had beaches there was no real point. We even came all the way from Easington to Seaton Carew to go swimming at weekends or during the school holidays.

We'd often see the sea coal wagons bombing up and down all day and all over these golden beaches. The sea coal men didn't seem to give a jot as they dug up half the beach looking for coal that had been washed ashore all down the coast from the pits to the North. Those wagons they drove were lethal. If you went plodging (sorry, paddling) you had to dive out the way from some of them. They were on a mission, and time to them meant money. They had to act and work fast before the tide came back in and so they scuttled like an army of soldier ants, each with his own particular task. One was digging, one shovelling, one piling the coal up, the other one directing and one of them was in charge of the choreography. It was impressive to watch. Some of these sea coal lads looked frightening and even Mike Tyson would have crossed the road to avoid them. The meanest of them were a cross between grizzled old Western Pioneers you'd see looking for gold and dragging mules, and those Orcs you've seen on "Lord of the Rings". We'd also see, but didn't take that much notice of them then, these footballers on the beach when the tide was out. My friend Steven Kilkenny reckoned it was the Hartlepool team practicing there, as the ground wasn't that far away. I didn't believe him as he was always making stuff up but, come to think of it, maybe he was right. Pools were really struggling back then and the current side are almost like Barcelona by comparison. One old boy, walking by with his dog, and who obviously watched Pools getting battered week after week, spotted them as the tide was about to turn and yelled out "Stop out there and do us all a favour".

The whole area around that part of Hartlepool and, virtually on the sea front, was a hive of industrial activity, just like huge swathes of the North East were then. As far as the eye could see, there was a huge complex of huge grey, incredibly noisy buildings, belching out thick columns of smoke, and a strong pungent smell that used to linger for hours. You'd hear whistles, the noise of machinery roaring, men yelling from inside these buildings, and a never ending din that went on from early morning to late at night. These buildings looked menacing and intimidating, and there must have been thousands working along there at these various ICI and local steel works plants. Today, they are all lovely covered fields with the odd smattering of housing, a nice place to take your dog for a walk.

Even the town of Hartlepool itself has been transformed down the years to such an extent that they even had the Tall Ships Race recently. Today, the Marina and surrounding area look like the south of France, apart from the bitingly cold North East wind whistling in off the sea. The rest of the town too looks positively upmarket, even though there are one or two areas that could do with a few quid spent on them. They are still waiting for the local council to decide what to do about the old Odeon Cinema. Alternative uses and suggestions are many, although if I were a betting man my money would be on a giant ball and chain for starters. There are still pockets of one or two back streets that are just so 19th Century, darlings. Apart from that, I have to admit the town is a million years away from the one I scuttled through on the way to that school for scoundrels, run by even bigger scoundrels. No wonder so many people from down South are moving up to the area. Keep it a secret though, as we don't want the whole of them landing overnight on the doorstep when they realise how good it is. By the way, if Hartlepool Tourist Board is reading this, I've just done your job for you.

That cold, draughty 1960s bus into Hartlepool from Peterlee used to go past the Victoria Ground, Hartlepool's home, daily. To call it a football ground then would be doing a great disservice and an insult to most of the other football league clubs who had grounds in much better condition. You could say they'd even have had grounds for complaint if you even suggested that theirs was the same as Hartlepool. Even then, as I caught the odd daily glimpse out of the window, I wondered what it looked like in there watching a match.

I had already been to see Sunderland play the year before, but just fancied the idea of watching someone else in the league. How silly of me to think that the experience would be anywhere near the first time I walked into Roker Park. But for me, it was simply a case of wanting to see my other local side, just watching somebody different. In later times, and all through my life to today, I've continued to go to matches there. It makes a real change, and a pleasant one sometimes (but not often) to watch what is now being called "real" football. By that, I mean "real" grassroots or traditional. In other words, what it must have been like years ago before the game became obsessed with greed and selfishness. Back then, though, watching Pools was very much unreal as I'm sure that bloke called Jeff Stelling will tell you.

It's hard for people to imagine but there are those who are totally obsessed with supporting sides like Hartlepool. I used to know years back a lad called Alan Stevenson. He was an ex-squaddie, raised in Plymouth by his dad who went to work in Devon many years ago. Young Alan was brought up watching Argyle but never really took to them. When his father returned home to Durham when Alan was 15, his dad took him to Roker Park thinking his son would soon feel the same way about Sunderland as he did. There was no reaction, nothing, not a sausage. It was Plymouth Argyle all over again. However, a week later, when young Alan and a neighbour went to watch Hartlepool in a Fourth Division bottom of the table clash against Rochdale in front of less than 2,000, he was hooked. It was all to do, as he told me, with that feeling of personal belonging, seeing players that he could virtually reach out and touch when they got a corner (or in Pools case, touching the home keeper every time he retrieved the ball from the back of the net). Even just to hear players shouting and swearing. It was like, he said, as if you were on the pitch and in amongst them. Never mind the small crowd. When Alan first stood in amongst the chosen few, by his own admission, he thought he'd found his own football heaven. He felt he belonged and had finally come home. It was also a strange feeling, he thought, watching a side that were in the Football League, but were so bad that you almost felt like they were outlaws from it.

Alan spent a fortune watching them home and away and could even tell you the name of the eleven who lost 4-2 at wherever it was on the last day of the 1989/90 season. One Friday night well over 20 years back, Hartlepool had a long away trip to Torquay. They travelled down to Devon early on the Friday morning, and as there were only seven supporters also travelling, the story goes that they allegedly hitched a ride on the team bus. A tale direct from Alan which I suppose would have made sense. After all, why pay to hire a separate bus when the team coach would presumably have had empty seats anyway, and who's to say those supporters just gave the bus driver their petrol money as a way of thanking him. I don't know if this was a flight of fancy by Alan, the hand me down football tale that you hear third hand from a friend of a friend, but that's what happened. After about an 8 hour journey down there and a quick stretch of the legs, by players and fans alike, it was time for the match and not surprisingly, after that slog, Pools were beaten soundly. The funniest thing, and one that made the journey there and back even more enjoyable (enjoyable?) for Alan and his mates, was that at the game itself, the seven of them who stood behind the goal segregated from Torquay fans, had the same number of police guarding them. "Imagine that" said Alan, "Our own personal individual police escort. What an honour. We felt like celebrities". I lost touch with Alan long ago and the last I heard he was working abroad. Wherever he is, you can bet that he'll be trawling the network looking for anything and everything surrounding his beloved Pools. Alan, real fans everywhere - including me - salute you.

Even Alan wasn't around when I first set foot in the old Victoria Ground. Just as well. He would probably have turned tail and fled back down Devon, offering apologies and a life-long allegiance to Plymouth Argyle when he got there. The ground from the outside was like something that had been lost in time for decades, neglected beyond belief. That's paying it a compliment. The surroundings and environment would have made Soweto look like Las Vegas.

The Victoria Ground then was a tip, and the four sides were basically corrugated sheets welded together. As an advert, not only for the club but also the town itself, they might as well have put up a huge sign outside saying: "Abandon hope, all ye who enter here". This would have been around 4BC (Before Clough). Hartlepool had always been the laughing stock of the League, although if you were a Pools fan then it was certainly no joke. The ground had not changed much since the 1920s. That's forty years of doing nothing, other than to watch it disintegrate even further, or maybe give the rust the odd lick of paint every close season. There was that much rust in some places, that wayward shots didn't clear the tin fences, sometimes they went through them. It's a good job they had nothing but bad luck, otherwise they would have had no luck at all (that's an old Blues song, isn't it?).

During the First World War the Main Stand (giant portakabin would be a more apt description) was hit by a bomb from a German Zeppelin heading out to sea. Hartlepool was one of the first places in Britain to suffer fatalities in the First World War when its Headland was bombed by German ships. An outraged Hartlepools Board wrote strong letters of complaint and sought compensation from the German Government. They asked for over £2,000 but fifty quid would probably have covered it, and heard nothing further. To add insult to injury, the same stand was hit by another bomb in the Second World War. Of course, by this time, Pools were getting used to it and decided not to waste any more stamps or paper writing further to those nasty Germans. So before and after two World Wars, that stand was still there in some form or other. That's what I saw when I rode by on the bus.

Pools were just one of so many teams that were destined to just drift through football history without any major honours, but looking on the bright side, at least they survived. Gateshead applied for re-election just the once and got the boot. If anything, down the years, Pools have achieved some kind of cult status in certain quarters because of this. They became that bad everyone wanted to see them. I'm surprised the monks from my old school didn't pay them the odd visit, a chance to see somebody even worse than they were. Their legend grew and spilled over down the years. When I worked in Newcastle many years later, I used to tell all my work colleagues that a day out watching them was a real treat. As Ken Dodd joked, it was very educational as it certainly taught a few of them who went a very valuable lesson. There are many teams like Hartlepool in the league who have survived, season after season, against tremendous odds. And we should all praise them. It's so very easy to be ultra-rich and finish in the top three or four, season after season. On the other side of the coin, it's enormously difficult to survive for years with no money and maybe having to throw young kids in,(kids who quickly become men), or players on loan that were drinking at The Last Chance Saloon when they rode into town. Today Hartlepool are a tight, well run outfit. They'll maybe never rise above where they are now, but they'll never end up in liquidation or administration and that's something that they should be rightly proud of. If you ran your home that way, or we had any Government in power that had the courage to run the country the same way, none of us would have sleepless nights wondering where the next penny was coming from. No, Pools were just one of those teams that were just fated to maybe provide the odd few results in a season, the odd cup upset that would make everything worthwhile. And can you imagine the shock of being dumped unceremoniously on your backside after being hammered at Hartlepool? Oh, the shame of it.

There were really bad times that far outweighed the good ones. Pools were that bad some seasons that they regularly used to fall off the football coupon. In the days before relegation to the Conference/Blue Square, when you were confined to oblivion rather than an unofficial Division Five, they must have had some real friends in football all over the place as they successfully applied for re-election over a dozen times. You can imagine some sense of warped honour and victory in achieving that record. "Nobody will ever beat that" you can almost hear some Pools fans gloat. "Not even Manchester United or Arsenal. So stick that in your pipe and smoke it."

.

I always thought that from the moment you are born then your future, or even fate, was already mapped out for you. Maybe that was also the case with Hartlepool. When they did join the league, the town had a strong Rugby Union following. Hartlepool Rovers had been around since 1879 and are still going strong today, and the football club really needed to go some to be able to win over the punters. It was a tall order, almost as impossible as Boyzone headlining at Glastonbury. Pools tried, and admittedly went pretty close, some seasons in the old Third Division North at a time when it was only one club that went up. Otherwise, they could have hit the heady heights of Division Two in 1957. Back then, they might just have been able to survive in the days when there really was a much more level playing field. Unfortunately, fate decreed otherwise. Sad as it may be, Hartlepool just isn't a football town. It just isn't. Of course, if they ever were to do really well they could easily pull in 6,000 plus crowds, but not much more than this in their current position. If they were ever to hit the heady heights of the Championship, they could probably pull in 12,000 for the big games, but probably no more. That would put them on a par with Scunthorpe or Doncaster, both of whom are punching well above their weight. They'd maybe average 8,000 going well, but if they really struggled it would be sub 4,000. That's nowhere near enough for sustainability. A lot of realistic Pools fans know that. For teams like Pools, though, there is always the glorious possibility of "what if?" If Blackpool, glorious Blackpool, can do it, then who knows?

When I went to see my first ever game there with my Uncle Jimmy and cousin Danny, there weren't many there but probably more than they get today. I seem to recollect that it was Southport they were playing, another side that went the way of many in the 1960s onwards. It was easy to compare the size of the crowd when you'd been to see Sunderland. I can't say I was that impressed, and the game couldn't have been much good as young Danny and I went wandering off round the ground. On one end, where the Mill House Stand is today, there was a big uncovered open standing terrace. This was the same basic, bog standard terracing you'd have seen at footy grounds all over the country from about 1920, and a lot earlier in some cases, right through to the 1980s. Only the best then would do for the elegant man about terrace. All you'd need to complete the picture would be spittoons for the fans. It was nowhere near the size of some terraces I was to encounter elsewhere and later down the years, but even then it would probably still easily have held 8,000 comfortably when full. That's more than the current capacity of Victoria Park today.

The pitch on that side of the ground was also a good twenty yards from the spectators. That killed the atmosphere completely but there was a plus side to this. This was handy, I thought, both for the players and spectators, especially when the game was bad and both could be kept the maximum distance away from each other. Maybe this was the original idea when the ground was built, a safety zone if you like, for the players well away from irate supporters foaming at the mouth. Directly opposite this end was the real piece de resistance. It was the wooden stand that I had seen only the top of from the upstairs bus window every day. When I saw it in its full glory for the first time it was jaw-dropping. You couldn't even call it a monstrosity and I just didn't have the words in my vocabulary, then or now, to do it justice. It looked like a wooden lopsided shed maybe 30 yards across with the front missing to expose a few seats on view. Nearly all were empty, but people were actually sitting in some of them. Today you'd need to pull it down to put up an eyesore. The roof looked as if it were made out of old tin cans. Either side of it, along the length of the pitch, was standing for about four rows of spectators. Behind each goal were what looked like two identical elongated bike sheds. One stand, the away end, was so deserted that I wondered if there were a load of kids hiding behind it having a sly smoke. Then there was the wind from the North Sea that could whip in at right or left angles, and came both at you and through you, no matter where you were standing. It was impossible to keep dry in the wet. The rain, not to be outdone by the wind, also hit you sideways and from all other angles. If the ground had been around in Ancient Rome they would have fed the people who built it straight to the lions.

As for the toilets, I couldn't vouch for what the ladies were like (although, to be honest, I don't think I saw any) but the men's comprised a four sided brick wall with an opening to get in -and quickly out - plus loads of scattered ashes (burnt season tickets?) where you could pee into. These toilets looked like recycled bomb shelters with no roofs on.There might have been proper loos elsewhere in the ground but I never noticed them. The game has come a long way since then. Even now, though, whenever I go to any toilet at half time in any ground, I nearly always end up in the queue behind the fans who've had about 14 pints each.

I always watched out for Hartlepool's scores after that, both on the telly and radio. There were some crazy results in those early days when dad used to get both the Football Echo and Hartlepool Football Mail every Saturday night. The Football Mail is sadly no more and gone the way of so many Saturday football papers. I recall Pools beating Barrow 10-1 in the very late 1950s and then losing by the same score at Wrexham in the early sixties. A certain Wyn Davies, later to be a cult figure at Newcastle, helped himself to four that day. You used to get some big scores generally then. One particular Christmas in the old First Division, Fulham beat Ipswich 10-1 and then lost to the same side the following day 4-2. Also over the festive period (not sure if it was the year after) Blackburn lost at home to West Ham 3-2 and then beat them 8-2 away.

My watching Hartlepool has been very sporadic down the years. If they were ever in London, or at home when I was in the North East and Sunderland were playing away, I was always down the Vic. Going there even once every six months was like visiting an old friend who always made you feel at home, no matter how long you'd been away. The only thing they can't do is put the kettle on for you as soon as you set foot in the ground, although their pies are still the cheapest I've ever come across. In the words of one of The Eagles' old songs; "I get a warm, easy feeling". They were, and still are, my second favourite team.

Just call me the Good Samaritan for giving them my money down the years. As an added treat, I'll sometimes drag one or both of my lads along, too. I think a lot of fans have that same kind of affinity to teams in their local area. I once worked with a lad who followed Bolton one week, and then went to Bury the next. It also broadens the mind seeing football at different levels of the League, as well as, more importantly, helping the lower league side with the extra gate money. If you haven't done it, do it today because that one extra person at the gate can make all the difference between survival or extinction. Drag a mate along, too. I've also seen some cracking games in the lower leagues. I've often been to Premier League games that were awful and then had my spirits raised a week later watching a seven goal thriller at Hartlepool. You never know what you might miss. A lot of supporters of sides in the Premier should think the same way and "adopt" a lower league side in this way. Just think what that extra revenue might bring them. Survival for starters.

I recall one really bad winter in 1967, my Uncle Timmy, me, plus a couple of his mates drove up to Newcastle for a derby match with Sunderland. Unfortunately it was called off just as we were walking to St. James' Park. We made our way back home, and then realised there was a match on at Hartlepool, a derby game against Darlington. Could we make it in time? We did, with minutes to spare and managed to squeeze in to the Mill House End. There were nearly 15,000 there that day and I bet a good 4,000 of them, maybe more, were Sunderland fans who must have gone there at the last minute, just like us (and maybe even a few for the first time too). It was a cracking game that ended in a 1-1 draw.

I was also lucky enough to see a couple of games during the Brian Clough era when he first came to Hartlepool. You sensed that there was something stirring in the air. That team then were playing with that little bit of extra confidence and an arrogant strut. To me, I thought that they were a bit cocky but I see now, in retrospect, that it was the first signs of the magic of Cloughie and his assistant Peter Taylor rubbing off on them. They always played well for Clough. They had to. Otherwise, as he also drove the team bus, he'd leave them behind. He was never ever going to stay at Hartlepool, that much was obvious, although I thought when he did move on to bigger and better things with Derby, Sunderland should have took a punt on him. In fact, Sunderland should never have let him leave in the first place. They could have given him some sort of coaching role and then, maybe, realised a year or two later that they had struck gold, just as Hartlepool did. I often wonder what would have happened if Sunderland got to him before he later began his happy wandering round the East Midlands with both Derby and Forest. I also bet there are a few thousand other Sunderland, Leeds and England fans thinking what he would have done for their fortunes as well. We'll never know and, instead, I'll just have to content myself in remembering how he was, as a player and manager

- confident, brash, cocky, and arrogant, but most important, supremely successful.

I also saw two players back then passing through onto bigger and better things. One was a gawky looking 16 year old called John McGovern, who the crowd used to give some real stick to, until he settled in and won them all over. That showed his courage. He was little more than a school kid but never ever gave up. He had energy to burn and used to run and run like one of those Duracell Bunnies. And then, in goal, there was Les Green, not flashy or arrogant or even that tall, just a really confident keeper who didn't know when he was beaten, and inspired defenders around him to play even better. If you had eleven of the likes of McGovern and Green in your side you'd really go places. And both of them did when they followed Clough and Taylor to Derby. Pools finished that season seventh off top, great for them considering their previous years of struggle. Clough had already left the next season when they were promoted with the nucleus of the side he and Taylor built, and they used to get some pretty healthy crowds as they charged towards the Third Division. There was one match against Swansea where there were over 11,000 in and what a racket they made. Who is to say it couldn't happen again?

Pools had some good players in those early years, too. One or two in the really early sixties came from just up the road at Sunderland. Willie McPheat, a big bustling forward who was never the same player at Roker after breaking his leg, and who scored his most famous goal in a 1-1 cup draw against mighty Spurs in 1961. He should never have joined Pools. Maybe after such a bad injury, it's always on your mind that it could happen again. I've seen plenty of players down the years that just don't seem the same when they've come back after a bad injury. They don't charge in with that reckless abandon they used to do before. This makes all the difference between just winning, or just losing a ball, and makes all the difference between even playing for Liverpool or Hartlepool. Ambrose Fogarty, a majestic Eire international forward, was Pools' record signing at £5,000 when he joined from Sunderland and the first time Hartlepool ever had a full international on their books. Sadly, the cut and dash of then Fourth Division football was not to Ambrose's style and the fans didn't see the best of him. He was one of those players-I think I saw him only twice at Sunderland- who thrived on better players around him. Fine when you were with a relatively skilful side, but Hartlepool at that time? Not a chance. Other players in the sixties that made their mark on me were Tony Parry and a big bull of a Welsh centre forward called Ernie Phythian, whose goals helped Hartlepool out of the wilderness to the Promised Land of the Third Division in 1968. The Promised Land wasn't all that it was cracked up to be, though, and Pools quickly made their way back to their spiritual home where they had resided in for so many years. That's better than saying they came straight back down, isn't it? There was also a Pools player, who must have gone from the scene by the time the sixties dawned, called Kenny Johnson. He had the rugged good looks of a film star. Anybody who wore a shirt and tie then looked like a film star to us street urchins.

Pools have had a few good players from both the North East's big two down the years. Ex-Sunderland cup winners Bobby Kerr and Dickie Malone both plyed their trade there in the twilight of their careers. There was even Peter Beardsley turning out at one stage, and even then he was capable of playing at a much higher level. One man who came from Newcastle United to Pools thinking his career was on the wane did end up going back up the leagues again. Joe Allon, Pools' very own Denis Law, rattled them in for fun as they once again stormed to promotion in 1991. Not long after, Chelsea came knocking and of course, Joe was off. He made quite an early impact at Stamford Bridge but the jump was the proverbial bridge too far for him. Not so, though, for one of the great forwards who turned out for Pools, Keith Houchen. He was an easy on the eye striker who was always in the right place at the right time, a bit like a taller version of Jimmy Greaves, the way he could sniff out a goal. Houchen went on to Coventry, where he scored that great winner in the 1987 FA Cup final against Spurs with a diving header. I don't know what all the fuss was about when they all praised it to the high heavens. He used to put them in like that at Pools on a regular basis. And as for Andy Linighan, just ask Arsenal fans. In the late 1970s, there was a big brute of a centre forward called Bob Newton who led the line. When the going got tough, Bob got going. He was always in the thick of it and if you'd fought in the trenches with this bloke you'd have followed him anywhere. He led by example, but sometimes had a bit of a short fuse and often went off on one. I'd liken him to a simmering assassin who, but for his temperament could have gone on to a much higher level.

Pools have nearly always had trouble attracting big crowds to the Vic, but when they have been on the verge of greatness - and by greatness in their case I mean looking like they could mount a challenge for promotion - the crowds have always come out. When Chris Hurley, brother of the famous Charlie Hurley of Sunderland, turned out for Millwall in 1965 in a Fourth Division match, nearly 11,000 turned out (I wonder how many were Sunderland fans?) and through the 70s to the 90s, when Hartlepool had the habit of claiming famous cup scalps (Derby County and Palace twice were both binned at the Vic) 9,000 plus were there. 16,000 rolled along to see Leeds but unfortunately they hadn't read the script. Poor Hartlepool got absolutely battered 6-2.

As current capacity is only just over 7,500, those days are long behind them but maybe, just maybe, in the future, if local teams start having to produce local players to survive -and Pools do produce some fairly good youth players - then there could be a surge to the Championship. I've got a feeling, though, that they'll never come as close again to the Championship as they did in 2005 in the play off final against Sheffield Wednesday at Cardiff. 2-1 up and only eight minutes to go, Nirvana in sight, then a man sent off, and a 4-2 defeat in extra time. Still, if they had gone up it would probably have been a really quick return. Pools' biggest game in their history? I think so, in terms of the stakes on offer.

There have been one or two others that have got the pulses racing. Older fans will point you towards the 4-3 defeat in the cup in 1957 to Manchester United, but coming a lot more up to date there was an intriguing game against Sunderland in the cup at the Stadium of Light in 2004. Obviously, I wanted Sunderland to win but if they tripped up, and they usually did when they were favourites, then I couldn't think of a better team to beat them than Pools. There were 41,000 there that day and over 10,000 made the short trip up the road from Hartlepool. Although Sunderland won 1-0, Pools were far from disgraced and made a real fight of it and in the second half it looked like they might even equalise. But it just wasn't meant to be.

One thing about Pools is that they are just like Forrest Gump's box of chocolates. You never know what you're going to get inside. It also shows the sometimes fleeting fame and fickleness of the Football League. No team, no matter who they are or what their status, should ever take their position for granted. I've seen many fallen giants down the Vic in recent years where you've thought to yourself: "What on earth are this lot doing here?" Last season it was Charlton Athletic, Southampton, Norwich and Leeds, sides who, not that long ago, were rolling Sunderland and Newcastle over with ease. In previous years it's been Derby, Burnley, Forest, Wolves, Fulham, Leicester, Sheffield United and Wednesday, West Bromwich and Blackpool. All once First Division greats who never dreamt they'd sink so low. Some of them have managed to claw their way back or are not far off it. There's a word of warning there to others about never taking life at the top for granted. If you don't watch your step, then see you soon at Pools.

What of Victoria Park today? The ground is set in plush, almost comparatively palatial surroundings. There's a Marina on one side, and a new town centre with shops and retail outlets in close proximity. The renamed and re-branded Victoria Park, with its still old fashioned floodlight pylons, is now a smart, functional ground with room for 7,500, more than big enough for the time being and, probably, for a long time to come. I hope I'm wrong. There are now covered stands at all four ends of the ground. There's the compact all-seater stand where once stood the main stand of years gone by. The Mill House terracing is still there but now there's some comfortable seats behind it. There's even a pub imaginatively named "The Corner Flag" near the corner flag on the Mill House side. If you are an away fan, don't be daunted. Those Pools supporters who go in there are real fans, good company, and if you buy them a pint, they'll even tell you how many you are going to win by. The last visit saw a Finnish couple, man and wife, Sheffield Wednesday supporters, approach both me and workmate Michael Oates. Straightaway, the talk was all things football and the half hour flew by quickly. I'm pleased their journey wasn't wasted as Wednesday won 5-0 in a canter. It was all over bar the laughing after only ten minutes as Wednesday raced into a 2-0 lead. We both bought a pie each at the kick off and that's the only time in my life the pies have lasted longer than the match. That Wednesday fan was also writing a book about FC Jazz, from Finland, so watch out for that one in the shops. It's sure to be a big seller in Hartlepool.

The Bike Sheds have long gone behind the goals. Behind the visitors' end, the old Rink End, there's seats for over 900 away fans (more if you sit on somebody's knee) and at the opposite end, the still terraced and brand new built Town End, where home fans congregate, you'll sometimes find me in amongst the real fans.

Here, even on the worst of days, both weather and performance alike, the banter can still get you through the most miserable of them. Best summed up for me by one moment of mayhem, and there've been many down the years. A classic, where Pools drubbed Notts County 4-0. Towards the end of the game, with Pools four up and the match over, a shattered Adam Boyd, who had been on fire all afternoon, began one last lung-shattering run from the middle of the pitch. He beat one man, then two, then three, in a jinking run and then spotted the keeper not far off his line. He just managed to majestically chip him from 20 yards before being clattered from either side. The ball hit the bar, came down, hit the right hand post then rolled agonisingly back out into play. There then followed a frantic scramble as Boyd, the keeper and two defenders raced to see who could get there first. With one last effort, Boyd was quickest to react and was up from the deck like a rocket, just managing to toe poke it into an empty net before being dumped again by another ferocious tackle. As the crowd already started to shout "goal" the keeper turned, and somehow flung himself backwards, just managing to tip the ball round for a corner. Everybody in the ground, including Boyd himself, was shattered, having watched twenty seconds or so of pure football theatre. We could have all been at the Old Vic, rather than the Vic, so brilliant was this particular play. All were speechless. All that is except one old bloke in front of us who yelled out, in pure frustration, the first thing that came into his head: "Boyd, you are a bloody disgrace!!!" The whole end just collapsed into a sea of laughter at this piece of authentic terrace verbal lunacy. So, too, did Adam Boyd, still lying in a heap about three yards in front of us all, gasping for air. Where else but Hartlepool?

Some things never change, though. On a warm day, always take an even warmer jacket with you. You never know when that wind or rain from our old neighbour, the North Sea, will come creeping in unexpectedly to welcome you to dear old Hartlepool.

CHAPTER 6
THE LONDON YEARS

When my family moved away from Easington to our new life in Southall, West London on 21st December 1962 I was the eldest of three. I was 11, brother Tommy 8, and my sister Margaret only a year old. Isn't it funny how you always think of your parents as really old and knowing everything, not realising, looking back as I do now, that they were still young and probably as nervous and apprehensive as we were. Dad would have been only 34 and my mother 32. I don't think any of us wanted to move to London but my dad had been out of work for a while and when he was offered not only a job, but also a house to go with it, he jumped at the chance. My father's uncle Terry had fixed up a home for us all. It was too good an opportunity to miss. Being on the dole was really like being on the breadline. There was a vast difference in lifestyle then between someone who worked and someone who didn't.

Although the mines could still have been an option for him even at that stage, my dad was one of many who wouldn't have gone anywhere near them, and who could blame him? He was only 22 in May 1951, two months before I was born, and working locally when there was a terrible disaster at Easington Colliery which cost 81 men their lives. They were always dangerous places to work and many would go nowhere near them. Only two of my granddad's five sons, Joe and Peter, worked there. Most pitmen would never want their own sons to work there either. My dad was no different and, besides, even if he had considered it, there was no way my mam would have entertained it. End of the matter!

Try as he might he just couldn't find work anywhere in the local area. Unlike the much more affluent South East, nobody really commuted to work in the

North East then because nobody could afford to. The roads, well before local motorways criss-crossed the region, were that poor that any bus would have taken you an age to get to work, and that defeated the purpose of the object as it would also have been poorly paid in the first place. The main workplace was hard, heavy industrial and back-breaking. You lived and worked locally near the shipyards, steelworks or local colliery.

The journey down to London was an ordeal, leaving at 9pm and arriving at Victoria Coach Station next morning at 7.30. There were no toilets on the bus so heaven help anyone who got on with a full bladder. You'd have to wait two or three hours before a designated stop. Then, next morning, after a virtually sleepless night, there was the walk to the Underground, the District Line to Ealing Broadway and then a train from there to Southall. It was nearly 10.30 am, a long 13 hours later, as we trudged through the snow and freezing cold, arriving at 49 Hartington Road, Southall, Middlesex. The house was cold, uninviting and, to cap it all, the furniture wagon hadn't turned up and wouldn't arrive till later that night. It was stuck in snow somewhere near Doncaster. I think we all wished we could have clicked our fingers and ended up back in Easington.

We were shattered and the three of us slept on two old chairs left behind in the house. It was pretty hard to sleep with the cold and it was a good three hours till a neighbour lent us a bucket of coal and we got the fire going.

Our home was very near to the Paddington/ South West BR line, adjacent to the local gasworks, and also near Heathrow. Wembley was also on our doorstep by bus in that crowded part of West London. When the wagon turned up, delayed even longer because of even more snow, I seem to recall some mattresses quickly being thrown down and we all just slept that first night on the floor. I was desperately sad and already missing home. That feeling was never to go away. My brother Tommy and baby Margaret, maybe because they were younger, found it much easier to adapt. Try as I might, that feeling of intense loneliness,and longing to be elsewhere, never left me.

We were soon settled into a routine of school and work. My new school was at the bottom of our street, Southall Grammar School. Initially it was all-boys and I very quickly made an enemy of a snobby English teacher who seemed to delight in ridiculing my accent from day one. That man, even to an 11 year old, was a disgrace to his profession. He thought it funny to tell the rest of the class that people from the North East lived in caves and still travelled by stagecoach. It was his idea of a joke. I think he took the hump when I said we had things called trains and that they were actually invented in the North East. I even let him know that the world's first and oldest railway line was built there between Stockton and Darlington. Good old dad with that Encyclopaedia Britannica set he bought. I knew they would come in handy. I learnt loads of useful, and useless, information from them.

Just when I thought the novelty had worn thin with him, he was at it again. This time, he had me up in front of the class as I made the cardinal sin of not pronouncing, southern style, "grass" as "grarss" and "glass" as "glarss". He asked if I could even spell the word, and to prove I couldn't, invited me up to the blackboard (or is that chalkboard?) ,gave me the chalk and waited. I remember trying hard not to bite my lip as I wrote three words on the board: Glass, grass, ass and then pronounced them all in a cut glass accent. "Glarss", "grarss" and then, when I got to "ass" I looked directly at him and said "arse". After he'd turned dark purple with rage, and the class had exploded with laughter, I was off to the Headmaster's office to explain my actions and giving cheek to a teacher. Happily, sanity prevailed. The head, Mr. Holroyd (I still remember his name) was from Oldham, and must have seen through what was going on. I still picture him giving me a wry smile when I told him the full story - caves, trains and all - and him telling me to get back to the classroom. Two things happened after the head had a quick chat with our English teacher. Never again did he pick on me, and never again did I give cheek to a teacher. The valuable lesson I learnt from this is that you should always stand up to a bully and, if that fails, "grarss" the coward up without even thinking twice about it. By the way, this advice doesn't work on a football field.

When the boys school later merged with a girls school a year later, I thought I was in dreamland. In our first mixed class, the seating arrangements were boy-girl, boy-girl and I had my first crush on a beautiful red head called Linda Wells. Alas, the feelings weren't reciprocated and I concentrated on my studies, watching and playing footy until I clocked another little smasher called Maureen Newman.

It's strange how the years just roll along very quickly even at that age . You think you have all the time in the world on your hands and, of course, you don't. A year is a year, and passes just as quickly for someone whether they are 16 or 60.The only difference is when you are 16 you still think you have a) loads of years left in front of you and b) that you can live forever. When you are 60 you know that a) you haven't and b) you can't.

My morning and evening newspaper rounds made me a bit of money and also gave me the chance to read all the match reports from each paper. Nobody ever got their papers on time when I did my round.

The summers usually found a whole mob of us walking to the nearby rec. for a game of football that went on from about ten in the morning till six or seven at night. There'd be about 30 of us all land at the same time. It was like a scene from "Gangs of New York" as the Walsh family, the Sheehans, Keays, Marinis, and Lightfoots descended daily for battle. Four jumpers down for goalposts and we were away. We were always joined by assorted strays from other clans who joined the line as the teams were selected. There were always two golden rules. The first rule was the one who owned the ball had first pick of the two sides and the second rule was never upset the one with the ball. Otherwise he'd bugger off home in the huff and the whole day was then a washout. Once the game was underway, teams could be added to or weakened accordingly as some went home and others joined from nowhere. Another rule was that a player entering the fray always had to join the losing team and if he turned out to be any good he'd be swapped for a worse player from the winning side to redress the balance, sometimes a humiliating experience for any young lad who thought he was a budding Bobby Charlton and then quickly realised he wasn't.

It was usually first one to 20 which then became 30 if you lost 20-18. 30 then became 40 if you lost 30-27, and so it went on. There were no obese kids back then - well, maybe the odd one - because it would be impossible not to partake in some sort of physical activity. If you went for a walk on your own through a park then, chances are, someone playing in a mass game of footy would yell across: "Hoy, you, get over here now. You're kicking this way!" And you had to. You couldn't walk, or waddle, away. You had to join in for at least an hour, or else. And, anyway, if you didn't join in you'd still get plenty of exercise as maybe ten or fifteen chased you right round and out of the park. There was compulsory exercise whichever way you turned.

To break the monotony of ten hour games of footy some days (you ached all over next morning), we'd go to the baths. Not the indoor variety but an outdoor swimming pool also in the rec. You'd stay in there all day with your bottle of pop. The pool was unheated and even on a blisteringly hot day you'd half expect polar bears to be in the water. It was freezing but once you'd broken the ice, literally speaking of course, and gritted your teeth for half an hour, you got used to it. Today you'd be fined for child abuse but, back then, we loved it. The secret, again, was that once in the water, you never got out again until closing time. Otherwise you'd have to endure that initial torture all over again.

I don't think anybody went on what we would call real holidays then, especially not abroad. You just didn't need to. We had our very own summer camp for six weeks that involved swimming, cycling, football, sunshine and occasionally the odd girl who'd join our company. We had it all and didn't even realise it.

Sometimes, as a real treat, we'd go up Southall Market during the week where they used to sell pigs off to the local butchers. Where the hell all those thousands of pigs came from in the middle of London was anybody's guess.

I found out very young that you were never far away from tragedy in your life when one of my class mates, a smashing lad called John McIntire, was killed during the school holidays in 1964. This was round the time that Spurs lost that great Scottish forward John White killed by lightning whilst sheltering from rain under a tree at a golf course. Whenever mention is made even now of that faraway John White incident, I automatically think back to the other John, John McIntire, an old school friend of mine, and all the years he never had.

During the summer, our family used to head back up North for a week or a fortnight. Those were the highlights of the year for us all. "Going home," just like all our other friend's families did too. Most of them headed to various parts of Ireland. The Marini family used to head back to Italy, confirming all our suspicions that they were somehow linked to the Mafia. Even the way they played football was sinister. I look back on those days and think that you wouldn't be able to afford to buy a holiday like that today. Most holidays today are a chore, a compulsory getting away for two weeks sunshine to find a bit of paradise. We took ours with us wherever we went. Dad even bought his first car, an Austin A40, and that meant that the world, or rather the open road, was our oyster. The journey from London to Easington then took roughly eleven hours. Eleven hours to do 275 miles. Dick Turpin could have done it quicker on Black Bess. It seemed to take an eternity but then pre-motorway travelling, apart from the A1, took you through congested towns all the way North. We had to go through Hendon, Baldock, Biggleswade, Grantham, Newark Ferrybridge and Stockton plus maybe others that have now escaped my memory. It was torture and I think the top speed on that car was only about 50 mph flat out with the wind behind us. We laugh now, but at the time it represented freedom to go anywhere, within reason.

In the first ever week we lived in Southall, dad wanted us to settle in quickly and as a treat took me and Tommy to our first football match in London. It was Brentford v Darlington in Division Four at Griffin Park. I took an instant shine to the Bees because they played in Sunderland's colours. Darlington's captain that day was Ron Greener, an old family friend and he recognised dad as the teams came out of the tunnel. He even stopped to talk to us as the teams made their way out on the pitch. Tommy and I were well impressed before Ron made his way out to join his mates.

The match was played on a brilliantly sunny but bitter cold December day. London didn't have the snow drifts we had left behind in Durham and I noticed that down the years what people in London thought of as severe wintry weather would have been little more than a light shower back home. Half an inch of snow had some southerners dressed up as Nanook of the North. Darlington won 2-1 but that didn't stop Brentford going on to win the league that season. We went there regularly after that and saw some cracking games and big crowds. Brentford were pulling in 14,000 towards the end of that season as they charged back to the Third Division. Hard to recall that less than 30 years before - a long time to us young bucks then but only like yesterday to any elderly Brentford fan on the terraces - the Bees were playing in the First Division and doing okay. We spent many happy afternoons at Griffin Park with our next door neighbour Colin Jones, and his elder brother Michael, who had followed the Bees for years.

We often rode our bikes - another bribe to help us settle in - from Southall along the Grand Union Canal all the way into Brentford on match days and some match nights too. That particular day, though, I recall the names of only two Brentford players that are probably still cherished by old Bees fans today. A swashbuckling fearless Tom Anthony, who, to an 11 year old, looked as hard as nails. Then there was Mel Block, an ex-Chelsea winger, built like the proverbial brick out house.

And so it was that Griffin Park became like a second home to me and sometimes my brother Tommy. If anything it was like a mini-version of Roker Park. There was a covered end behind one goal and open end behind the other. It resembled so many stadiums around that time in all four divisions. Two big ends behind each goal, one usually open for the fresh air fiends, and one covered, plus the standard main stand on one side with seats and directly opposite usually another standing paddock. And you could walk from one end of the ground to the other so that you'd maybe always have the same packed home fans at both ends of the ground in each half.

There was also always the unmistakeable heavy smell of liniment near the players' tunnel when the sides came out. I think it must have been fashionable then to bathe in it before hitting the field, as well as then hitting the supporters' nostrils. At that time Griffin Park could comfortably hold over 30,000. How sad that later, the capacity not only at this ground, but all others too, would be slashed dramatically as the health and safety regime moved in. This was inevitable for so many reasons. Brentford used to get really big crowds round about 1964 to 1967. They regularly pulled in over 15,000 and in two glorious cup replays against Oxford United and Burnley they topped 30,000 and lost both of them. Little did we know it then but this was the end of an era as far as this level of support for The Bees, and many others, was concerned as crowds in general were on the wane. Then, as now, there were other distractions creeping into the game. Why go to footy on a freezing cold afternoon when you could stay at home in the warm and watch the wrestling on telly on Saturday afternoon? Or better still, there were highlights sometimes of lower league games on the box the following afternoon. Laughable now but then it was supposed to be the start of the death knell of the game. For some poor sides it actually was. They would have had you certified if you told them then that in 45 years time you would be able to watch your team live on telly in a pub on the other side of the road from the ground on a match day. That's another thing Brentford had, too - a pub on every corner of the ground.

At the end of the sixties and early into the seventies, hooliganism began to emerge into the fray. Looking back, it was a wonder the game wasn't finished off altogether. It was bad, really bad, and sometimes ridiculous as pitch battles involving hundreds sometimes just erupted in the back streets, before and after matches. At Stamford Bridge round about 1969 in the height of the skinhead craze, police made a whole army of these skinheads take their Doc Marten "bovverboots" off before they were allowed to enter the ground. At Fulham, in a match against Millwall, the entire game became meaningless as it developed into a series of skirmishes off the field. A baying mob of Millwall fans used the entire 90 minutes to goad, harass and threaten anyone who dared cross them. One man, trying to remove his hot dog cart, ran for his life chased by over a dozen of this scum. I cheered like hell when justice was done on the pitch and Fulham won 2-0, which led to even more running battles. It was absolutely and utterly senseless behaviour. What was starting to happen then reminded me in later years to come of a much smaller, and less serious, version of Heysel. Thank God those days are behind us now. And if they aren't, and are still simmering away somewhere, then this time it could be a step too far for the game.

Those happy days down Griffin Park were the start of a very strange love affair with Brentford that still lasts to this day and as long as Sunderland, Hartlepool or Brentford win then I'm relatively happy. It's an awful day when all three get turned over, and I've seen that a few times. I've also cleaned up at the bookies when I've had a treble on all three to win. Mostly, though, I've been out of pocket down the years chasing this particular treble.

Brentford had some good players passing through their ranks. Maybe we took them for granted, or maybe we were just way too young to realise who they were. In the mid to late 60s, there was Ian Lawther, ex-Sunderland inside forward, who used to be a real crowd favourite and used to find the net regular, John Dick, ex-West Ham centre forward, Mel Scott, ex-Chelsea defender, Welshman Dai Ward, a cunning forward, and Jimmy Bloomfield who was a real majestic mid-fielder way too good for that level and who eventually played for West Ham in the First Division. Then there were what I prefer to call the dependables, players who trudged on and never let you down. Every team had them, even now. I recall the name of Gerry Higgins, who played the same style, match after match, resilient, tough but fair and who always had a smile on his face as he launched a player into touch. There was an old full back called Ken Coote who, even then, looked like he'd been round the block and back a few times. He'd played for Brentford since 1948/9 and was nearing the end of his career when I saw him. He never missed a tackle, never flinched when he got whacked and just got up and got on with it. A real old fashioned full back with greased back hair and a wise, kindly looking face. No wonder the crowd loved him.

We once saw a night match against Wrexham, Division Three, in November 1963 when the Bees won 9-0. We arrived late as the old lady who let us park our bikes in her garden for a penny each was still out doing her shopping. We heard the noise for 1-0 just as she let us in round the back. It was one of those nights where everything came off for them. Then there was another game with Port Vale who had a player manager called Billy Bingham, ex-Sunderland (although I never knew this at the time) who later went on to manage Northern Ireland. Brentford beat them too, 4-0. Notts County with a very young Tony Hateley up front came, saw and were beaten 4-1. Then there was Derek Dougan, of Peterborough United but soon to be Aston Villa, who must have played one of his last games against Brentford in the Third Division before moving. I think he scored twice that night. He was like greased lightning in and around the penalty box. And as a reminder never to leave a game before the end, there was a match against Luton. Brentford 2-1 up, 15 minutes left and dad telling me it was time to nip off to beat the traffic and get the bus home. Whilst we were homeward bound, Luton's secret weapon Mark Lazarus (who won a League Cup winners medal with QPR in 1967) ran riot and we got back in to find the final score Brentford 2 Luton Town 6.

We also regularly watched our local side Southall who played at Western Road, a 16,000 capacity ground. They also played in red and white stripes, so watching them too was to become a must. This thing with red and white stripes seems to be a family trait. My brother Tommy played for his local junior school, St. Anselm's, Southall (red & white stripes) and then in later life he and wife Sue moved to live in a lovely little village called Hemingby in Lincolnshire. His local side are Lincoln City who –you can guess the rest. My brother was a great footballer in his youth and we regularly used to watch him grab his usual five or six goals a game at schoolboy level. He later played for Southall and had trials with Fulham. Southall at the time had the likes of Alan Devonshire and Gordon Hill coming through their ranks and both of them went on to play in the First Division later. Tommy was on par with them, maybe better, but unfortunately he was distracted by a female (weren't we all?) at the time and it just wasn't to be. I'm reminded of that classic line from the film "On The Waterfront" where Marlon Brando looks back on wasted opportunity and the fact that he never made it to the top as a boxer. And the classic line: " I could have been a contender". Well so could you Tommy, so could you.

There was a whole gang of us used to knock around together when we watched Southall. On the way to the ground there was a sweet shop where you could buy packets of broken crisps for a penny a packet, and that was one old penny, too - 240 of them to the pound, Because the crisps were broken into tiny smithereens, the packets usually held and weighed five times the amount of a normal packet that cost four times as much. Even then I could spot a bargain, and we used to get through four or five packets each watching the match. Now, of course, the newsagent would be visited by the Health & Safety Gestapo where he'd lose his licence for selling non-EU prescribed broken goods to minors, be evicted from his shop, and also be hit with a £15,000 fine. Still,a small price to pay for keeping the public safe. After the match, both Tommy and me used to run back from the ground like Olympic sprinters to our house about a quarter of a mile away just in time to get the classified results and usually find that Sunderland had gone down the pan again. There was also the classified football paper on Saturday nights, the London Evening Standard, long gone now. There are not many cities left, apart from Sunderland, and the last I heard Portsmouth and Liverpool, who still have the football pink on a weekend. And I wonder how long before all that becomes history with the advent of the internet.

We had some great times and laughs at Western Road. Southall played in the Athenian League, true amateurs, and used to get nearly 1,000 per home game. In local derbies against Hayes and Hounslow, there would be maybe 2,000. Some of the teams who visited were like amateur nectar on the tongue: Walton & Hersham, Windsor & Eton, East Ham United, Corinthinan Casuals, Grays Athletic, Sutton United, Wimbledon, Leatherhead, Hillingdon Borough and Carshalton. I think the closest they came to a an FA Cup appearance was in 1965 when they actually reached the Fouth Qualifying Round and drew away with Walton & Hersham. We were so naïve that we even brought a home made banner along for the replay with "Southall for the Cup" written on it which made front page in the local paper the week after. Sadly, by then Southall had lost 4-0 and were out of the cup. Our dreams of a trip to nearby Wembley cruelly dashed for another year.

I did once break ranks from watching Southall when dad and I went to nearby Hayes to see them play then famous amateurs Crook Town in an Amateur Cup quarter final game. That must have been round about 1964 and there were about 9,000 there that day. Crook held them and won the replay. Those size crowds at that sort of amateur level would just never happen today.

Back in the very early 1960s, Southall were respected members of the League. They got to the Amateur Cup quarter finals one year round about 1963 and held then non-league Wimbledon at home to a 3-3 draw. There were 8,000 there but defeat in the replay saw the end of those golden days of the big attendances, and they slowly, but inevitably, drifted away into obscurity. Wimbledon, well run and well-supported, were already on a roll that swept them onwards and upwards. Southall went in the opposite direction. Now the ground is no more, along with the pub that used to stand at its entrance, The Halfway House. Poor old Southall went the way of so many. I checked recently and found that the name does still live on and they ply their trade some four or five miles away in a local park. I've never been back to find out.

For some reason, I cannot truthfully remember any Christmases spent in Southall all through my teen years, perhaps because I wanted to be somewhere else. My one abiding and cherished memory of a great day out with my dad again evolved around football. We often used to share a pint together but this one was really special .It was the World Cup final 1970 with Brazil playing Italy. The pair of us, on a blisteringly hot afternoon, popped out for a quick drink and then another. The match had just started and so we stayed all afternoon, and both got pleasantly plastered in the appropriately named Bricklayers Arms watching Pele and Company tear Italy to pieces. I don't know what it must have been like watching the game sober but, blind drunk, Brazil were playing football way off the Richter scale (a bit like the pair of us that day). Were they the best Brazil side ever? You better believe it. I didn't even realise it at the time but those days at 19 when you are young, fit, working and don't have a real care in the world, safe at home with your mam and dad, your whole life ahead of you (as my father often used to try and drum into me) really are the happiest of your life. And I was too busy feeling sorry for myself to know it.

When my father died aged only 59, in November1987, I was already working back home in Newcastle and when I went down for the funeral, there were fireworks being let off all over Southall. It was Diwali Night, an Asian festival, and the skies were all lit up. It all seemed so perfect. I thought it was just like a celebration and commemoration of his whole life, arranged especially for him. I also thought how was it possible for life to go on as normal, everybody still laughing and joking, when he was no longer part of it. Our last game together before he died was against Burnley at Griffin Park, and he was typically in fine form that day. We found a pub full of Burnley fans next to Griffin Park on one of the four corners and, after a couple of jars and a swift introduction, he had about a dozen Burnley lads rolling about laughing with a selection of some of his finest jokes lasting well over an hour. We were all crying with laughter and I think one or two of them were even keen on staying and ignoring the match altogether. We even stood with them on the terraces, two unofficial members of Burnley FC Supporters Club (Sunderland Branch). Whenever I watch Burnley or see their result on the telly I automatically think back to that afternoon so long ago. Just three days before he died, I rang him with the usual match report having seen Sunderland demolish Southend 7-0 in a Third Division game at Roker. My mother never really got over it. She lived on for another 18 years but didn't adjust to life without my father. She never really smiled like she used to after dad went. Just before she passed away, I caught her shouting at a framed picture of him telling him off for leaving her so soon. When she eventually moved back North to live near her family, by that time all her friends in Southall had all left and returned to Ireland and all their old roots elsewhere. Ironically, my mother died in London where she had been visiting my sister. Afterwards, clearing out her little bungalow, the last ornament we found, hidden behind a wardrobe and wrapped up in brown paper, was a small wall-plate with various pictures on it. The name on it read "Southall", the place she always referred to as her real home.

I eventually returned North in February, 1976, and dad and I watched our last ever Southall game on a miserable Wednesday night. I can't even remember who they played or what the score was. That night I wasn't remotely interested in football. I was going back home and felt as guilty as sin that I had somehow let my dad down by leaving. I stood there thinking back to how both my parents worked so hard to make a better life for all three of us, and did it with very little money, too. They never owned their own home and rented all the time they lived down there. Buying or owning property wasn't something my dad was ever really into, or thought important; he never believed in such materialistic things. As long as he and mam had enough to pay all the bills, and see everybody happy and smiling, that did them.

Living in West London meant that we were spoilt for choice and had Brentford, Fulham, Chelsea and QPR on our doorstep. I was a frequent visitor to all of them, along with trips to North London for Spurs and Arsenal who were the two glamour teams back then. Chelsea, too, had their heyday in the 60s and 70s. Crystal Palace and Charlton were further out in South London and I visited both whenever Sunderland were in town. And then there were the trips to the magical East, the East End, to take the odd look at Millwall, West Ham and Orient. These grounds seemed a long way from our West London home, especially Millwall which was then, and now, a pretty intimidating place to visit. The original Den was aptly named because it was just like stepping into one whenever we went there. Those grounds still standing since I first went there have changed out of all recognition and are virtually brand new stadiums. Highbury and The Den are no more and even Tottenham, West Ham and little old Brentford will soon be moving on. It's sad but also inevitable.

Those who moved on to bigger and not necessarily better stadiums have probably left behind an army of old fans who might be thinking just as I am today. Whenever I see a match on the box from Spurs or Chelsea or other London sides, I am back there, whisked on a Magic Carpet through the miles and the years. There was the opulent splendour of Highbury, visited for the first time in August 1965. To a little lad who had grown up on the terraces at Roker Park, entering the plush confines of majestic Highbury was the equivalent of going to the Ritz. This was no disrespect to Sunderland. It was just that Highbury had the feel of a place that looked like it meant business both then and in the future. I wasn't too far wrong as it later transpired. Roker Park was just as big and a hell of a lot noisier but it was raw and our best days were way past and belonged to the 1930s when Sunderland and Arsenal were what you'd call rivals in the real sense of the word.

Before gallivanting round all these places I needed the money to do it. Whilst I was at school I had my parents to subsidise me, but it was made plain to both their two sons that once we had left school we had to stand on our own two feet. Work or do without. What a slogan that would be today on billboards everywhere, especially aimed at those who won't work and don't want for nothing either. They'd have got a shock spending a fortnight with my mam and dad, but one that would have pleasantly changed their lives for the better.

When I left school at 16 in 1967, with my precious five GCE "O" levels, that automatically guaranteed me instant access into the Civil Service the following April. Why join the Civil Service? The best advice my dad ever gave me was simple. "No matter who you vote for, the government always gets in. Work for them and you'll never be out of work" Some advice,eh? I heeded his words but, unfortunately, I had to wait nine months before starting. What could I do in the meantime? Perhaps put my feet up or nine months touring Europe? No, get a job, any job, till then and so I started work as a naive, green as grass delivery assistant - that's a van boy to you - at Walls Meat & Handy Foods in Southall. I wasn't green for very long working with some of those drivers. They'd have put Fagin and the Artful Dodger to shame with some of their scams. We used to deliver sausages, bacon, bacon joints and pies round Supermarkets and local shops and stores. My area was Wimbledon and it was hard graft. My job was loading up the van each morning and making sure everything was on board before we left the yard. We'd then set out in the early morning light delivering, and not getting back till six at night. It was back-breaking but I loved the fresh air, outdoors and the adventure. It was just like being a pirate on the high seas, in more ways than one.

I never missed a shift in nine months and that made me unique compared to the rest of the lads. Some of them never put in two days running. Half of them would be off sick with a broken flask. I was in demand and ended up getting all the plum rounds. That wasn't before I'd had the delights of doing Poplar, Peckham (rough wasn't the word), Worcester Park (very posh) and Watford (too far out and stuck in traffic all the way there and back). It was a great job in the summer but in the winter with no heating in the van, and frozen packets of bacon to handle, you had to force yourself out of bed thinking about the ordeal that lay ahead. We got to know other delivery men carrying all sorts of stuff on board. Ice cream, Mars bars, Crunchies, cooked chickens, the lot. There was something for everyone. It was a bit like swap shop as we traded our stuff for theirs. One box of Crunchies traded for 12 packets of bacon, and so on. I don't want Walls coming after me after all these years so let's just leave it at that. My mam always said that, even at 16, I was already bringing home the bacon big style. We ate well and I think I put about a stone on in the time I was there. Mind you, I was still nowhere near the Sumo style lot kicking around today. I would have been an amateur by comparison.

When I eventually joined the posh sounding Ministry of Housing & Local Government, I worked in a former Victorian hotel in Tothill Street, Westminster directly opposite St James Park Underground station. Built in 1888, Queen Anne's Mansions was a horrible, dirty looking, quadrangular grey monstrosity. It was a 14 storey high block of former flats that must have been hastily transformed for about a fiver into offices 1960s style. Our office was next to one of the original non-refurbished hotel toilet blocks on floor seven with all the original fixtures and fittings. They would have been worth an absolute fortune today. Thomas Crapper would have been a proud man to have seen it, knowing it had survived from the 1880s right through to the 1960s.

There were long dark narrow corridors with very little light even during the sunniest of days, and narrow spiral staircases used as short cuts that took you up and down different floor levels. There was room for only one person at a time to go up or down between floors and you half expected Vincent Price or Christopher Lee to be coming down the other way as you went up. We even had a lift that was operated manually by some poor bloke who had to sit there all day long. Otherwise how else could it work?

There were even rumours that the building was haunted and if you worked there you'd know why. Your imagination would be working overtime, along with most of the lazy buggers who worked there. If you were working in there late on a dark winter's night, or even during the day, you always imagined that you were being watched by someone from one of the deserted rooms across the dark court yard. In the ten months I was there before it was pulled down, there were at least three ghostly sightings. Of all the toilets in that building, one sighting just had to be in the loo right next to our office. The other two were on the spiral staircase on floors eleven and twelve. I used to take a 100 yard walk - or sprint if I felt a bit jittery - rather than go in the next door toilet, and as for the spiral staircases? Not a chance.

Round that time I'd also learnt how to drive and passed my test when I just turned 17. The lessons were only a quid each although my driving instructor, Tottenham Ted, a big Spurs fan (how did you guess?) gave me two lessons for one pound ten shillings, provided I kept quiet about the extra lesson. The extra ten bob went into his pocket, not the driving school. Dad thought that if I had a car I would feel less homesick as I would then be able to drive the odd weekend up North. The first car I ever owned wouldn't have got as far as the next street, never mind the North East. The first-and last- car I ever owned in London was a 1959 Hillman Minx with column stick gears that cost me £35 and it lasted about 6 months. My dad had seen one costing £95, a Ford Zephyr, but the cost was way outside my price range. I could cry even now when I think about the hours we both spent together looking for the perfect set of wheels so his son could make the odd weekend getaway. After spending a fortune trying to keep that heap on the road, I gave up on owning four wheels and went back to the bus. Today that car would have been a collector's item with its whitewall tyres and genuine leather seats. It just needed a new engine, floor and a gearbox, that's all.

As well as my love for football I loved my music too and it had to be live and loud. Th 1960s was a great time for that, too. We'd already seen the birth of The Beatles and The Rolling Stones, and in 1968 we were all feeling old enough to start venturing into pubs. There were loads of them in Southall, virtually one on each street corner, and many up and coming bands used to flog their puddings on a weekend, all hoping to become as big as The Who. Some were really good, others were dreadful, but even the bad ones were better than listening to the jukebox, or even worse today, karaoke. Simon Cowell would have had a field day back then listening to real talent although he probably wouldn't have recognised it if it bit him on his backside. Exactly like today, really.

There was one pub called The Northcote Arms, just off Southall Broadway, that used to put the newer bands on each Sunday night and it was only a quid to get in. We were spoilt watching the likes of Led Zeppelin, Free, Rory Gallagher, (no relation to Noel and Liam; this Irish Blues Rocker was about ten times better), King Crimson, The Groundhogs and many more. We even got to see the old Bluesmen like Howlin' Wolf and John Lee Hooker. Watching these old black masters was like watching old time footballers teaching their tricks to a whole new generation of up and coming white rock and blues bands. Nobody did it or copied it better than the Stones and Led Zeppelin, still massive today to a whole new generation of pimply young rockers. We also used to go up West to see the more mainstream bands like The Who and The Small Faces plus The Kinks. I listened to all kinds of music. I even went to see Desmond Dekker, the old reggae star, but once you'd heard his first two songs, you'd seen his whole act, a bit like rap and hip hop music today. The greatest of the lot, though, was Jimi Hendrix who we saw in 1968. Comparing him to the rest of the bands and acts I'd seen then was like comparing the Real Madrid team of 1960 to Halifax Town. Nothing I've seen before or since could get anywhere near him. My music always came first with me after football. I still like some of the modern rock stuff but find most of it strangely bland, even after I've turned the volume up full blast. My younger peers actually tell me to turn it down, just like my mother used to say to me in years gone by. I find that strange. With the modern stuff, there are no guitar solos and complicated riffs not because, as my niece says, they are old hat. It's more because most bands today can't play that sort of stuff. It's too difficult for them to pick up. Or maybe they are too lazy or not good enough to learn them. It's a bit like playing football without real width. Dull and it won't get the crowd going.

Working in Westminster brought me into contact with loads of workmates who followed sides all over London. In the building were fans from Spurs, Arsenal, Chelsea, Brentford, Palace, Leyton Orient, West Ham, QPR and Fulham. Even a Millwall fan, Stan Wheeler, who looked as mean as the team he followed. I was the only one following Sunderland - plus Brentford - which gained me some kind of grudging respect, as well as funny looks. It was really easy to get around then all over town on fairly empty midweek tubes after 6pm and so, during the week, I 'd often go, with assorted workmates to watch Fulham Chelsea, QPR or even nip up to Tottenham or the Arsenal.

You paid at the gate, none of this all ticket nonsense, and it was relatively a lot cheaper than today. I was only on £9.00 a week at age 17 in the Civil Service back then but it cost only four shillings (20p) to get into the Bridge or Craven Cottage. That was less than 3% of my weekly wage. Today a 17 year old in London would need to be on maybe £1500 a week, perhaps more, to go to watch Chelsea at the same cost comparison. And my wage then wasn't even a great one compared to some of my mates who worked on the building sites and pulled in £20 a week. You do the maths and shake your head as I still do now. One game at Chelsea, I didn't have enough money on me and only had half the admission price. I sold a programme to make up the difference. That's how cheap it was Pre-Terry, Drogba and all. You'd also have a real good natter on the terraces with the real fans back then. Many of them were Scots, probably because Chelsea used to have a fair smattering of them in the side, as well as Tommy Docherty, the manager. I wonder how many of those supporters still go today. Try talking to some of the new wave lot that get to The Bridge now and they'd think you were either a fruitcake or trying to chat them up.

During the period I lived in London, between 1962 and 1976, interspersed between many return journeys to the North East and back, I often visited Highbury and often went there with workmates - and even a girlfriend - to watch them. I was hooked on the history and tradition of the Gunners and, as a neutral, loved watching them. Even then, they played some lovely one-touch stuff. You'd get some laughs as well. In a North London early season derby there were 66,000 packed inside on one of the hottest days of the year in August. We were roasting nicely in the middle of the old North Bank when, to our right, we caught sight of a rather large man who had passed out with the heat. When I say large I am being diplomatic. This bloke was colossal even by modern day standards. If you'd have half a side of him in your freezer, you needn't have had to worry about running out of meat for two years. The objective of the crowd, themselves under considerable duress, was to get this poor bloke down to the front to the St. John Ambulance crew. There was no way they could reach him and they were yelling for him to be passed forward. There were cries of "Heave!" as the fans, already sweltering, tried to raise this enormous, unconscious, weight up and over their heads. It wasn't a pretty sight as the huge man, easily 25 stone, slowly bobbed down to the front, often disappearing under the waves, and then suddenly popping back up above surface again. First his money went from his trouser pockets, then his shirt, followed by his shoes with the tremendous effort needed to get him down to sanctuary at pitch side. Finally, with one huge effort, he was there. It took an eternity and I remember little Geordie Armstrong of Arsenal, hands on hips, pausing to take a corner, just in case the crowd surged forward if Arsenal scored from his kick .By the time Buster Bloodvessel came round at pitch side, he had lost all his dignity - plus his trousers - as the ambulance crew managed to cover up his modesty. You can laugh about it now but he could so easily have died that day, and not just of embarrassment, if that crowd decided to just leave him there. I still don't know how they managed to get him to the front. Again, today, he'd probably be suing everyone in sight from Arsenal FC downwards for loss of dignity under the Human Rights Act, or whatever, and winning his case.

There was another 63,000 in against Derby County in a cup game and what made this all the more remarkable was that it was played on an afternoon due to power cuts in the early 1970s. And then another 62,000 for a Sixth Round cup replay in 1973 against Chelsea, with Sunderland awaiting the winners. The Gunners won 2-1 and I had a strange feeling making my way home to Southall that night that Sunderland could beat them. I even travelled up to Hillsborough for the semi-final on the Arsenal trains, but jumped on a bus to Sunderland after the match to celebrate. I just knew Sunderland would win the cup after beating Arsenal, too. They played in an all white strip that day, and next morning in County Durham, there was a white blanket of snow to wake up to. Somehow it seemed almost like divine intervention and that even the heavens were with us. By then, also, I was really smitten with a pretty Southern girl called Marie, but I think the main reason that it was never going to work was because I always knew I would go back home one day and Marie just didn't fancy it.

She came up North with me a couple of times but couldn't take to the North East ways. What she mistook for nosiness was nothing of the sort. It was the genuine warmth and friendliness of the people she met. I could never have settled down and lived in the South. As for the North/ South divide, I heard some old feller tell me the perfect definition of the difference between them. In the South, the weather is warm and the people are cold; in the North it's the other way round.

My last trip to Highbury was quite sad, too. Some bugger pinched my wallet. Unluckily for them, though, the wallet was worth more than what was actually in it.

If you took a modern fan back to Stamford Bridge in the very early 60s, they'd be hard pushed to tell you where they were, and not because it was amazingly cheap to get in. Then it was a huge mainly uncovered bowl on three sides with mountainous terraces. You'd need an oxygen bottle, with Sherpa Tensing as a guide, to walk to the back of the steepest parts. Along one side there were the usual bog standard seats, 1950s style, plus terraces. And then in the corner, the most ridiculous looking thing you've ever seen in your life. A stand on stilts completely isolated from the main one which seemed to defy gravity. A throwback to the 1930s, and if you saw it today your first reaction would surely be: "What the hell is that?". Your second reaction would have been to demolish it before it actually toppled over. It only held about 1500, all seated and today they'd have to pay you to sit in there. The Bridge back then had a dog track running round it and sometimes the football was that bad you'd wish they'd set the dogs loose to watch instead. There was always a buzz about the place and it was what I'd call a real football ground. The only trouble with Stamford Bridge was that a 35,000 crowd (what they usually pulled in round about that time, although obviously much larger for London derbies) was totally lost in this vast arena. You could get 60,000 in easily, and still have loads of room to escort some 30 stone fan, who might have fainted, down to the front in a wheelchair.

Loftus Road was the home of then Third Division QPR in the mid 60s. In 1967, QPR, with a young Rodney Marsh, beat West Bromwich in the League Cup Final at Wembley 3-2 after trailing 2-0 at half time. Back then, you could have just gone along on the day. I saw a couple of games at Loftus Road that season and the ground was only one step up from being a glorified pigeon loft. QPR's ground record is only above 35,000 and they must have used a few shoe horns to get the last 15,000 in.

It had one tiny main stand and even tinier open terraces on most of the rest of the ground. There was a small tin shelf behind one of the goals that masqueraded as a roof. It was totally useless on wet days as it only provided cover for those lucky few in the last six rows at the back, provided the rain came straight down and not at an angle. Size wise, using Stamford Bridge as a guidemark, it was like comparing a Yorkshire Terrier to a St. Bernard. Everywhere else provided not one jot of protection when the rain lashed down. I once saw a local derby there against Brentford on a foul Friday night which the Bees won 3-1 in front of 11,000. The atmosphere was electric and I was soaked to the skin before the game. By the time I got home on the 207 bus from Shepherds Bush to Southall Broadway and walked the rest of the way, I was sneezing like a snuff addict. I spent all day Saturday and Sunday in bed with the flu.

West Ham was a real jumping joint too in the 1960s and still is today. Although home games were a long way away (nearly 30 odd stops on the District Line from Ealing Broadway), Upton Park was always a great place to visit. It was a real proper old fashioned sort of ground. Their fans were the London equivalent of North East supporters. They were fiercely loyal, with not much to sing about at the best of times, and had a real knowledge of their team and got behind them. I was impressed and have always had a soft spot for the Happy Hammers and the way they play the game, even in defeat. Sometimes it isn't just about the winning. West Ham were more popular than the likes of Leeds United ever were, and that was partly down to the way they played the game - with a smile on their face, rather than a scowl. They were approaching their golden era when we first set foot there, FA Cup winners in 1964, European Cup Winners Cup winners in 1965 (try saying that one after eight pints) and World Cup Winners in 1966. West Ham fans will never get sick of telling you that last one.

Apart from the majestic Bobby Moore, Hurst and Peters, they also had some other great characters too. Harry Redknapp(a better manager than he ever was a player), Budgie Byrne, Brian Dear and Alan Sealey. Jim Standen, the goalkeeper, was also one of the rare breed who played both league football and County Cricket too. Howzat ,then? And then there was the now long gone Chicken Run. It was like an elongated bus stand and I'd never seen anything like it since my early days watching Hartlepool. In fact, maybe Hartlepool sold it to them. It must have been built in the 1920's, if not before, and I bet even then the builders left town quickly once they'd finished the work and been paid. It was no real surprise when that particular beauty was pulled down.

Then there was the absolutely enormous Valley where a 40,000 crowd would be lost in the vast surroundings. I was there to see a Cup Replay with Chelsea in the 1970s with 70,000 comfortably fitting in there. Again, it was like scaling Mount Everest trying to get up the steep embankments to the top terraces once you'd got through the turnstiles. And once you'd got your breath back, and cleared the excess mud off your shoes, way below in the distance you'd see the Valley pitch itself. From the back row it would have been like looking down on a Subbuteo game, even with binoculars. The sheer scale of it had to be seen to be believed. It was a real shame when those mountainous terraces were slowly whittled away and the ground redeveloped like so many others. You'd have had to have been there to judge the size of the place. A bit like you telling some bloke about the monster fish you once caught. Until he saw it for himself he just wouldn't believe you. One December afternoon, with the snow swirling down, against Sunderland in a Second Division promotion game (1963), a crowd of over 42,000 was just absolutely lost in the place. Again, dad and me climbed up this huge muddy steep embankment before the match, up and up and up until you reached the very last row of the terraces. And then down, down, down to the waiting pitch below. And after the game, the same trek in reverse. It was like one of those Japanese game shows, again, where the poor contestants get humiliated for the fun of it. This definitely wasn't fun though. In the dimly lit way out, one poor bloke lost his footing and must have slid a good 50 feet downhill slalom style on his backside in the thick mud, rolling and tumbling until he slowed down at the bottom of the bank, skittling over a couple of lads eating hot dogs. He was covered from head to foot in mud, and goodness knows what else, but got up like nothing had happened and walked off into the dark. How they let him on a train or bus that night, I don't know. He had to have lived nearby and probably had to strip off stark naked at his front door before his missus let him in.

Then there was White Hart Lane with the huge shelf. Why did they ever get rid of that? It was worth a goal start to Spurs when the opposition ran out and clocked eyes on it. Some of our mates in Southall, John, Michael, Peter and Richard Walsh, all used to follow Spurs and we tagged along often. This was in the days of Greaves, Gilzean, Mullery, Jennings, Knowles, England and all. White Hart Lane was another ground where the team used to have to lift the crowd, rather than the other way round. I suppose you could argue, though, that if you had a team that could only turn it on when the crowd were at a thousand decibels, then that team couldn't be much cop, could they? Spurs were, though, and on their day could turn anybody over. The trouble was they lacked the consistency to do it on a regular basis. Looking back, if you had been a Spurs fan watching their fabulous double team of 1961, then anything after that must have been a terrible anti-climax. They really were that good.

Craven Cottage was a quaint, friendly ground right on the Thames and sometimes you'd half expect a butler to meet you at the main gates with a glass of Pymms on the way in (and definitely a stiff brandy on the way out). When I saw it for the first time it always struck me as a welcoming Olde Worlde establishment. An open end behind one goal and also alongside the Thames Embankment (all standing of course), and a covered end behind the other goal. There was the obligatory Main stand along the other side and there in the corner, the cottage itself that housed the dressing rooms. It was a lovely view in the summer, but in the winter that cold wind would fairly whistle up the Thames. It was still the Bahamas compared to Hartlepool, though. When the footy was really bad, which was quite often as Fulham battled gamely for First Division survival in the 60s, we'd often turn our back on the match and watch the rowers going up and down the Thames from the back row of terraces. It was marginally more exciting although, unlike Fulham, we never saw anyone sink beneath the waves. In spite of that, Fulham always had some good players who would have graced any team in any era. There was Johnny Haynes, of course, George Cohen, the much under-rated goalie Tony Macedo and even a youthful Bobby Robson. Not enough, though, to eventually stem the tide of relegation that saw them drop into the Third Division in consecutive seasons. I even saw Hartlepool beat them many years later 2-1 at The Vic, just before Kevin Keegan worked his magic on them on the long road back. It's nice to see them doing okay again and Johnny Haynes would be proud of them and the revamped Cottage. And for only 25,000 of them, they make a real nice racket.

Selhurst Park was another ground that was a bit far out for me, but I used to pop across whenever Sunderland were in town. Palace was another team that used to remind me a lot of Sunderland, a great, noisy support and very little end product. They'd be up, then down, then up, then down. Just like Sunderland and Leicester City, they could well have been nicknamed The Yo-yos. But, as any fan will tell you, if you never experience the pain and heartache of relegation, then you'll never experience the sheer joy of going back up again. Mind you, after about the fourth or fifth time of experiencing both, the novelty does tend to wear a bit thin. You do wonder, though, what the long term future of sides like Palace will be. The longer they are outside the top flight, the harder they will find it to actually stay there on a long term basis when they do get back. Selhurst Park was a spacey ground with big stands and a nice playing surface. When they went through to the First Division in the late 1960s, they were promoted with Coventry and I always thought that Palace would be better suited to do well in the top flight. How wrong was I? Coventry soldiered on, season after unspectacular season (a sore point with Sunderland fans) and Palace quickly dropped back down again. Even so, Palace had a fantastic support then and pulled in 30,000 plus in the Third Division, and 35,000 or more in the Second Division.

Brisbane Road, with apologies to Orient, has always remained an enigma to me. I remember visiting it for the first time in 1964 and thinking "How the Hell did this lot pip Sunderland for promotion to the First Division two years ago?" I was naively comparing the size of the ground then to that of Roker Park and the respective fan bases. It doesn't work like that, though. Leyton Orient gained promotion because the eleven players they put out on the pitch over 42 league games had been more consistent than Sunderland. Orient deserved their promotion - end of story. Never mind the fact that it was their one and only season in the top flight in 1962/63. They were cannon fodder nearly everywhere they went, but still deserved their brief stay in the sun. I always found Brisbane Road and their supporters a really friendly, welcoming lot. Sadly, the last 4 times I have seen them has been at nearby Hartlepool and, even here at third tier level, they look as if they have found their comfort zone. I remember them in their glory days when they used to get "only" 15,000 in the Second Division (what would they give for those gates now if they had a ground big enough to hold them?) and they mixed it with Liverpool, Sunderland, Leeds, Newcastle week after week-and succeeded sometimes. As for Brisbane Road itself, it was a lovely little ground, that once attracted 35,000 in a cup game against Arsenal that I remember watching on a Thames

Telly Footy Special. There were two main stands plus two open ends and a pitch that used to cut up easily. Sometimes it looked like a ploughed up field, and that was early season. I used to dodge along with a Leyton Orient fan I worked with called Johnny Johnston (not the one who played the piano on all of Chuck Berry's classic hits) a couple of times. Johnny lived just round the corner from Brisbane Road with his folks and had been indoctrinated by his dad when he was nine. He remembered the "glory days" when there were never less than 8,000 going along.

Last and certainly not least, put on your crash helmets, take a deep breath and join me on a white knuckle ride as we very, very carefully embark on an ever so slow, careful walk to that most intimidating of venues, The Den. The original Den, Cold Harbour Lane, in East London. Whatever you do, don't look or stare at anyone, not even that old feller on the corner over there, who's eyeing you up and down. Be afraid and you might come out of it in one piece. I'm sure things are much better now and Millwall have done wonders in trying to move well away from those dark days. (I know they have as I had the privilege of spending a few hours with some proper Millwall fans prior to them beating Sunderland 1-0 in an FA Cup Semi Final at Old Trafford). However, in the 60s and 70s, I am not exaggerating when I say that absolutely and positively nothing compared to The Den for a frightening 90 minutes, regardless of which team you were. I'll say this for their fans back then. They were not biased and had no real favourite visitors and teams. They hated all of them with equal venom. Win, lose or draw you were always looking over your shoulder. No one, but no one - unless they were insane or bordering on the suicidal - wore their colours down there. Even home fans used to scrap with each other when the Lions were losing, and they used to lose quite regularly. Wearing a scarf or badge was like a red rag to a bull-or should that be an angry lion? I once saw two geriatric dockers belting the hell out of each other in the safe confines of the seats I was in, when Burnley had the audacity to go into an early lead there. I suspect that both thought the other was a rogue Clarets fan and so, naturally, this triggered off the appropriate response. This was only natural at Cold Harbour Lane. There was no real joy at all in going there. I've seen Sunderland win 4-1 at The Den and sat in absolute silence on my hands for the full 90 minutes. I was 23 at the time and took my two much younger cousins, Danny and Dean, with me. It was terrifying, and they were under strict instructions not to talk to anybody, both before and after the game, and that, for God's sake, don't cheer if Sunderland score. It was a surreal experience as Sunderland could have hit eight that day and the three of us just sat there like a trio of tailor's dummies for the full 90 minutes. It was only when I was a mile away from the ground that I punched the air in triumph, checking carefully, of course, that there was no one within 50 yards of me in all directions. Still, at least we managed to sign Charlie Hurley off them in 1958, so who's laughing now, eh?

There was no Wimbledon then, at least not in the Football League. The Crazy Gang didn't come on the scene until later and are sadly now no more. I don't count MK Dons as their successors. No, to me the "real" Wimbledon - that's AFC Wimbledon - are currently in the Blue Square League (Conference) and I, along with thousands of footy purists, will raise a glass to them when they return and take their rightful place in the Football League and playing back home in Wimbledon. Wouldn't it be ironic if they ended up playing themselves in the not too distant future? MK Dons v AFC Wimbledon. There'll be sparks flying that day when it happens - and it will - the way AFC Wimbledon are progressing.

London grounds then compared to now? For those of you around then, or maybe not even born, if you are asking if modern stadiums are better, then the obvious answer is a simple "yes". They are safer, cleaner, more customer friendly, comfier, and much less dangerous places to be in. But they do not have a tenth of the passion or atmosphere of their old counterparts.

We must have been stark raving mad at the time, us 13 and 14 years olds, who went with our mates and braved the crush, the swirl and sway of it all. In retrospect it was dangerous but, to a daft youth, it was exciting and somehow you always felt that if you got out of your depth then there was always some older bloke or blokes ready to pull you out of the maelstrom and get you to safety. They just would. It was all part of some wonderful camaraderie that made football then a unique experience. That has now gone. Unless you have stood on packed terraces (and packed like sardines) at The Valley, Highbury, Stamford Bridge, Craven Cottage, White Hart Lane, Upton Park and even Griffin Park, then you couldn't possibly make comparisons unless you were there. You can make a potential judgement from the safety of a reference book or have a gander of an old clip on "You Tube" but you just had to have been there to have really known.

I suppose now I was incredibly lucky to have been brought up in London during the Swinging Sixties (even the word "swinging" has different connotations today!). My first ever visit to Wembley was to see a Schoolboy International in 1963 when three of us cycled there to see England beat Scotland in front of 93,000. In 1966 we got on our bikes again and pedalled there from Southall, to stand outside and listen to the noise. Fair enough, it wasn't the same as being in there, but to a 15 year old and his mates it was the nearest thing to actually being there. And how many others got that close to the greatest era ever in English football, standing outside Wembley and listening to that noise telling everyone that England were World Champions? We did. We thought we were the three Musketeers (well, four really) standing on the edge of a great battlefield and safely hearing and breathing in the noise and smell of it all. I wonder how long it will be before we ever see it again. Sadly, I suspect, not in my lifetime, nor maybe even my two children's, Marty and Dan. They get annoyed with me now as I show an increasing disinterest in watching England today. In truth, if England were playing in my back garden, I'd shut the curtains on them. In the past, it was fair to say that through an appalling choice of management selections by the FA, it really was scandalous that a man like Brian Clough was conveniently overlooked. Had he got the job, it would definitely have been a case of a Lion led by donkeys. Now it's even worse. We've graduated to a donkey led by even bigger donkeys.

As the 1960s grew to a close in London, the lure of the 1970s just didn't seem to evoke the same kind of passion (1973 apart). Perhaps it was because I was growing up and becoming a lot more cynical - or should that be realistic? By then the magic was beginning to wear thin on my southern adventure. Dad was right when he said that my choice of employment as a 16 year old would be the best move I ever made. He was always right. It would enable me to return home to the North East where I have lived to this day.

CHAPTER 7
SUNDERLAND IN THE 1960s

As an old History Teacher once told me many moons ago, "if you don't know your history, then you have no idea about your past. And if you don't know where you've come from, you'll have no idea where you are going". To a naïve 13 year old, as I was then, I thought these were the words of a boring old fart. And at the time they were. Now that I am older and graduated to that same sensible level of understanding (it's only taken me forty odd years to get there) I know exactly where he was coming from. It just took a while for the penny to drop. Perhaps if he'd just said simply "Ignore the past and it'll come back to bite you on the bum" it would have made much more sense.

That lesson applies to nearly everything in life, especially football, and to both teams and fans alike. Never has it been more appropriate than today where your modern football fan is cocooned very much in "the now", that awful patronising place where ignorance and smugness reign supreme. I know because I've seen it in grounds all over the country and in bars all over the world.

We live in a time where generally people couldn't give a monkey's cuss what happened ten years ago. It's gone, history, and should be confined in the bin. How many times have you heard someone say, usually one of the telly pundits or "experts", that five years is a long time in football? No it isn't. The people who say that are just issuing sound bites, words to cover up their failings or naivety about something they have no grasp of. That's my opinion, and as these experts will so pompously tell you that football is really all about opinions then I've given you mine. Five years isn't a long time in anything, least of all anything as insignificant or unimportant - on the scale of things in life- as a game of football. Some footballers don't change their style or attitude over a lifetime of them playing football so how can five years be "a long time"? A long time compared to what? Five years is just a grain of sand on the beach of time. A little speck of nothingness that all too quickly becomes part of your past and it won't even dawn on you that it's gone. We are all just briefly passing through, and whether you are 13 or 93, we are all just so far along the road. Just as someone might not have been around in the first 40 years of your life, you won't be around in the last 40 years of someone else's. It's what you do with it that counts. To dismiss the past as irrelevant is folly. Besides, it always comes round again to tell you where you went wrong the first time, so just be ready for it.

I shrug my shoulders when I hear someone say that nobody really cares anymore about teams that have won nothing in the last 20 years. If they are speaking for themselves and the well rehearsed script they are reading from, then they are probably right. But they definitely don't speak for me or thousands of others out there. It's all part of this daft "living in the now" attitude that's been around for years. It will always be around, too. Teams that have won absolutely bugger all for the last hundred years, never mind twenty, must be doing something right all this time to please and hang on to their fans. They must have provided the odd moment that kept them all going in the dark days. Even kept you dreaming of when they were going to do it all over again.

Do these oracles speak for you when they come up with this tripe? If they do, then football really is in a right old state and we might as well pack it all up now, switch off and just go home. They might as well just say: "Don't bother going to the match anymore, there's no point. You'll never win anything so just give up on your side no matter who you and they are".

There are 92 teams in the league and only four of them can be champions each year. Even now that's become devalued as they'll also tell you that the Premiership is still the only one that counts. They'll tell you that, and virtually drum it into you. As a result, all the other leagues are totally second class, or so the experts will have you believe. The Championship, Leagues One and Two and beyond? "They're all Mickey Mouse". As for the FA Cup and League Cup, they are the sole domain of Manchester United, Chelsea, Arsenal or Liverpool provided they can stir themselves from their lethargy long enough once these competitions have reached the semi-final stages to go on and win it.

You do get the odd shock in the cup, granted, but they are now becoming few and far between and as rare as hen's teeth. Just as Sunderland in 1973,

Southampton in 1976 and West Ham in 1980 won the FA Cup for the old Second Division and Sunderland, again, plus Cardiff and Millwall reached the final from a lower league status, this shouldn't have happened. It wasn't in the script. You'll never again get a Derby County or Nottingham Forest winning the top league title. Those days are gone but not the dreams of the typical footy fan who still clings on to both his season ticket and prayer mat, anticipating and still dreaming of the day when his side come through on the rails to capture The Holy of Holies. If they take your dreams away, then what's left?

There is now a new wave of footy fan sweeping in, as the old ones bow out. Born in the mid to late 80s onwards, they generally don't even know the history of their own club let alone anyone else's. They haven't got time for any of that nonsense. They will openly scorn and deride both old and young alike who cherish things like history and tradition. They'll tell us it's all an irrelevance and unimportant, right? Wrong!

Every side in the league - and I mean every side - has at some point in their history had their own moment of glory. In some cases it might well have been before the birth of the Mighty God Sky, or even telly itself, with stories passed down from father to son. Ancient black and white clips, fast fading through the ravages of time, might well still be around to verify authenticity and above all this, there is always one wise old prophet still wearing the tatty woollen scarf and proudly announcing: "I was there!"

What you might well need in the future (tongue in cheek) to stop the rot of indifference could be the return of the old fashioned 11+ certificate exam for all young supporters of a club. You'd need at least a 60% pass before your dad could take you to the match, and before you'd even be allowed in anyway as a fully fledged supporter. If you fail the test, then you'd need to retake it at a later date. In the meantime, your studying could be carried out on the terraces of a club nearest your home address, but obviously not the club you support. That would be cheating. Not only would you get a decent education as you learn about the team you intend to slavishly follow for the rest of your life, you'd get plenty of fresh air and plenty of time to reflect, too, as you studied your homework at maybe lower league level. Genius or what?

I mentioned terraces there, too. I meant seats although there are still plenty of grounds where (lucky) fans can still stand. The beauty of the terraces even now is that you can slowly and safely walk away from the local loudmouth or village idiot whose actions you don't agree with. You certainly can't do that in all-seater grounds, unless you spot an empty seat elsewhere, pretend you're off to the loo and slowly and discretely walk away, never to return. What am I saying? Of course, you'll be able to find an empty seat. There'll be loads of them in grounds all over the country in the future the way the game's heading.

As I meander down Memory Lane, please don't groan. After all, it won't be long before you find yourself going there as well. I often ponder on early incidents involving games from my past and they always centre round me standing either in the Boys End (did we have a Girls End then? I don't think we did) or in front of the barriers. I've learnt to bite my lip down the years and be a good loser watching my team in action. I manage to see beyond my own allegiance - or maybe that should be blind devotion - towards my side whenever we've played others. I also don't cry anymore when we get beat as I used to when I was really young. Good job, too, as I'd be forever wiping my eyes. But I can still shed a tear with the emotion of it all in some games. You'd be a fool not to, wouldn't you?

Football is a strange game and if she were your wife or girlfriend, you wouldn't trust her an inch. I've seen us batter the opposition for 90 minutes and then lose 1-0 and, at the other end of the scale, seen us play bloody awful and come away with a 4-1 win. And I've always thought the same: "How did that happen?"

If you've got a great memory, like I have, then you'll even be able to store the games away in your mind in alphabetical team order, and refer to them as points of reference many years later when you are playing the same team again. You can even use this technique to impress your friends, or win bets in pubs or at parties. I'll show you what I mean. G is for Grimsby and very early in the 1962/63 season (or was it 63/64?) Sunderland played them near Bonfire Night, November 5th. We won 6-2 and the only way I recollect this was the headline in that night's Sunderland (Footy) Echo:

"Roker forwards let their bangers off and Fishermen's net bulges with rockets"

At another game at The Stadium of Light (and years away from dear old Roker Park) I watched Sunderland throw away a late winning advantage to Portsmouth who did the same thing to us many years previously. I was walking home full of hell and had to laugh at myself when I realised the absurdity of what I was muttering. "That's twice those buggers have shafted us in 15 years". If only life was that wonderful that all we had to worry about, no matter what was thrown at us, was somehow getting stitched up twice every decade and a half. That's when the words of my history teacher came back to me, walking home, just after Pompey had ruined my weekend. I wouldn't have picked up on this absurd irony without my memories. If I'd forgotten the past, then I'd miss out on the irony of it all. Both of them would have counted for nothing. I wouldn't have had the satisfaction of killing that long walk home thinking about how the past can come round to bite you all over again. Simple, isn't it? Or do you want me to run that one by you again?

I look back on my childhood like it was yesterday. It was on the scale of things. 40, 50 or 60 years is just the blink of an eye. As for old, I'll tell you what old really is. Try the Grand Canyon and those fossils dating back 50-60 million years. That's old. 13 or 14 year olds will laugh, but they'll find out quicker than they think. By my reckoning, nostalgia kicks in round about the age of 21, or even earlier if you've been jilted in love as a daft teenager. At 17, you'll yearn to relive those magic last five months - usually the length of time the doomed relationship between you and Waynetta lasted - and you'll get teary eyed and pine for those good old times. That's nostalgia. That's the age you wish you could relive those last few months of bliss and that's when you are already on that "Memory Lane" treadmill. At 30, you will long for being 21 again, and at 40 you'll wish you were 30. And on it goes as time just flows on, and behind you, at a rate of knots. And the worse thing about all this inevitability is that there's bugger all you can do about it. Pick this book up in 20 years time, covered in dust, and you'll nostalgically think: "He was right".

My Uncle Joe, an ex-miner for so many years now, took me to my first ever football match in 1961. Now in his late 60s, but forever young in my eyes, he was then a cross between a young Elvis and Marlon Brando in "The Wild Ones". Joe had a motorbike kept in my Grandma's back yard and I still have a photo of me and him posing on the back of it. Not many years later, he graduated on to the more fashionable Beatles look with nifty jacket to match but, in truth, just like football, I preferred the old look rather than the new one.

It was Sunderland v Norwich City at Roker Park and only three years after Sunderland's relegation from Division One for the first time ever in their history. I didn't know this at the time, of course, but I quickly learned my Sunderland history along with my ten times table when I started to get interested in the game at that junior apprenticeship level. Joe also set me exam questions which I tried to get the right answers to as I made my way backwards and forwards to and from the fish shop doing messages for him every Friday night.

On the day, and because his mate's car had yet again broken down, we got the train to Sunderland and walked across Wearmouth Bridge to Roker. There was the first sight of those now old-fashioned, long gone, massive floodlight pylons coming into view as we rounded the corner into Roker Baths Road, followed by the huge concrete structure that was the Roker End. It was awe-inspiring for a nine year old, but that was nothing to what lay ahead once I first stepped inside the ground. It must have been the equivalent to the feeling an Ancient Roman might have had when he first stepped foot inside the Colosseum.

Once I'd made my way past the kiosks selling the pies and Bovril, and gazed up at the darkness of the mass concrete above, it was like emerging from the underground into daylight. A bit like a miner must have felt getting out of the cage into bright sunshine. The first thing I noticed was the lush broad green pitch then the massed banks of terraces already half full. Then, when I turned round to look back, I saw a huge bank of terracing going backwards and upwards for what seemed forever. Then I was standing directly behind the goal, and fighting for a vantage spot along with hundreds of others. I was told my reaction would either be one of two things - I'd either love it or hate it, no in betweens.

No prizes for guessing which way it went with me. The crowd, the noise, the build up to kick-off, the buzz of the masses that got louder and louder, the little old man at the front in his white jacket yelling: "Peanuts-tanner a bag" and, to cap it all, the huge roar at five to three as the teams came out and my first sight of the colours of both sides. Sunderland used to run out in those days to the sounds of "Z Cars", still associated this day with Everton. To a nine year old too young to understand anything about the vagaries of plagiarism back then, it didn't matter. I used to love that record and still do whenever I hear it, usually when Everton are on the box. When I think back to that first match, I genuinely believe that was the exact moment when I must have first started the habit of associating everyday things with a specific match in time. To prove it, 50 years on I can still picture my uncle Joe wearing black winkle pickers, blue skin tight jeans and a light grey top. He was also desperately trying to catch a bag of peanuts being hurled towards him by that little old bloke in the white coat.

It was a brilliant sunny day, warm and lazy, and I can still see now the striking contrasts in the colours of the two sides. Norwich played with their yellow shirts and green shorts, and Sunderland in red and white stripes and then white shorts. Because of that day, I have always had a soft spot for Norwich. I even remember pestering my dad that Christmas to buy me a yellow footy shirt and green shorts but don't think he had much joy getting them. Instead I ended up with a blue & white striped Sheffield Wednesday shirt (or was it Hartlepool?) and black shorts. Near enough, as far as dad was concerned.

The game itself seemed to pass like a blur, and at breakneck speed. It was as if Sunderland had planned the day especially for me and no one else as they took an early lead and went on to a 2-0 win. But I also recall the crowd groaning and squealing in both panic and agony as Norwich had Sunderland on the ropes before a second goal calmed things down near the end.

I was well and truly hooked after that and it was plain sailing as to where I wanted to be every other Saturday afternoon. I used to cry on the rare times it wasn't my turn to go and my brother Tommy went in my place. By then Joe and his mates were the talk of Easington as they graduated to a reliable car and there was only one spare seat available.

Money really was tight in those days as well, even though it was only relatively cheap to get in, and you learned to share good things. Besides, it would have spoilt us if we got things that easy early on. My mam just couldn't afford for both Tommy and me to go so that was the end of it. Nobody went berserk then or rolled around the supermarket floor till they got their own way. You just got on with it. After wiping away the tears, I devised a way of making sure that next time, with or without Joe, I'd be able to make my own way there.

I quickly learned how to earn my match day money along with my cousin Steven Brown, by shovelling in loads of coal that were dropped in the backstreets of Easington. This was a regular ritual all over the many collieries scattered across South East Durham, and everywhere else in the North East coalfield, too. Each house had an outside coal hatch which opened so you could then fill the coalhouse in the back yards. With a big shovel you could probably put in a full load in maybe 20 minutes, less if there were two of you. For that you maybe got two shillings which got one of you into the match. We used to end up pitch black at the end of the day and if you were lucky enough and fit enough you'd maybe get to do five houses in one day. Exhausting work, but it kept us well out of mischief and taught us the early values of hard work.

Once we shovelled in a load for this old miner who promised us a special treat when we finished. Expecting a big bonus, we went at that coal at break neck speed and then imagine our surprise when he gave us two slices of jam and bread each when we'd finished. We were that miffed, we waited till he sloped off down the local boozer, climbed into his coalhouse, and spent nearly five times longer shovelling the whole lot back out onto the street. Mind you, we still ate the jam and bread. If you asked kids to do that today for pocket money you'd end up in court for child cruelty and abuse.

What made it all the more laughable was that I'd be on holiday at the time flitting back and forth from London with mam and dad. There wasn't much in the way of sightseeing or sunbathing to be done in the Colliery, so I just made my own entertainment. No music arcades around so I just shovelled coal as part of the then 1960s Healthy Schoolchildren Initiative Programme. I'm just surprised that they haven't reintroduced it today for 12 and 13 year olds. Much more fun than tweeting each other, and whatever else it is they do.

Following Sunderland in the 1960s was a golden period as far as both crowds and players went. Ask your dad, or maybe your grandpa, and they'll endorse what I'm saying. They'll all have their own memories, their own favourite matches and moments, but they'll all roughly tell you the same thing. We had the terraces and if you weren't lucky enough to have stood on some of them, then you've never really watched English football in its truest and rawest sense. Looking back now, maybe you were lucky to have been spared this experience, but at the time we just took it for granted.

The sanitised setting of, in most cases, modern all seater stadiums is now the vogue, although there are still a few fleapits out there even today. The modern stadiums are appreciated by many but there is something wrong somewhere today when a few hundred away fans can usually out shout and out sing a 40,000 plus home crowd. When you see this happening it's as if football is, in some way, selling its own soul, its own identity on the cheap. I suppose this is an inevitable consequence after Heysel, Hillsborough and Valley Parade where something clearly had to be done.

It's strange how games from over 45 years in your past happened as if they were yesterday. When we first moved to London to start our new life it was like we'd all moved to another world. Everything down there was different to what we had grown up with. The culture, the language, everything was alien. Now it's nothing, with motorways and all, but back then it was like moving to a foreign country. Some people today still think London is. It was the winter of the big freeze with bad weather lasting for months on end and it caused chaos across the country. There were snow drifts 12 feet deep in parts. Now, if there's six inches the whole country is paralysed. Even in the bad weather, I used to get back home to the North East often enough on the "Magic Bus" from Victoria to Sunderland. It was a lifeline, and the closer I got to my old stomping ground the happier I'd feel.

There were games too numerous to mention, good and bad, but mainly good as far as I can recollect. Teams then seemed to go out to win games, home and away, and weren't content to merely go out looking for a point, and this was when it was two points for a win. The temptation to claim half the spoils would have been a lot more desirable then than today, you'd have thought, but that wasn't the case then. Sides just went gung ho in some cases for that one extra point, not two, for a win. They'd be out of the traps like greyhounds and naturally this made for some fantastic games. Scores like 5-5, 4-4, 7-2, 5-4, 4-3, 5-3, 6-6 and even 8-3 used to appear often on the box. Today, they'd be sacking managers twice a week at some clubs with results like that. This reckless, maybe naïve, approach to a game was great to watch sometimes. Sunderland used to win a lot more games in the old Second Division than they ever did in the First. But then again, so did everybody else that stepped up from the wide open spaces of the Second to encounter the elite forces of the First. There was always a massive gap in class. I was way too young to recollect their last great glory days pre-1958, and even my own dad was too young to remember their golden age of the 1930s. Hand on heart, and as sad as it is to say this, I think those days are gone forever. I could be wrong, of course.

There were memorable games for an excited 10-11 year old, including an away trip to Ayresome Park. Sunderland waltzed into an early 3-0 lead over Middlesbrough then had to cling on for a point in a 3-3 draw. There was a night game at home against Newcastle played in a blizzard. Sunderland and a very young Brian Clough won 2-1 in front of 56,000. I was frozen but that warm glow afterwards as I thawed out slowly in front of a roaring coal fire at my nan's, then making my way up to bed to relive every kick in my dreams.

By far and away, the most dramatic and memorable of them all was in March 1961, FA Cup Round Six with Sunderland home to the then mighty Spurs on their way that season to the double. As a treat (a treat?) dad decided that he would take me along. Brother Tommy, then only six, was deemed too little to go, and this time it was his turn for the tears. I felt sorry for him as we left the house but if I'd known the ordeal that lay ahead for both my dad and me, I think I would have gladly swapped places with him there and then, and stayed at home with mam.

Tottenham had a fabulous side that season but I still think that for one moment of fate, Sunderland would have beaten them that day. The gates were shut with 61,000 inside, but looking back now, I think there were even more in there. In all the games I've watched since then, it was the only time in my life I was ever really scared inside a football ground, and I've been in some pretty frightening crowds down the years. The instructions I got from dad were very simple - hold on to his hand tight once we got inside and don't let go. I wished almost instantly I was anywhere else other than in an already nearly full Roker End. It was terrifying and it was still nearly two hours before kick off as we tried to find some safe point on the terraces. The front end was already packed beyond packed, and so that was one cunning plan by my dad that went right out of the window. The Roker End used to hold well over 20,000 in its heyday before being reduced to a shadow of its former self in the 1980s. When full, and in full voice, it was an awesome sight (think of The Kop at Liverpool) and it was already full at 2pm, with thousands more pushing, shoving, trampling and forcing their way in. It was impossible to get a decent spot to see and I was clinging on for dear life to my dad, in front of a barrier one moment and then the next I was just swept from him by a swaying, surging sea of people.

Those safety barriers that day were anything but as people pushed, shoved, squeezed and punched their way to a relatively secure position. But there wasn't any. I looked on helplessly, the panic rising in me, as my father drifted further and further away. I couldn't breathe properly and then almost immediate sanctuary as two men, realising the danger, lifted not just me bodily, but three or four other shrimps, above their heads and up and away down to the front and the cinder track behind the goal.

Today there would have been some bloke with a clip board watching all this from a safe security point somewhere, carrying out a risk assessment analysis before deciding whether to intervene. But back then, it was a case of "get the buggers in" and then "get the buggers out again" when they saw the danger signs. I really think people could have been crushed to death that day, and the sad thing is, I saw many more scenes like this down the years in many grounds elsewhere.

It was also my introduction to the Roker Roar, the first time I had ever heard such a deafening noise. I was never again to experience such a noise or atmosphere anywhere and this includes London, Glasgow and Manchester derbies. I'd heard and read about it in the papers but it meant nothing to me as a young lad. Besides, until you've seen or heard something yourself, you don't tend to believe it, do you? How best to describe it? It was a cross between spine tingling, deafening and uplifting, with just a pinch of petrifying thrown in to add to the effect.

I still get goose bumps just thinking about it and still maintain, even at my tender age then, that Sunderland would definitely have won but for one moment of madness by the crowd. When Sunderland levelled in the second half to make it 1-1 after trailing so early in the game, that signalled a mass pitch invasion by hordes of ecstatic fans, no doubt fired up and in a state of delirium by the incredible explosion of noise. That pitch invasion was also the start of a new trend too. Back then it was unheard of, but I suppose the sheer exultation of that equalizer, after enormous pressure, was like a dam bursting. The people - and the noise - just exploded on to the pitch. I'll never forget seeing, from the safe confines and comfort of the cinder track, the look on

Spurs captain Danny Blanchflower's face as it happened. Even the normally composed and laid back Irishman had a look of shock and bewilderment in his eyes, as he screamed and pushed his team into some semblance of order. They were like a boxer on the ropes, hanging on for grim life and praying for the bell to ring, to stop the pounding they were getting.

The delay caused by that pitch invasion gave Spurs vital time to rally round and recover. Had the referee restarted the game quickly then they were there for the taking. They were out on their feet, gone, mesmerised and, I think, beaten by the intensity of it all. But those two or three minutes of mayhem allowed them to regroup, get their breath back, and just about hang on. Even then there was pandemonium as Spurs desperately defended a last minute corner, with the roar by then at maximum decibels. Taking all this in, and all at once, left an indelible mark on my mind. You cannot begin to even know where to start to describe such things to anyone of another generation, or indeed, even anyone who was around at the time and didn't get in that afternoon. Football memories are a highly charged personal thing and the excitement and pandemonium of that one afternoon meant that Sunderland had their claws into me for life. They had already beaten Arsenal 2-1 at Roker and then Second Division Liverpool away 2-0 in earlier rounds, and another upset looked on the cards. I think that if we'd edged past Spurs, the momentum would have carried us all the way to Wembley. Who knows we might have been the first Second Division team since 1931 to win the Cup, a full twelve years earlier than we actually did in 1973. Fate decreed otherwise. I remember reading Blanchflower's autobiography a good few years afterwards when he referred to that particular game. He described it quite simply as the most incredible and deafening experience he had ever encountered in all his playing days anywhere in the world.

While all this was going on, my dad was frantically yelling at me to stay where I was. There was no chance of me leaving my safe haven, and certainly not joining in with the rest of the cavalry when the stampede began. It was odd seeing my father trying to combine looking out for me and watching the game at the same time. We both waited till the ground was well and truly empty after the final whistle and, even then, there were loads of people doing the same thing. I think all of them just wanted to get down off cloud nine that they all must still have been on after watching that hour and a half of pure theatre. I was reunited with him long after full time and we both made our way home back to the bus station in a stunned kind of silence. I don't know about him, but I was well and truly shattered. Fresh air never tasted so good after getting out of that packed madhouse. I fell asleep all the way home on the bus.

We both listened excitedly on the radio (no telly coverage then) the following Wednesday night for the replay in front of an even bigger, but much quieter, 64,000 crowd at White Hart Lane. What a terrible anti-climax that night turned out to be for Sunderland. Spurs won 5-0 and, to be honest, it was easy for them. I think Sunderland had well and truly shot their bolt in the first game. It was all or nothing for them at Roker, and nothing was all we had left for the replay. I often wonder what would have happened, though, if that last minute header from a corner at home had somehow squeezed in. If it had, I suspect the crowd would probably have celebrated a famous day by taking half the ground home with them as a souvenir.

Most of the 1964/69 years were spent watching Sunderland usually getting thumped all over London, my new home. But with dad in tow, there were still some sparkling moments, a few laughs but usually tears. I wore my heart well and truly on my sleeve, as well as the red and white rosette on my chest. In those days, Sunderland always had a bit of magic about them. It seems hard to believe, but it was true. They were well respected in the capital, and had massive away support then as now. They were a bigger draw at the time than our North East neighbours Newcastle up the road. And that was a fact. It's worth remembering also that in the glory days of the 1930s, only a brief 30 years before, Spurs and Arsenal's ground record crowds were both set against Sunderland. In that era both Sunderland and Arsenal were North/South rivals. Those things stick in the minds of real, hardcore, traditional fans and never go away if you are an older fan. And these fables would, no doubt, have been passed on in legend to the next generation of younger fans, sons and grandsons, too. It was the same reason why fans my age remember the mighty Wolves side of the 1950s.

Looking back it was easy to see why Sunderland still had this allure. We had only ever played in the top division right up until 1958 from the days when the league was founded. Promotion in 1964 after six years in the wilderness must then have been regarded as the return for keeps of the proverbial prodigal son. There was a real shock in the football world with Sunderland's relegation in 1958. If only we had a crystal ball in 1964. We've been up and down like a fiddler's elbow ever since although hopefully we might now look forward to a more stable time in the Premier.

One of our first games in London after the return to the top flight first time was at Highbury and although we lost 3-1, we played some great stuff. The Arsenal crowd loved it and for a good half hour we had them on the rack. Unfortunately for Sunderland, the Gunners did what we couldn't. One run by

George Mulhall, Sunderland's flying winger, was worth the admission money alone. A scorching 50 yard burst beating man after man, the inch perfect cross to little Nick Sharkey's head and the ball just waiting to hit the back of the net. Except that it didn't and went straight over the bar. Never mind, I was naively thinking, it's only a matter of time. And it was - for Arsenal.

There was the nightmare of an 8-0 thrashing at West Ham in 1968 where Geoff Hurst could have taken a shot at the corner flag and somehow it would have found its way into the net. I knew it was going to be a bad day when dad and I got there late for the kick off after being stuck in an underground tunnel just outside Plaistow. By the time we got into Upton Park we were already 2-0 down. We thought this Hammers fan who told us was pulling our legs. When we realised he wasn't, we should have left there and then but, ever the optimists we waited for the fight back to begin. Sunderland once beat the Hammers 3-2 at Upton Park earlier in the 60s after trailing 2-0 and we clung on to the belief it could happen again. There was no chance of it that afternoon. It was a bit like Custer at the Little Big Horn waiting for the Indians to run out of arrows. Worse, a lot worse, was to follow, as Geoff Hurst went on to score six. I took scant consolation in definitely thinking that one of the eight was handled into the net by him but it was all academic. At 6-0 down, even Jimmy Montgomery, years later to make Wembley's greatest ever save, had a huge grin on his face as yet another West Ham chance went begging. At least I think it was a grin on his face. It could have been shock. At the end, as we debated the shambles, we thought that West Ham would have beaten anybody in the division playing like this. A week later, I think they got turned over 3-0 by one of the bottom sides. That was West Ham, alright.

For some reason, it was always dear old Fulham, the real poor relations then of London, who always used to turn us over at Craven Cottage. Dear honest, trustworthy, ever so friendly and ever so dependable Fulham. They only averaged about 20,000 gates and that was poor back then by First Division standards. Even Third. Division Brentford nearly got more than that. And it was always the same bugger, over and over again, who stuck it to us. The late and unbelievably great Johnny Haynes. What a player he was. He used to do all the damage whenever we met. In the late 70s and early 80s, he'd have been a stretcher case in the first ten minutes of the match, but in the mid to late 60s silky skills reigned supreme. And Johnny Haynes was both skilful and supreme. How he never played for anyone bigger than homely little Fulham I just don't know but players round that era were incredibly loyal. Their only reward, long after their playing days ended, was to be remembered, loved and revered. There were so many of this type of player back then, motivated by home town pride rather than money And how many can you say that about today?

In one end of season game, where Fulham made an impossible escape from relegation that even Harry Houdini wouldn't have pulled off, Haynes beat Sunderland on his own 3-0. Tony Macedo, the Fulham keeper, could have watched the game at the other end sitting comfortably in a deckchair for 90 minutes. I should know because I was standing right behind him waiting forlornly for him to be called into action. The busiest he got was picking loose crisp packets off the pitch. I think he spent the second half counting pigeons on top of the main stand roof.

Then there was the sheer majesty, magic and cheekiness of the one and only Jimmy Greaves, who on his own absolutely slaughtered us at White Hart Lane. We lost 5-1 and it could have been 15. Although I should have hated him, I was absolutely mesmerised by this little goal-moocher, this genius who flitted in and out of the game just like the Artful Dodger picking pockets, and helped himself to three - or was it four? - goals from four touches. My favourite opposition player ever and if you'd seen him that afternoon he would have been yours, too. Win, lose or draw, he always played it the right way and always with a cheeky grin on his face, plotting who to stitch up next. He was quick, lethal, crafty, cunning, deadly, and accurate. Everything you'd ever want in the perfect forward. If you get the chance to read any of his books or even see him in person, then just do it. He's as funny off the field as he was the smiling assassin on it.

QPR briefly appeared in the old top flight in the mid-60s but not for long. The only First Division game Sunderland played there was a 2-2 draw on a wet and very loud Wednesday night. Then there was Chelsea who were the darlings of the London set back then (and a bit like now really). Through a youngster's eyes, they represented football's answer to the aristocracy, and a then painful reminder of the heartache of why the likes of my father had to leave the North East and look for work in London. Isn't it funny and a bit ironic that 50 years on, and for different reasons, Chelsea are still arguably London's biggest club. We usually got nothing there in terms of league points, with 3-1 the usual type of score we got beat by. But I do remember seeing another little gem, a bloke called Bobby Tambling, a smashing forward who seemed to find it so easy to beat our defence over and over again.

I still find it odd as to how you can remember games from so long ago like it was last week, and games last week just seem to vanish from the mind. It must be some kind of football dementia or perhaps selective forgetfulness. Maybe when you do get older they don't seem to have the same significance or importance. Maybe you just can't be bothered by it all. I do know that when I was only nine I spent so much of my time down my nan's in Easington before we headed down South. I compare Easington then to the way I think of football today. Back then, Easington Colliery was a thriving busy little pit village, and today it seems little more than a ghost town, with huge swathes of streets now gone along with that strong and proud community spirit. Every time I drive through there it's the nearest thing you can imagine to going back in time. They even used it to film "Billy Elliott." They didn't have to spend much transforming the place either.

Many proud and identical pit villages in both Durham and Northumberland went the same way. Some might call it progress that all the dirt and belching chimneys spewing out smoky coal fumes have now long gone, but many more would call it a downright shame. They may have been dirty and old fashioned but they'd never turn their back on you.

My earliest end of season memory in Easington goes way back to season 1961/2. That was the birth of the modern Liverpool as we know them now, as they steamrollered their way out of the Second Division with some Scottish manager called Bill Shankly. Little did we know at the time but that man was laying the first foundations and building blocks that are still around today. They were way too good for the division and I laugh now when I recall how Shankly always reminded me of James Cagney. At one stage I was convinced they were one and the same person - until I first heard Shanks on the radio. James Cagney never spoke with a broad Scots accent. Another childhood illusion shattered. Liverpool would figure prominently throughout the sixties for this particular Sunderland fan, and they were nearly all unhappy memories.

Sunderland got thumped twice that season by them, 4-1 at home and 3-0 away. Even then, it looked like it was us that were going to go up with them in second place. I'd have settled for that. Even Plymouth Argyle came into the promotion frame that season and they have never been so close to the top flight since. The only other club who were near us for that magical second slot were Leyton Orient and they couldn't possibly get promoted with crowds of only 15,000, could they? There were no play offs then and only two points for a win. Goal average, not goal difference, used to also be taken into account. So you'd have the daft situation of some team pipping you for promotion because their goal difference was 1.75435 whereas yours was only 1.65843. No wonder I was so good at Maths back then as I studied the Saturday night League Tables.

The last red hot day of that season saw us sitting next to the pit yard wall at the bottom of Camp Street, Easington with a portable radio on full blast next to our ears (technology or what?). Neddy Ball, an old man who lived opposite at the bottom of Camp Street, did his bit and he had his radio on full volume for additional support, and the back door open. It was Sunderland away to Swansea Town (they hadn't changed their name to City then) and Leyton Orient at home to Bury. Leyton hadn't dropped their first name then either and when they finally did it took some convincing trying to tell my young brother Tommy that they were actually a London club and not from the Far East.

The maths that day was quite simple (no they weren't!). Sunderland had the better goal difference by something like 0.232 of a goal (and they call the game daft today) and if both they and Leyton won, then Sunderland would be promoted. No ifs, ands or buts. That was it. I listened intently, me and seven others- eight pairs of tiny lugs all pressed round one brick sized radio. The reception was that poor you'd think the commentary was coming from Mars, but we exploded in joy collectively when Sunderland went 1-0 up but then discovered Leyton were leading 1-0 as well. That didn't matter, though, as long as the scores stayed the same.

The minutes dragged on and we were told by the expert at Vetch Field that a second goal looked on the cards as Sunderland dominated. And then just as things couldn't get any more tense or exciting, we lost the reception for what seemed an eternity. Then, suddenly, the radio spluttered back into life again but something was horribly wrong. Why did the man on the radio - this expert - tell us that Sunderland needed to score again if the two results stayed as they were? Then the horror as it dawned on us all that Swansea had equalised while we had all been stranded on the dark side of the moon. I still remember the man who scored it as well. Brayley Reynolds. We listened in agony to the last fifteen, ten, then five minutes as Sunderland missed chances to go 2-1 up and get instant promotion. A yell on the radio of "It's in - oh, it's kicked off the line!" had us filled with false hope, and then suddenly it was all over. Leyton Orient had won 2-0 and they were up. And we weren't. I felt tears rolling down my cheeks, but at least I wasn't alone. It seemed like the end of the world but of course it wasn't, although having to wait another year before we could try and get up again seemed so unfair.

If you don't believe that lightning doesn't strike twice in the same place, then you'd be wrong. The following year, 1962/63 and a year to the day, Sunderland knocked on the door yet again. And just like the previous year, it was a three team fight. If football is theatre, then that season Chelsea would be cast as pantomime villains.

Stoke City were the team that everybody wanted to beat that season, maybe because they had the star of the show in a 48 year old Stanley Matthews who had returned there from Blackpool. The only time I ever got to see this great man play was actually at Stamford Bridge when dad and I just managed to get in before they shut the gates with 66,000 crammed inside. Wherever Matthews and Stoke went so, too, did the crowds. There were 62,000 at Roker Park to see Sunderland beat Stoke 2-1 and I'm sure that Matthews never played that day. I don't think he often figured much for Blackpool either, come to think of it, whenever he and they came to Roker Park. Of course, you wouldn't dare tell the punters he wasn't turning out until they had all paid to get in, would you?

At Stamford Bridge, where the main priority that hot day in the middle of a packed Shed, was to actually breathe for 90 minutes, a very young, and very nervous, Chopper Harris played against Matthews. He still put in a couple of crunching tackles, nervous or not, which Stanley shrugged off with a smile. Stoke won a pretty drab match 1-0 and the magic of Matthews rubbed off on his team. Those two games both occurred over the Easter weekend and I stupidly, again, believed that those results meant that both us and Stoke were going to go up at Chelsea's expense.

It was the season that seemed to go on forever and ever, and the harsh winter paralysed football for 12 whole weeks. You had teams still not past the Third Round of the Cup who, because of postponements, actually ended up in the Fifth Round draw. It was crazy. Can you imagine today, for example, seeing a cup draw as follows: Blackburn Rovers or Burnley or Plymouth Argyle or Crewe Alexandra v Tottenham Hotspur or Arsenal or Sheffield United or Brentford. That's how daft it was. And then, of course, if there were replays in any of those games it prolonged the agony even further. Games could even go to a third or fourth replay. There were no penalty shoot outs deciding matters back then. That season went on way past its sell by date because of it all. Today all the drama would have been removed by probably just tossing a coin to settle the matter.

On the very last day of that very long season Chelsea went to Roker Park in an almost impossible situation. I actually felt sorry for them before the match. They were four old points - that's two wins - behind Sunderland but with a much better goal difference. Chelsea had a game in hand and it was Sunderland's final game of the season. Everything was stacked against Chelsea. All Sunderland needed to do was draw at home and that was it. Game over, they were up. It was even simpler than the year before and not a Brayley Reynolds in sight to do any damage. Chelsea not only had to win at Roker, but then win their final home game against Portsmouth, to pip us. However, I should have known that day that this wasn't going to be any ordinary showdown due to a series of events that tilted the match Chelsea's way.

The weather that afternoon in the North East was absolutely awful with a deluge of sleety rain (or was that rainy sleet?) driving in from the North Sea. It was absolutely freezing. You wouldn't have sent a dog out in it but we were still in the ground for 2 o'clock. For some reason, rumours swept round the town and outlying areas that the match had been called off. Local Radio Stations added to the confusion and advised a "wait and see" approach. But many people must have assumed the game was going to be postponed because of the weather (I wish it had been) and never bothered to get along. As a result "only" 47,000 turned up. Still a good crowd but it would have topped 62,000 if it hadn't been for the Chinese Whispers. That extra 15,000 might just have tipped the scales Sunderland's way that day. They would have been swept to promotion by the noise. It is little things like this that can make the difference between winning and glory, and losing and disaster.

It was one of those games where you knew, just knew, that Sunderland weren't going to score. They threw everything but the kitchen sink at Chelsea and dominated from the off. But the state of the pitch slowed down the game and suited Chelsea's heavy handed tactics. Not only was the ball clogging in the mud, Chelsea were also clogging into Sunderland. Their game plan was to disrupt the flow and also kick the crap out of Sunderland. They succeeded. Poor old Charlie Hurley was one of the early victims. As the crowd started to go quiet, so Chelsea also started to menacingly hit Sunderland on the break. Late in the first-half, the smallest bloke on the pitch, little Tommy Harmer, deflected a shot in from a corner off his backside to put Chelsea 1-0 up. The Roker Roar turned into absolute silence in a split second as reality started to slowly set in. I thought back to Swansea the year before. It couldn't happen again could it? It could, and it did. Try as they might, Sunderland just couldn't get the ball in the net. I learned something at that match, too, that still applies to this day. You can have the best team in the world, the best players, you can dominate from start to finish and create chance after chance but if your luck is out, you'll not win. It was Grayfields playing field in Hartlepool all over again when our school team failed to do the business and snatched a defeat from the jaws of victory.

There was one astonishing incident when an equaliser looked certain. Peter Bonetti (at least I think it was him) dived the wrong way and the ball just clipped him on the heels and went out for a corner. You can't legislate for that sort of luck in football, and just to think also that if the ball had hit Tommy Harmer on his right buttock and not his left one, Chelsea wouldn't have scored. Oh, the cheek of it.

Of course the local Football Echo tried to be optimistic that Saturday night. Chelsea still had to win their final home game against Portsmouth but we knew that the game was up, in more ways than one. It was like that Spurs Cup game all over again. I was hoping against hope that dear old Pompey would do their bit and help us out by getting a draw. With prayer mat in hand, I listened in on the radio midweek. Sunderland could still go up. Chelsea didn't just win the match. They annihilated Portsmouth 7 – 0.

The following year was the year when we finally won promotion and the last home game against Charlton was almost an anti climax as we won 2–1 in front of 51,000. Even then, the team we went up with, the incredibly popular and fans' favourites Leeds United, went on to much greater things in the top flight than we ever did, but at what price?

However, the real highlight of that season, and there were many in the 1960s, was an epic FA Cup sixth round battle against Manchester United. Sunderland had already battered the then league champions Everton 3-1 at Roker in an earlier round in front of an ecstatic 62,000, a match that was all but over at half time as we raced in to a 3–0 lead. Bristol City were also beaten 6–1 but their fans did them proud with loads of noise. The replayed game against Man United at Roker should never have happened though. In the first match at Old Trafford, Sunderland were 3–1 up with only five minutes to go. Then, as now, they treated the fans to their familiar Japanese Suicide act routine. Somehow, this time they managed to snatch a draw from the jaws of victory. Charlie Hurley hammered in a wonderful own goal past a bemused Jimmy Montgomery with a shot that Bobby Charlton would have been proud of, and another one quickly followed from George Best. And the rest, as they say, is history.

Still, never mind I thought, we'll finish them off at Roker Park. After all, it was only Manchester United with Charlton, Law, Crerand, Best and all. At 3 o' clock onwards in Sunderland that midweek afternoon, over 100,000 people started to converge on Roker Park. Thousands from the local shipyards and mines left work early, many with compassionate notes to bury their dearly departed grandmothers .The crowd congestion around the ground was that serious that some of the Sunderland players staying at the nearby Roker Hotel on the seafront were forced to walk to the ground and even when they got there they struggled to get in.

The official attendance that night, after gates were smashed down enabling thousands to rampage free into the ground, was given as that magical figure of 47,000 again. Anyone in there that night and lucky enough to get out unscathed would tell you that the crowd was probably well in excess of

70,000, and probably nudging towards Sunderland's record ever crowd of 75,000 against Derby in the 1930s. It was absolutely heaving. If it had been cattle in there, they would have called out the RSPCA and shut the place down, but then it was just part of being a footy fan. Anything in the way of you was trampled as you fought to get in, and then out again. People lost all interest in the game in some sections of the crowd and were punching each other just to try and get out. If you actually fell or fainted in the crush that night then you would probably have ended up a fatality. Sadly, people now realise that in those type of crowds, this wasn't wild exaggeration, as Hillsborough was later to confirm in devastating circumstances. Over 20 years before that particular tragedy though it was just a way of life. People who yearn for the return of the terraces might have had a real rethink if they had been in there that night. It was the equivalent of bobbing about in the middle of a raging, mountainous sea without a lifejacket, and not being able to swim as an added handicap. You just wanted the game to end so that the crowd could just ebb away and let you feel safe again.

Sunderland took the lead twice and each time got pegged back as the game finished 2-2 in extra time. Two draws and both times we had the game won. I thought it would be third time lucky as I tuned into the midweek radio yet again. No penalty shoot outs then, and so it was off to Leeds Road, Huddersfield for the second replay. Sunderland started like an express train and when we quickly went 1-0 up, I thought: "this time we'll win". We didn't, and lost 5-1. That night they actually showed the highlights in black and white on Sportsnight. Of course, had Sunderland managed "Mission Impossible" and won, you just knew that the camera men would have lost the film on the way to the TV studio.

In truth, that was just about it in terms of excitement for the rest of the 60s. Our first game in the First Division in 1964/65 was home against Leicester and a 3-3 draw. We went into that match with the youngest top flight player ever in goal for us - goalkeeper Derek Forster aged 15 years 185 days. And at the opposite end, there was Gordon Banks, England's greatest ever keeper. Banks gave young Forster a friendly hug and scuffed his hair as they exchanged ends at the start of the game. It was a debut covering three games and ten goals conceded by Forster that effectively ruined the rest of that youngster's career. He was barely heard of again. That's how cruel football can be.

1964/65 and the following seasons saw us as little more than perennial strugglers and those fans who thought that the glory days were just around the corner would quickly become disillusioned and vote with their feet, with gates dropping to round the 20,000 mark. There were still some fantastic memories though.

One match, in particular, left me and my brother with a bitter/sweet experience. On Boxing Day 1965 we went to Roker to see them play Liverpool. I don't know what possessed us but that day there was only two of us going and we went on the bus. The pair of us had on the standard gabardine mackintoshes and short trousers. By the time the bus trundled through Easington Colliery delayed by both snow and ice, we should have realised it was going to be yet another one of those days. We were like two blocks of ice getting on the bus, and the slow journey through to Sunderland didn't thaw us out at all. We then had to walk over a mile from the bus station to the ground and get in early for a good spot down the front. There was a long, long wait for the kick off. No roof, a biting wind, sleet and snow in the air and an hour and a half before the teams came out. If I could have wished the pair of us back home in front of the fire there and then, there would have been an instant two empty spaces on the terraces. We were freezing and there was no way on earth me and my ten year old brother were going to last till twenty to five. It was now an hour to kick off and with the cold unbearable, we were like two little penguins dancing up and down trying to keep warm and huddled together for warmth. I don't think I've ever been as cold as that since.

At five minutes to kick off, the teams were out for "shotty in" and Liverpool were at the Roker End for their warm up (warm up?). My one abiding memory of that day was a fierce looking Bill Shankly, collecting tracksuits from his team, whilst barking out what were obviously last minute instructions. He passed behind the goal less than a yard from us with a lovely, warm smile for all those hundreds of tiny frozen faces. And much more than this, he held out his right hand as he walked slowly round the touchline on his way back to the dressing room, trying to reach as many of those excited youngsters hands as he could (a bit like the high five routine you'd see today). Both Tommy and me were ideally placed and both of us got a fleeting touch of a warm hand against our own two frozen ones. Tommy only vaguely remembers that incident, but when I told him years later whose hand tried to warm his that day, his eyes just lit up. That was the magic of Shankly, even to a Sunderland supporter.

And then the match was off with Liverpool attacking the Roker End, and both of us hoping for an early goal for Sunderland to at least try and warm us up. It didn't happen. Liverpool raced into a 2-0 lead right in front of us .Two sucker punches with two identical goals from corner kicks, two flicked on back headers by Ian Lawler to find the head of Ian St. John who nodded in twice on the six yard line. And that was even before some of the stragglers had even got into the ground. That was enough for the pair of us. In tears with the cold, I made an executive decision and we must have left after a quarter of an hour in. We couldn't take any more, and I don't mean the score either. All I wanted to do was to get the pair of us home and we both hobbled slowly all the way back over the bridge to the bus station, every step agony on our frozen feet. Even today, I still watch programmes on telly about people stranded in snowstorms suffering from hypothermia and think: "I know exactly what you're going through".

The feeling of relief and joy as the pair of us eventually got home that day from our very own Ice Station Zebra! The absolute luxury of getting in and sitting on the mat in front of that big banked fire - you can keep your gas central heating - as the feeling of warmth, accompanied by pins and needles, ever so slowly returned to our grateful feet. And as for the match, Sunderland did come back to 2-2 but not for another fifty minutes. We'd never have lasted that long. Then a third sucker punch from Liverpool to win 3-2 near the end and that put paid to that. No Match Of The Day, no goals on telly so we had to rely on match reports. One crumb of comfort was that Sunderland went to Anfield a couple of days later and drew the return fixture 0-0. Our feet had just about thawed out by then.

I suppose there were other crumbs of comfort to keep us going through the rest of the sixties. Sunderland's promotion in 1963/64, the build up to that and the cup run that season, left an indelible impression on young minds. There were big crowds every home game and when you've been standing in them, ranging from 42,000 to 62,000, then it's a bit of a come down to see them dip to only around the 20,000 mark, as they did regularly when the magic started to wear off. It was pitiful to watch. There was always, though, just like life itself, something or someone to come along and lift your spirits. Someone a bit like Bill Shankly making our day, and leaving one small memory to last a lifetime, when all he did was "shake hands" briefly with me and brother Tommy. For me, that's right up there with seeing Jimi Hendrix live (and even briefly stopping to talk to him). I'm still dining out on both those two stories.

And perhaps it was rather prophetic - or perhaps pathetic - to describe Sunderland's last performance in the First Division that brought down our 1960s curtain on the big stage with Liverpool again the visitors to Roker Park in the 1969/70 season. It was a typical Sunderland scenario with us needing to win to stop up. But many fans then must have thought "Stop up for what? Yet another slog over nine months?"

There was really a general feeling of apathy both on and off the field around that period. Only five short years earlier in the Siberian conditions that me and my brother endured, the crowd at Sunderland nudged 50,000 for Liverpool's visit. The attendance that night was only just above the 30,000 mark. That's 20,000 missing, totally disinterested fans. I think many who had been disillusioned by empty promises had just given up. Even then, I think that Liverpool came along that night determined to do their bit to keep us up and send Crystal Palace down instead. That's how a lot of us felt and how the script would go. Instead we limped almost apologetically and weakly out of the top flight and back to the Second. It would have been maybe a fitting and almost apt way to say goodbye to the swinging sixties if we'd put on a barnstorming performance, still lost, and were relegated. But we didn't. It was like watching paint dry, a bit like sitting in the pictures and thinking "Isn't this where I came in?" all over again. Sunderland, never one to disappoint you, lost 1-0 to a Liverpool team who seemed to bend over backwards to let us stay up. It was embarrassing to watch at times as Liverpool slumbered and laboured to make Sunderland look good. We were that bad we couldn't even take advantage of it. There was one defining moment when giant Ron Yeats somehow lost an easy header to Sunderland's tiny Nick Sharkey in the six yard box. A certain goal, but, no, the header drifted about three yards wide. At the finish Liverpool must have thought "Aye, aye lads, we've been rumbled" and went up field and tried to make it look like a real game. And when a feeble shot by Chris Lawler found the net, I honestly thought along with others that the poor lad, in embarrassment, was mouthing the words "I'm sorry" to a shocked Roker End.

And so Sunderland's second reign in the First Division came to a sorry end. Not so much a defiant, snarling, spitting, fighting back- breaking performance with shots coming in at all angles against a battling Liverpool side. We couldn't even be bothered to boo them off at the end of a disastrous season It was more a resigned white flag of surrender and one that deserved the ultimate silent accolade. The following season really did test the patience of Sunderland's loyal but shrinking army with crowds dipping to the 15,000 level and even lower sometimes.

But there's one thing about football, as well as life in general. There's something very strange about adversity. No matter how bad some things get, there is always something or someone waiting to pull you up, to either shock the life out of you, or excite you beyond belief. It was typical of Sunderland that only three short years later, in 1973, they were to provide both these emotions at the same time and become the darlings of the nation when much travelled Manager Bob Stokoe rode into town.

No wonder my favourite ever saying, both on and off the field, has always been: "You never know what's round the corner".

CHAPTER 8
THE TIMES THEY ARE A' CHANGING

When you watch football today, in its safe, ever so bland, clean, risk assessed surroundings with stringent health and safety checks around every corner carried out strategically to the umpteenth degree by an army of various co-ordinators, you can't help feeling deep down that somehow you are missing out on something.

There is nothing more depressing, for example, than being in a ground that's half empty even with 15 minutes to the kick off. There's no atmosphere, certainly not in the home section anyway, nor anybody getting in early that can even stoke up the crowd. And if there was, there's nobody to stoke up anyway. In the days of the terraces you'd need to be in by at least 1-30pm to make sure you got a barrier down at the front, or a good spot in The Boys End. Today, no doubt under the Sex Discrimination Act, you'd not be allowed to have or display a notice saying "Boys End". Who knows what signs they'd put up in case they offended anyone and it led to a compensation claim on the grounds of hurt feelings or whatever. No, today you can walk in at bang on 3pm and know that there's a place, or rather a seat, just waiting for you. Never mind those who have got there earlier and are inconvenienced by having to get up, then sit down and get up and then sit down to let you through. Today you get the complete stranger, doing his or her annual pilgrimage, who doesn't know where their seat is and accusing you, a fully fledged season ticket holder who's been in the same seat for the last five years, of sitting in the wrong place, and then standing there expecting you to move. ("No,mate, yours is back there - Row 22 seat 345, This is Row 20, seat 345"). And not as much as an apology as they slope off.

At least it provides some moments of merriment, especially if you score a really early goal and someone is still on the way in, and sheepishly tries to slide past without being noticed. I can't resist winding them up. "You should have seen it, what a belter" or the more biting: "It's still one nil, but it should have been three". And then they look at you as if you're something they've just scraped off the bottom of their shoe. It's as if it's your fault that they've missed it. They'll come back with "Yes, I know what the score is, thank you very much, I can see it on the scoreboard." And that's when you go for the jugular: "Can you see the time on the scoreboard as well? You've missed the first ten minutes". By the time they've thought of a response it's too late. Even if is witty or patronising, then you totally ignore it, or if you bite use the good old "broken record" routine: "Just sit down; some of us are trying to watch this".

Then there are those buggers who feel it is necessary to have eight or nine pints before the game in one of the stadium bars. They'll stroll in 10 minutes into the game, instantly trying to whip the crowd up into singing along with them or taunting the opposition fans with a highly original chant of "Who are ya?" (They're Sheffield United fans, mate, they're from South Yorkshire, and they know who they are, but they're not quite sure about you). Then 15 minutes before half time they're up again ready to either hit the bar early (I wish someone with a bar would have hit them earlier) or go to the loo. Then it's the same nonsense again in the second half. I reckon they must see only 40 minutes of an actual match. I'm surprised that some of them haven't written to the club asking for discount on their ticket on the grounds that they only watch half the game.

Of course, all these shenanigans and all this puerile nonsense would never have happened in the first place when we had all standing. Then, you'd be able to slide in pretending you'd just nipped out or, ever so slowly, inch your way away from a potential hotspot and save your blushes or maybe someone else's. All of it very civilised. That's because people moved about on the terraces all the time, usually to get away from the iconic loony (every club had one and if you were Millwall, there'd be loads of them, nearly all of them violent and nearly all of them very near you). Then there'd be another quick swerve away from the local loudmouth Foghorn Leghorn or the bloke who'd just dropped his guts right beside you after devouring four pork pies, three pints and a pickled egg.

Unless you've ever stood on the terraces (in today's modern society it's probably the equivalent of an ASBO for real football hard nuts) then you'll never really understand what it was like to experience that feeling of belonging, of companionship with people you might never have even seen before. Within minutes, though, you'd feel you'd known them for years. You were never alone or lonely on the terraces, unlike that daft old advert years back for "Strand" cigarettes. You don't know what I'm talking about? This 1960s advert featured some sinister bloke leaning against a lamp post about midnight smoking a fag. The advert never worked for one simple reason. It implied that it was only extremely sad loners who would stand on deserted street corners at midnight smoking "Strand" ciggies. What a real own goal for the advertisers and probably an early bath for the poor genius who came up with the idea. It wasn't a good selling point for a cigarette. This was certainly not the case on the terraces. You were never ever alone on the terraces, even if you were smoking a Strand at the time.

How could you or anyone else possibly be alone or lonely watching any match? Unless you were rather a strange cove or stunk to high heaven, then a conversation with anyone came as second nature within moments. It was as natural as breaking wind and glancing suspiciously at the man in front of you to avert the blame, or asking the bloke on your right did he have a light (something else that has also, pardon the pun, gone up in smoke). If you were henpecked, or just plain hated the missus altogether, it was the ideal escape for just a few precious hours, a few moments of quality man-time.

It wasn't all fun and games, though. The secret of not losing credibility with those around you was not to overdo matters. You could do this quite easily by condemning or criticising your own team or player far too early or too easily in a match when things weren't quite going your way. We've all been there, haven't we? You feel on top of the world and are looking forward to a good win ("No bother today; this lot haven't won since January") and then - bang. Before you know it, you're losing 1-0. It can't get any worse, can it? Yes, it can. Bang again. 2-0, and that's when the explosion starts in your head. A maniac starts ranting that the manager hasn't got a clue, his tactics are crap, time he went, and he starts raving on like a demented mad man. And then you realise, to your horror, that maniac is actually you. Someone to the left retaliates: "There's plenty of time, man. Give them a chance. They'll get back into it". If they do get back into it and claw back to either win or draw, then you end up looking a prize idiot with egg on your face. If they go on to get beat 4-1, then your outburst is justified and you can bizarrely claim some kind of warped moral victory. You might even traipse home with a slight smirk on your face, knowing that you were right, even though you had just been battered 5-1.

The next home game you promise yourself that this time you'll express caution if you go a goal down early again. After all, you don't want those around you to think you're a miserable, moaning sod. Then you breathe a sigh of relief when, this time, someone to your right comes out with virtually the same outburst you did a fortnight before. And then you find yourself uttering these classic words to them: "Give them a chance, man. They've only been playing five minutes". And thus it goes on, game after game, month after month, season after season, with a scapegoat or sacrificial lamb always within easy range of you. It's the circle of life, or should that be strife? That kind of fellowship, camaraderie, or just plain looking for a mug to have a cheap shot at is well and truly gone.

That is exactly what it was like to be on the terraces, no matter whether it was Oakwell watching Barnsley bounce back from 2-0 down to 2-2 , then win 4-3 or Victoria Park watching Hartlepool bounce back from 3-0 down to pull it back to 3-3 and still get beat 6-3. The same scenario repeated week after week everywhere. And who said all grounds and their fans were different? They weren't. Not on a match day. No matter whether it was Gillingham in the South East or Carlisle in the North West, they all went along with pretty much the same dream, the same breaking point, the same roar when they were back in it, the same groan when they knew they'd blown it, and the same sense of resignation or anger when they spotted the offside flag waving to chalk off that last minute equaliser. And they all followed the same route home that they always took after the match, and they all thought that things would be so different the next home game. Sometimes they were, but usually it was very much a case of deja vu.

You'd never understand any of this unless you were brought up on the terraces which happily still exist at some grounds in the lower and non-leagues. There you can get a chance to go back in time, only in your mind, and remember how it was for your club before they went all-seater, or moved on to pastures new. It really is refreshing to stand there as a neutral and just listen, observe and even join in. The banter and wisecracks are entirely different when you are standing as opposed to sitting and if you don't believe me, then why do you suppose they have the saying "sitting target" for? Because that's effectively what you are when you sit. You are trapped in the confines of a seat, sitting on you hands and not daring to make a nuisance of yourself. And if you do then just wait for that icy retort from a nearby smart arse: "Shut up, you silly bugger!"

It galls me sometimes - no, it galls me a lot - to hear the theorists or modernists (whatever you want to call them) dictate to you that we are all so much the better for having the comfort of all-seater stadiums as opposed to being on those old cramped, dirty terraces. Much the same way, I suppose, that those two musical gurus Louis Walsh and Simon Cowell can say a new version of an old classic song (justified by them calling it "contemporary") is much better than the original, when you know full well that it isn't. What do they base these assumptions on? Do they draw on their own personal experiences, or is it more smugly based on their need to change things for the sake of changing things? It's just the same in football. Do they have unique individual evidence affecting each club to arrive at their haughty decisions or is it much easier-and safer- to just impose a blanket ban on the whole lot of them? If that were the case, then it's unfair on all those clubs who, down the years, have imposed their own in-house stringent safety checks only to be told that it's much easier having a "one size fits all" approach. You know what I mean by all this, don't you? It is a twisted kind of logic that would work in much the same way as if you had a dog that happened to pee on your best carpet. Don't bother trying to train it not to. It's much easier, and more cost effective, to just have it put down and then you've solved the problem.

I do admit though that sometimes, only sometimes, when I'm sitting in a nice, comfortable safe seat protected by the elements on a freezing cold afternoon(notice I use the words "nice, comfortable, safe"), I think that we've come a long way. But even then, I've often been to a game played under these conditions where the atmosphere has been quite good and I know it would have been ten times better with the noise from the terraces roaring them on. This is a view shared by many. Maybe issuing punters with a loudspeaker each on the way in might prove to be the best way forward in the future. We have come a long way in terms of comfort, visibility, environment, ambience and amenities but these seem to have replaced things like atmosphere, excitement, comradeship, pandemonium and noise. All these words don't fit collectively together under health and safety rules. There are advantages and disadvantages when comparing both sides of the argument. I do know this, though. If it were possible to whisk my "pre-terrace"16 year old nephew Liam off to a night game at Roker Park round about 1964 I know which way he'd vote.

It is strange speaking to younger supporters, some of whom weren't long out of nappies when all-seaters started to creep in, when they, too, harbour a secret desire for some kind of standing area at the match. It would certainly create a better and still safe atmosphere. Those of my generation still long for a return to those halcyon days of the 1960s. Those even older can go back to the 1930s ("You call the grounds packed in the 60s? You've seen nowt to what we stood in").

We all know now of course why change had to come, but did it have to be so drastic? The tragedies of Hillsborough, Heysel and Valley Parade escalated the need and demand for safe and better conditions in stadiums for the fans.

That demand, though, was an ignored voice in the wilderness from many fans themselves going back well over 40 years before these disasters happened. Capacities in several big grounds could and should have been decreased substantially in the 1960s and 1970s. No ground should have held more than 60,000, regardless, and no ground should have had fans penned in like they were. That was shameful and all our concerns were conveniently ignored by the then experts. Now we have another lot of modern ones telling us what's good for us.

Although it was admittedly exciting being in huge crowds like that, it was also both dangerous and frightening. What we really wanted back then was some sort of happy compromise. We wanted not only a chance to stand on the terraces, but also to stand in relative safety. That request went unheeded until it was too late. Being in a ground holding 66,000 where the safety limit should really have been some 10,000 less was no laughing matter. There was nothing remotely romantic about it, either. I envisaged a disaster happening because of this way before Hillsborough. I'd nearly seen it happen on several occasions well before that black day. When some bright spark actually decreed that fences should then be erected to actually prevent people from spilling onto the field when it got too congested, then you knew that the game was well and truly in the hands of lunatics. Clubs for years scrimped and scraped when they were getting thousands through the coffers in a day when players' wage bills were next to nothing compared to turnstile takings. That was the time for action, not when people died through negligence and incompetence years later. Tragedies will always occur in history. They have in the past and they will in the future. There is no escape from that fact. What about the fact that we all knew even decades ago that some tragedies could and should have been avoided? That's the biggest tragedy of all.

Today there are still countless debates and arguments going on (keeps them in all in work, doesn't it?) for retaining even part of a stadium for standing, and a chance to keep all the ones who like to make a noise in one area. If we do live in a real democracy, as we are led to believe and are reminded about all the time, then why can't we exercise this particular right to freedom? That's the right to stand rather than sit down. It could even be included as part of a Government Healthy Standing Initiative (they've got titles for everything else). Of course this would have to be part of a stringent health and safety check but surely, if clubs were able to abide by this, why couldn't they be given the option of choice? Or is the answer likely to be "No" because it's all part of some Nanny State syndrome designed to protect but really strangling us all? They now tell us what to eat, what to drink and obviously the dangers of standing that are also bad for us. Standing is allowed in some parts of Europe, so why not here? After all, if we are meant to be part of a single Europe then, again, why is it always us that appear to be the only ones singled out to abide by EU rules when the rest of Europe very conveniently, and sometimes sensibly, ignore them? I am not advocating the return to the type of footy ground that I frequented in my youth. Not on your nelly. The thought of cramming 60,000 into a 45,000 capacity ground might well be cosy and very intimate but it was a recipe for disaster. 53,000 sardines and 7,000 seats does not make for a happy 90 minutes viewing. I'd be more minded to take a current 30,000 seater, retain 22,000 seats, take 2 blocks of 4,000 seats behind each goal and turn them into standing areas for both home and away fans. The result would be an increased capacity from the original 30,000 up to easily 40,000 and a much better atmosphere all round. And it would provide freedom of choice. Go to a match today and what happens anyway when the game occasionally livens up? Everybody sitting automatically stands up. It's only a natural and human reaction to do so.

I think that they have the balance right at lower league level. I've touched on Hartlepool and cite them as an example of how to accommodate the best of both worlds. They have plenty of seats on three sides of the ground and they still retain the terraces both behind one goal and also in the paddock. It sometimes makes for a cracking atmosphere even with crowds of only 3,000. Those few hundred, especially behind the goal, make some noise win, lose or draw. When there have been over 6,000 in there for visits of Leeds or Sheffield Wednesday in recent years, the place just bounces. It's like sitting next to one of the speakers at a U2 concert. Compare this with a Premier League game with 10 times as many in and if the match is flat so, too, is the crowd. That's exactly why some Division One and Two fans still standing will tell you that for real football and real passion, it's the only way to see a match.

I have been to matches with 35,000-50,000 in where the only noise in the stadium is coming from the away end, even when they might be getting beat. This is partly because it's a day out for them and a chance to show the home fans how noisy they are. It's also a territorial thing, designed to let their team know that, although there isn't many of them, they have travelled all this way to lend their support and the extra noise might be just the spur for them to win away. It's much harder than winning at home, of course. When you are playing at home you tend to leave it to your team to do all the work. It's their job to lift you. After all, they have the advantage and should use it. They get paid enough to do it without your help and, besides, I'm too comfortably settled in my seat to do anything about it.

It's ironic that the more successful the team, the more their fans will turn on them at the drop of a hat. It's understandable of course. Fans can be like spoilt brats demanding the best at all times and when, on the rare occasion they don't get it, they resort to wailing. No wonder Roy Keane had a pop at some segments of the Old Trafford crowd. Having been brought up watching my team through thick and thin, I can't get my head round it all. I sometimes question whether they are real supporters at all. I wouldn't like to think I was in the trenches or battle zone somewhere with some of these lot by my side. They'd be off out of there as soon as their tea wasn't stirred properly. I couldn't believe a Chelsea match where they were actually booed during the match - they eventually won 2-1 after being 1-0 down - and it looked like they were on their way to a second home defeat in 148 matches, or whatever it was. What would they do if they hit hard times (it's happened before, it could easily happen again) and finished mid-table or even relegated? My heart goes out to those poor dears who obviously watch the game on some other astral plane to the rest of us. Humility even amongst football fans is a wonderful thing and will make you a lot more friends. Nobody likes the arrogant and sarcastic variety.

There are many today who are getting brassed off and are even on the verge of revolt. A close family friend of mine used to watch Chelsea in the 1970s when you could just go along on match days and pay at the gate. He was priced out of it just after the Abramovich revolution kicked off. A new wave of Chelsea fan swept into the club, not knowing their Arsenals from their elbows, and he was very conveniently brushed to one side. He tried to keep up but had to call it a day, the final coup de grace being delivered when he forked out some £80 for him and his boy to watch a drab 0-0 draw. With drinks fares, eats and programme his day out cost him nigh on £120. This type of once loyal fan is being removed from the game. I know families in this neck of the woods, and probably yours too, who could survive for a fortnight on that sort of outlay.

When Roker Park was demolished in 1997, I counted myself very lucky to have had two sons who were old enough to have experienced the old fashioned atmosphere I grew up with there. We were all sad to see its demise but when you saw its capacity being stringently reduced on health and safety regulations down the years from 45,000 to 38,000, and then 30,000 down to a paltry 22,000, you knew there was no alternative but to say goodbye. It was like watching an old and loved friend slowly dying. I stood there for the last time in a friendly against Liverpool, who were the first ever league visitors there in 1898. I'm not ashamed to say that I cried that night as I walked out of there for the last time. Both my two sons were born too late to have witnessed the great days of 60,000 plus crowds and can only wonder what it must have been like. I've told them, of course, but it's not the same, is it? By 1990 when they both took an interest it was down to a meagre 30,000 and still falling. The massive Roker End had been half demolished already and was a sad mocking reminder to us all, for years, of how the game was heading. Even after its closure, I couldn't keep away and even watched the quick, painful demolition during those summer months of 1997. I was quite optimistic as our new 42,000 home (increased later to 49,000) neared completion at the nearby former Wearmouth Colliery site. I thought it quite appropriate, and ironic, that the new ground was built on the very site where miners once toiled their whole lives away. Sunderland's fan base was built on the backbone and lifeblood of thousands of miners, and their descendants and families, many of them from the nearby Durham coalfields. Not forgetting, too, and equally important in the development of the club, were those thousands of shipyard, glassworks and steel workers who lived in the then biggest shipbuilding town in the world back when the club was born in 1879. Today, the ghosts of them all look down on the gleaming Stadium of Light, sitting on the edge of a now quiet river that was once full to the brim with ships.

Nostalgia affects all fans everywhere. At the far end of the country, and still looking like something from a bygone age, is Fratton Park. It was sad to see the sudden demise of Pompey resulting in their relegation from the Premier League but I often wondered how they managed to punch way above their weight for so long. The Premier League takes no prisoners for both teams and grounds alike. Had Pompey been able to pull in 40,000, instead of their full houses of only 20,000, they might have stood a chance. Now we see how it all went horribly wrong for them as they bit off more than they could chew in an attempt to not only keep afloat but also compete. I hope they bounce back on more solid foundations, mainly because their fans and ground remind me so much of those of Sunderland.A friend of mine who went down there a couple of seasons back told me that when he walked in just before kick off, it was like a surreal blue and white version of Roker Park circa 1985. The noise and passion hit him right between the eyes. He had to pinch himself to check that he hadn't wandered through some time portal. Some grounds do affect you like that. You either love them or hate them. Portsmouth's ground is a classic example of how they can take away the terraces, reduce the numbers coming in, but never diminish the spirit. It wasn't that long ago in the late 1980's that they used to pull in 30,000 in both the old Third and Fourth Divisions on their way back up the ladder. A potential new home may offer them more chance of success than at Fratton but will never emulate what they will leave behind.

It's inevitable, but understandable, I suppose that for the same reason – greater ambition and more financial clout - the likes of Everton, whose ground is very similar in style and design to both Portsmouth and the old Roker Park, is now in need of an extreme makeover. Difficult if not impossible when you consider the geographics involved. Many grounds built in the early part of the 20th Century, or even built in the latter years of the 19th, are now hemmed in by back to back streets and impossible to develop. With the advent of the all-seater and relocation costs involved, some clubs might well have decided to stay put and reduce capacity drastically from maybe 58,000 down to a paltry 36,000. Still a good crowd but just think of all that lost revenue with a 22,000 drop in gate money game after game, month after month, year after year.

One hundred years back, fans didn't have cars or motorways to get to the match. The ground had to be central for all of them to get to and many would have walked there. Some of the really old grounds probably had horse parks before the car parks came along. Everton have done well to keep in the top seven recently but they know that realistically they need to compete and to do that they need a bigger home. In the 1960s they could pack in 60,000 into Goodison and that's the sort of crowd they need again - and would nearly get - with a new home. The issue, though, is would they be prepared to share a ground with Liverpool? It could come to that in the current economic climate.

A visit to White Hart Lane in the early 60s would have seen you regularly mixing it with 63,000 others. The difference between then and now in both atmosphere and noise levels is as wide as a mile. Tottenham's huge shelf required an oxygen bottle and binoculars from the back row. It was the same for Liverpool and the former Kop.

Stamford Bridge is also unrecognisable from when I first stepped foot in there in 1963. Chelsea against Grimsby in the old Second Division (the year they went up) and they came from behind to win 2-1. These were the days, pre-Osgood, of Bobby Tambling and Ken Shellito, Frank Bluntstone and a very young Peter Bonetti in goal. Even though I was only 12, the names stuck. The Bridge then had possibly 90% of the ground devoted to standing. Only the rich - or so we thought - used to sit in the seats, and at Stamford Bridge then, there appeared to be very little of them. When you consider that the ground record was once over 84,000 you have an idea of how big the place was. It was the original super bowl, years before American Football brought us the other version. Today 42,000 is a full house and you have to wonder when they, too, like so many others will outgrow their home. There's no real room to expand and accommodate a capacity of even 60,000, never mind the 75,000 they could probably pull in if they carry on in the present vein. I also remember it being a lot, lot louder than it is today.

Going back even 20 years and looking at how grounds everywhere were then you'd be forgiven for thinking you'd been whisked off to some alien world, certainly a third world country. Primitive would describe it perfectly.

Wembley itself, once England's pride, looked tired and jaded even 20 years back. You would, too, if you were knocking on for seventy. Just like getting old, the joints start aching and creaking and, although you think you haven't changed and can still cut the mustard, you can't. And neither could Wembley. I still think, though, that getting rid of the twin towers and all they symbolised was an act not far short of vandalism, and certainly rank stupidity by the powers that be. My theory as to why they went is simple. When Wembley was built it was simply called The Empire Stadium, Empire denoting everything Britain stood for in the early 20th Century. As our Empire faded and died, I think somebody wanted to get rid of the last remnants of any links to the Empire, by then an outdated and not so cool word. Far better to have something more in keeping with our fine modern, multi-cultural society and so "Empire" and Wembley just had to go. It was just so last century, as the twin towers were sacrificed just like Britannia on our coinage. It was a link to a bygone era and not relevant to our future. It didn't matter a jot that the majority of true fans wanted them to be retained as a feature of the New Wembley. They were old and so had to go. I think if the towers had been retained, then they, alongside the colossal statue of Bobby Moore, would have shown the whole world just how magnificent the home of football past, present and future, and all it stood for, actually was. The Bobby Moore statue provides a fantastic link to 1966. The inclusion also of the twin towers would have provided an equally impressive link also. And besides, who was it hurting?

The new Wembley, magnificent though it is, sums up much of what is wrong with the modern game. With its vast swathe of red seats, half filled at kick off time by mainly corporate clowns, it lacks atmosphere. Impressive it is but noisy it definitely is not. The old Wembley had a real feeling of togetherness. I look at the new version and see real diversity, alright. Only this diversity is a division between the masses and the classes, those who are there for the occasion and enjoyment of it all, and those in the seats always in range of the cameras and seemingly full of people who look like they'd rather be somewhere else. A small price to pay for modernism? I don't think so.

My favourite neutral ground of all was Highbury, so magnificent that, unlike Roker Park, it was far too good to pull down when Arsenal moved on. You don't demolish stately homes when the owners either die or do a moonlit flit. You preserve it for posterity and that's just what happened. Now it's been converted to fabulous, luxury two and three bed apartments, each of which are probably worth more than the original Highbury cost to build. If I were an Arsenal fan and related to the Getty family, I'd have bought one, too. Living there, you'd still be surrounded by history and still only a short walk to The Emirates. You could just visualise the ghosts of Herbert Chapman, Alex James, Charlie Buchan and all those countless other Arsenal greats still lurking around old Highbury, never wanting to move on. The Emirates is a really impressive replacement but lacks the style, grace and atmosphere of Highbury. The rooms may be bigger but the family who moved in there don't make half as much noise as the folks who lived in the home they left behind. Even a dull game at Highbury was made acceptable by the ornate surroundings and 1930s stands. Today they'd justify them being old by giving them the chic name "retro". If you want a definition of that word in a dictionary, and how it's been ambushed, it would have to be the following:

"Invented by a lazy sod who can't be bothered to think for himself, and so just plunders a fabulous, stylish thing from years gone by and justifies its newness by calling it "retro".

When I was young my dad used to take us on days out to all the big museums in London and maybe that's where I got my early appreciation of all things old. Even at an early age, works of art and buildings centuries old were so much more stylish and grand then their bland, modern counterparts. I still wonder that today in some modern stadiums, and some modern music critics.

Arsenal fans were just as noisy as any others in London, although when I first starting bobbing up there from Southall in the late 1960s they hadn't then hit the heady heights that they enjoy today. Maybe the excessive noise was just loud groaning and general shouts of anger. An angry mob makes a hell of a lot more noise than a happy crowd. When things are going well, then there's no earthly need to scream at the top of your voice telling everyone how blissfully delirious you are. You just have a warm glow and a sense of quiet inner peace. You'd even smoke a cigar if you were allowed to. However, when you are 3-0 down and playing like you don't give a damn, then that sense of outrage will have you screaming your head off along with 50,000 others. Perhaps that's why in recent years Highbury was known as The Library. What could their fans possibly have to moan at? It also possibly explains why both Newcastle and Sunderland's crowds are generally so volatile. When you've not really won anything of note since 1955 and 1973 respectively, one tends to get a bit irate at it all.

Bolton Wanderers' Burnden Park holds a lot of happy memories. Once having a capacity of 60,000, it was another ground that slowly saw its capacity whittled away. When I drove past it, they'd even built what looked like a supermarket at one end of it. Handy I suppose if you were doing the stocktaking in the back of the shop and spent a sly hour and a half watching the match. My last visit there was in 1976 when both they and Sunderland were going neck and neck for the Second Division Championship. Bolton won 2-1 in front of 48,000 but even then there was the evidence of the slow decay of this once grand old stage. I saw it at many other grounds as well. Clubs, even until the bitter end, generally thought that fans would show up regardless, season after season. Some of the grounds were more like hovels with crumbling terraces, stinking cesspits that passed for toilets, and no shelter from leaking roofs. Entrances onto the terraces, once inside, sometimes comprised a slippery slope which quickly turned into a muddy quagmire in the wet. Nowhere was this worse than Springfield Park, home of Wigan Athletic. There was one part of the ground where away fans could go sledging, without the sledge, down a slide made of pure mud - just like they did in the film "Woodstock."

There was also a terrible laid back attitude by police and the authorities in general towards anyone attending football. For all they cared, it didn't matter whether you were a doctor or an office worker. If you stood on the terraces then you were scum; simple as that. I saw this in evidence at Bolton that day, just after Wanderers scored a goal. Not surprisingly Sunderland fans were unhappy bunnies. You always feel frustrated and angry when you are losing - a human reaction - and you'll always get someone getting a bit too loud and abusive, but never violent. But this was not an excuse, surely, to drag them out when common sense would tell you that seconds later they would have calmed down and just got back on with watching the match. Then it was a case of taking pre-emptive strike action. It's a bit like a footballer wanting to get his retaliation in first, in advance of the actual foul on him that hasn't yet happened.

As Burnden Park eventually slowly disintegrated, so too did the fortunes of Bolton until they eventually turned the corner with the new Reebok Stadium. Their days by then of 45,000 plus crowds had long gone and their new capacity was set at a reasonable, understandable and very sad sub-30,000. I don't think I have ever seen it at full capacity, not even when away fans took their full quota. A 26,000 crowd is usually as good as it gets. Ask any Bolton fan for his favourite moments and great games and nearly all of them would involve games at Burnden Park. They'd also probably tell you that they would have welcomed some sort of say when their new ground was named. But it could have been be worse. York City currently play at the wonderfully branded Kit Kat Crescent. Can you imagine their fans inspiring them on to victory with the Kit Kat Roar?

Hull City's Boothferry Park was another grand old gaff in its heyday. When I was watching Brentford, in the 60s, the Tigers regularly used to pull in 35,000 plus gates whilst they were a Third Division side. When I saw them play at Griffin Park they must have made up well over half the 22,000 crowd, and effectively turned it into a home game. They had someone called Chris Chilton who tore Brentford to bits as they won away 3-1. They were on the way to the top flight on the back of massive support and a side that would apparently sweep all before them. You can see where this is heading, can't you? They were so ambitious that they even talked about having a private rail line that would take their fans direct to Boothferry Park, all as a result of this phenomenal support. Such was the atmosphere and reputation of the place, that in 1967 Leeds United and Sunderland played out an epic FA Cup Fifth Round second replay there in front of a capacity 51,000 (another game I listened to on the transistor radio). The match ended up in a near riot, a notorious battle between two warring sides who, over the years, never really got on with each other. When Leeds were awarded a hotly disputed penalty late on, all hell broke loose. Worse was to come at the final whistle as some of the Leeds team, 2-1 winners, then began Round Two of the battle with Sunderland in the dressing rooms.

Hull's promised rise to the top was all heady stuff to an adolescent like me. However, always heed the warning about whenever you hear that something's too good to be true, it usually is. That's when the wheels usually fall off. They quickly did in Hull's case. I don't really know what happened. Maybe they overstretched themselves (a dangerous thing to do in football or any other business) but the ground, team and support crumbled away ever so slowly. At one point, poor Hull looked like they were heading for the knackers yard altogether and it wasn't all that long ago either. I saw them lose 3-0 to Hartlepool in a Fourth Division game in front of no more than 2,500 and I couldn't believe how bad they were. They made an equally poor Hartlepool look like world beaters. I thought back to their game at Brentford in the 60s and it was a valuable lesson about never taking anything for granted, even in football. Just when you think you've cracked it, someone comes along to pull the rug from under you. Alternatively, just when you think everything's against you and you can't go on, something or someone comes along and gives you a lift. Happily for Hull, this happened to them. It's only in the last ten years that they have awoken from the nightmare and clawed themselves back. I wouldn't have given them a prayer for them even surviving in the league the night I saw them at Hartlepool.

When they moved to their new home at the KC Stadium - named after the lead singer of that fine legendary American band from the mid-1980s, KC and the Sunshine Band - with a modest 25,000 capacity they could never have dreamed where it would quickly lead. The stadium is typical purpose built and does make a loud noise when City are on song. Very soon it would house Premier League football. The problem that Hull had then was that the ground was just way too small. The city of Hull is a big place with a huge catchment area and no real competition for miles (sorry, Grimsby Town, maybe one day). They had already proven in the 60s that they could easily pull in 30,000 and probably nudge 40,000 in the top flight. Maybe they'll mull over that if they get back up there. If they do, I suggest that they act double fast. Don't even think about the increase and while they are on with that, lower admission prices to go with it. That way you'd fill it up even faster. They're a passionate lot down there and it would be a win/win for them. Remember also another ex-Premier League outfit Reading who decided on extending their 27,000 Madjeski Stadium capacity to 38,000. The only trouble was by the time they got round to actually doing it, their particular Premiership bubble had burst. Now that they are back down in the Championship, the extension, along with the champagne, look like being on ice for a few years to come. What's that they say about striking while the iron is hot?

Teams should reach for the sky when building a new stadium and instead of thinking low, they should aim high. Rather than have the initial problem of how to fill a 20,000 capacity stadium when you've only ever averaged 10,000, think big. Build a 30,000 seater and then work out how you can turn that 10,000 gate into, say, 25,000 by letting everybody in at half the cost or even lower. It's going to be the way forward anyway as more and more clubs are faced with more empty seats. Better still, plan for the future by letting youngsters in for a quid, and maybe senior citizens in for free. They've earned the right. What have they got to lose? I'm always minded of that Kevin Costner film "Field of Dreams". If you build it, they will come - but only if the price is right.

That simple philosophy should one day apply to all teams in the country no matter what division they play in. A unique experiment carried out some two years back by Mansfield Town, of the then Vauxhall Conference in a match against Gateshead paid real dividends. Rather than charge standard admission prices, Mansfield tried a bold approach. "Come through the turnstile and pay us what you think we're worth". A quid, 50p, a fiver - let the fans decide. As a result some 7,700 people turned up- Mansfield's biggest crowd in years - with the kick off delayed 20 minutes. Some Mansfield fans, who got in for nothing, might have asked for a refund when Gateshead beat them 2-0. The away team were obviously more inspired than the home team so there's always the sting in the tail. Sunderland Reserves tried a similar experiment a few years back in a reserve game against Liverpool at The Stadium of Light. It was free admission and money for charity thrown into blankets before the match and 33,000 turned up that night. Obviously you couldn't do this all the time but wouldn't it be lovely if just once or twice a season, a team gave something back to the fans by contemplating something such as this when they know that they'll not be expecting a big crowd.

There's optimism and there's optimism, however. When Darlington played at Feethams not many years ago, they and then Chairman George Reynolds had a bold vision for the future. Feethams was a lovely, little stadium in beautiful surroundings and ideally situated for the people of Darlington to get to. It could easily have been converted into a practical and modest 12,000 seater, big enough for any ambitious outfit to contemplate even Championship football. Given that Darlington's gates at the time were never above 4,000, then that would have been enough for them to gradually increase and maybe climb slowly to perhaps 8,000, or more, once the Championship beckoned. This would have been a more realistic vision for George, the club and the fans, and a steady way of pushing things forward. What I'd call baby steps. This would even have allowed for having to put in a brand new pitch with poor drainage which had been the bane of Darlington for years.

Unfortunately George, just like Moses years before him, must have seen a vision of the Promised Land. In his case it was the Premiership in five years and a 27,000 seater on the outskirts of the town which he envisioned bursting at the seams. He even modestly named it after himself, and sat back waiting for the crowds and the cash to roll up. Unfortunately I think he may well have put the cart before the horse. He'd built the stadium before first developing the team. The result was a workmanlike, efficient but nowhere near good enough outfit making their debut at their new home in a Third Division fixture against Kidderminster Harriers. The public of Darlington responded magnificently and over 12,000 turned up on that opening day. Because of safety concerns, sections of the ground were never opened and that's still the same to this day. I'll give George this, though. It was and still is a fantastic looking ground and teams in the Blue Square, turning up there, must think that they've taken the wrong turn on the motorway and ended up at Old Trafford by mistake. The only thing giving the illusion away is the missing hordes. And so, a genuine state of the art, all-singing all-dancing, white elephant was born. The home team were inspired by all this on the first ever game, but so too were the visitors who won 2-0. The season was a wash out with George making the mistake of thinking that all he had to do was to provide the perfect setting and the town would turn out in force. Maybe they would have done if they had a team to match the stadium. Meanwhile, their local rivals not far down the A66 in Hartlepool, initially envious and perhaps nervous at the thought of being totally eclipsed by this sudden and gigantic transformation, must have collectively breathed a huge sight of relief and then thought to themselves "We're quite happy with our 7,500 capacity and 4,000 gates".

Hartlepool could never have contemplated such a move and that's why they remain one of the thriftiest teams in the league. They may never pull up trees, but at least they won't be buried under them. Darlington now ply their trade in the Blue Square Premier League where they pull in less than 2,000 weekly and their very existence is debatable. It would be nice to see them going for promotion and then getting maybe 4,000 coming along but I bet they wished they'd stayed at Feethams.

The lessons of Darlington are a lesson for all teams not to be too over ambitious. Some dreams take longer than others. Some never get there at all, or if they do, they quickly turn out to be nightmares built on foundations of clay.

Anybody that ever ventured to Maine Road on a wet murky Saturday afternoon in Moss Side would have known that they were in for a rough, bumpy ride and a real blood and thunder, sometimes thud and blunder, affair in a traditional English setting. Maine Road was never one for the faint hearted, especially if you were daft enough to give Manchester City an early lead. Set right in the heart of Moss Side, where even the pit bull terriers used to knock about in threes for safety, Maine Road would rock with the noise when City were in the lead. City fans traditionally always used to regard themselves as the real club in Manchester. Sir Matt Busby even spent his playing days there and Manchester United played there while Old Trafford was being put back together following war time damage. It's hard to imagine the sense of camaraderie that existed then even amongst the fiercest of fans. There was no segregation because they didn't need it. I doubt if such generosity would happen today if refurbishment work at one ground meant using the home of your nearest and dearest for a few months. Fans would be up in arms but then unity was strength in the real sense of the word.

The lure of a brand new home, purpose built and much bigger than Maine Road, following the end of the Commonwealth Games,was too good to be true. With no hefty mortgage repayments, and more room to raise a bigger family, it was easy to leave Maine Road. In its day it could accommodate with ease 60,000, and leave room to swing a cat, but when someone offers you the chance of a luxury upmarket move with no money down, then what can you say? The answer was simply "Bugger tradition and all the history attached. How soon can we be off?" Besides, with Maine Road's capacity now down to 34,000, who would possibly turn down such a deal? Some teams just land on their feet and City were certainly one of them.

Whenever I think of Stoke City's former Victoria Ground, not to be confused in the 1990s with Hartlepool's ground of the same name (although I'm sure you'd be able to spot the difference) I automatically compare it with Roker Park. Both were relics of a much bigger bygone era, and both grounds slowly deteriorated along with the sides themselves, until both the stadiums and the teams inside were a pale imitation of their glorious past. In an ideal world, both stadiums could have been mothballed after closure and made into living, breathing working models to commemorate the places where industrial hard working males frequented every weekend for the past century. Stoke City's ground could have been carted off and rebuilt at nearby Alton Towers, and Sunderland's to nearby Beamish Open Air Museum. They could both have been re-branded as 19th Century sporting arenas. Of course, they would have to be given a modern name such as "retro stadiums". They could even have been tourist attractions like the Colosseum in Rome, but without the murderous past. Totally preposterous of course, but one day, and it won't be many years from now, school kids of the future, in their thirst for knowledge, are going to ask what a coal mine or pot kiln was, how pottery was made, how were ships built, and also what did a football ground look like with terraces and barriers, and old fashioned turnstiles. By then, they'll be able to visit one, courtesy of a virtual reality trip, or whatever, and picture it just like it was. There'll even be scope for a virtual Colosseum with virtual lions and virtual spectators. They could even make a day of it with a picnic and virtual egg and tomato sarnies. They'll be virtually there in their imagination but couldn't possibly translate the feel of that emotion into the real thing. Far better, in the case of football stadiums, and much easier and more cost effective, to knock down - obliterate even - the old dumps and rebuild them with tasteful housing and ever so thought-out designer names such as Turnstile Drive, Half Time Close, Offside Boulevard, Peanuts Tanner A Bag Lane and Can we sing a song for you Road. A brilliant concept, don't you agree?

You can't virtually replicate the feel of standing at The Victoria Ground in 1976 for a cup game with Sunderland with 42,000 hemmed in there, or the replay four days later at Roker Park in front of 47,000 (all they'd then let in). Both had a rip-roaring noise and incredible atmosphere. It may have been progress to demolish and move on and abandon the old ways, but it was enough to make a grown man weep at the loss.

Both The Britannia (there's me thinking the name Britannia was so un-PC and last century) plus The Stadium of Light are much more modern, safer, state of the art, and can also produce a fearsome and intimidating atmosphere, but only under certain conditions and circumstances. In the days of the terraces, shouting from the first minute to the last was regarded as compulsory, something you did as naturally as breathing. Today it is more of a voluntary effort and a case of looking around in your seat to see who might be staring at you. A little bit like having afternoon tea at your Auntie Ethel's when you were a nipper and not daring to take that last piece of slab cake she'd baked in case your mam gave you what for.

As for Wigan's new stadium, I hark back to what I said about Darlington. I fear for sides like Wigan who have tried to reinvent and re-brand themselves as something new and exciting. It only works if you were ever old enough as a league club, to remember those golden days of the 1930s when you actually were new and exciting in the first place. Springfield Park, their previous home, would have made Hartlepool's Victoria Ground even 45 years back, look like The Emirates. Clearly they had no option but to move. The local jokes about pulling the place down to put the slums up just about summed things up for them, but their new home, just like many others, was soulless and lacked any real identity. The trouble is Wigan never had much of an identity or history to reinvent. What they have achieved in such a short space of time is amazing and their stint to date in The Premier league really does defy logic. They are an inspiration to many sides in lower leagues who must think "if they can do it so can we". They are the perfect role model. You do wonder though what will happen to them if they really do have a bad season. They have to play out of their skins to keep a crowd of 16,000 – and falling - on board, and that includes away support, too. My only amazement is how they pull this many in when they never had a real fan base in the first place. Where will it end if they suffer the ultimate fate of relegation? I can easily visualise them dropping like a stone if this were to ever happen. To be successful and lasting, I think there has to be solid foundations that have endured down the years. Burnley, Portsmouth, Hull City, Bristol City and Cardiff have them. These are teams who you just know could take off and rocket if they got things right. I don't, and never did see this, at Wigan. They have punched way above their weight for years. One day they might take one punch too many that knocks them out permanently as far as the Premier is concerned.

As an example of how the game has changed so much in the last 20 years alone, and that's no time, move outside the cosiness and luxury surroundings of the Premier League. Out here is where you'll still find the majority of fans watching their teams, and telling you defiantly that this is the real heartland of the modern game. And as proof that they can compete, too, and that their game is also thriving and has something to offer, all these clubs have moved on to pastures new: Cardiff City, Colchester United, Chesterfield, Coventry City, Derby County, Doncaster Rovers, Huddersfield Town, Leicester City, Middlesbrough, Millwall, Northampton Town, Oxford United, Reading,

Morecambe, Rotherham United, Shrewsbury Town, Scunthorpe United, Southampton and Swansea City. And apologies to any I've missed or who might even be drawing up plans to move as you read this.

As for the rest, every ground bears little resemblance to how it might have looked in the early 1990s. I got a shock seeing Griffin Park, record capacity once 39,000, some 35 years after I was first there. It was a brand new ground. It looked so tiny to what I remembered, and how did they ever manage to fit 30,000 in on the two magical cup nights I was there? Remember, too, that if you were going to a game round about the mid 80s, even early 90s in some cases, you'd have seen very little difference or changes to those grounds as they would have looked 40-50 years before. In a way we should be grateful for all that's happened. Would it have happened at all, or happened so quickly, though, if it hadn't been for horrendous circumstances that forced this change?

As I sit in my own personal seat in the Lower North West Corner of The Stadium of Light, I look up in warm comfort as the driving sleet and snow swirl around the covered giant roof way above that protects me. In just the blink of an eye, I think of bygone days where I stood maybe an hour and a half before kick off, in the uncovered Roker End, a hostage to the elements, huddled together with others trying to keep warm, a hot pie in one hand and a cup of Bovril in the other. Sometimes I'd curse myself for not wearing an overcoat when the snow or rain started lashing down, or that bitter cold wind hit you off the nearby North Sea. It wasn't just Hartlepool it visited, you know. You'd hope against hope, just as you always did, that Sunderland scored an early goal, maybe two, just so that you'd have something to think about other than that your feet were numb with the cold. I wonder now how we ever put up with it, week after week, still turning up even when we once went nine games without so much as scoring a goal, or 15 games without a win. But we did. It was all part of growing up, following your side and maybe thinking what would happen if I never went today and they ended up winning 5-0? That blind faith and plain eternal optimism kept you going. A self inflicted initiation ceremony that went on and on until you had achieved full honours and graduated as a certified football fanatic. As I bask in the warm glow of my lovely snug seat, and all these fine new surroundings, I laugh inwardly. And I very nearly cry too. So how can I sum up these very personal feelings?

If you like your music, as I do, then go on to "YouTube" and listen carefully to Neil Sedaka's "Hungry Years". It's a sad, poignant song about a man who has achieved so much in his life. And, yet, for all his riches and success, he longs for what he calls "the hungry years", a time when he had nothing but desires and dreams to succeed. Having worked so hard, and climbed so far to make it to the very top, he now discovers it's all been done. He yearns for those hungry years of his youth when hard work, and dreams, spurred him on.

I miss the hungry years too.

CHAPTER 9
A FAN'S VIEW

A few years back, Sunderland in the then Coca Cola League One (or fizzy pop league as it was fondly called) were up against Dario Gradi's Crewe Alexandra, then a smart little club that always played football the right way. They also provided a conveyor belt of good players that were conveniently picked off by vultures further up the food chain. That's how teams like Crewe have to survive. Their attitude to the game is very much like West Ham except without the big crowds, history and trophies. My young son, Daniel, now a strapping hulk of 25, was having a quiet chuckle at some elderly looking Crewe fan in his late seventies, who, from a distance, seemed to be covered from head to foot in badges. When we got closer, this old gent was festooned on both his waistcoat and shirt sleeves in hundreds of badges, collected down the decades watching his beloved Alexandra. He was wearing them with as much pride as an old soldier might have worn his War medals on Remembrance Day.

My son thought it sad that anyone would want to advertise the fact that they were crackers about Crewe. I told him he should be privileged to see such a sight. There in the flesh, was a real football fan, a rarity, probably even born in Crewe and obviously watching them before even I was born, growing up on the terraces at Gresty Road and following them all round the country year after year. Not for him the bright lights of Old Trafford, Highbury, Goodison and other First Class stations. He would have been watching most of his football at lower league level as Crewe were on a par with sides like Hartlepool, Darlington, Halifax and Rochdale in terms of football prowess. And he would have been there treading round all these glamorous grounds long before any football was ever shown on telly. There wouldn't even have been so much as highlights, or should that be lowlights, at that level.

Early on in his life he could so easily have binned that waistcoat and all the badges accumulated and just did what so many other fans from provincial towns up and down the land used to do. Merely jump onto the latest bandwagon and sworn life long allegiance to Chelsea, Liverpool, Arsenal or Manchester United (subject to contract renewable every five years depending on success of the individual club concerned). Perhaps he could even have taken a sideways step up the road to nearby Blackburn when they won the Premier League; that might have proved a more tempting distraction at the time. But not for him the shallow allure of the latest flavour of the month outfit. He would have been tortured by the thought of some tempting fly by night side stripping him of his dignity and leaving him with a lifetime of guilt. He was stuck with Crewe and obviously loved it. If I had more time, I would loved to have stopped to talk with him but, it was very nearly bang on kick off time and the opportunity was lost. It was no more than a cursory and admiring look, a quick word, and then off into the stadium. In days gone by, when you'd be off to the old stadiums, you'd have been able to stop to have a real natter. The advent of the all-seater stadium now means that now all you have to do is turn up almost bang on kick off time to a waiting seat and see away fans in quick passing.

I wonder if he had been at White Hart Lane one night for a Cup Replay against Crewe back in 1960. Crewe actually held Spurs 2-2 at home in a Third Round game and must have fancied their chances big time in the replay. They were 6-1 down early in the first half and went on to lose 13-2. Crewe fans getting in to White Hart Lane even 10 minutes late would have seen their side already 3-0 down and the game over. You would never get that score today mainly because once a game is safe teams tend to just shut up shop. Back then, you had a duty to the fans to entertain for the full 90 minutes. Today, Spurs would probably have either fielded a weakened team, took their foot off the gas after about 4 or 5 goals, or made maximum changes once the game was safe. In 1960, it would have been a fabulous full strength Spurs side, no substitutes, against the minnows of Crewe. Great for Spurs fans but really frighteningly unlucky for Crewe.

I have seen all too often the folly of switching horses, or in football parlance, abandoning your team for a better one that happens to be riding alongside. I heard one daft young female on a Saturday morning trendy football show actually say that she used to follow Chelsea but was now a massive Arsenal fan. Staggeringly, nobody on that show thought it even worthy of comment, or even pulled her up about it. Not one of them told her she was talking through her backside. I'd have used one of those old fashioned giant hooks (the ones you used to see on those comedy shows when someone was dying on stage) to drag her off the set and tell her to come back when she'd grown up. The irony is that now she will have found that the football wheel has turned full circle. Her five year contract at Arsenal would have lapsed, and she'd have looked at what they'd won compared to Chelsea, her side previously. The obvious solution for this fickle blonde beauty would be a transfer. A switch of allegiance back again to those Stamford Bridge boys. Lucky them and a might relieved Arsenal to get her off their books. Maybe somewhere out there she is still on the airwaves, and if so, still no doubt spouting her nonsense. She may even have an army of young fans hanging on her every word. Tell me this isn't a generation thing, and the state of things to come. If it is, then we are all doomed. If you are in your twenties, or whatever age, and you feel exactly the same way as I do then there might just be hope. Maybe that's just the way it works in terms of allegiance today and modern fans can switch sides much the same way as I change my socks (I don't change them once every five years by the way).

Perhaps it's something to do with the modern quickness of change and living in a seemingly shallow world with its up to date, and then quickly out of date, ever expanding and changing technology .You can be in and out of fashion in a matter of weeks now. That might have something to do with hollow attitudes and where image is absolutely everything at the expense of everything else. Maybe this nonsense has spread to football too. Certainly the old feller from Crewe, assuming he's still around today, would have probably had a quiet word in that pretty girl's ear, gave her the benefit of his wisdom and experience on the vagaries of the game, past and present. And if that failed, just gave her a friendly clout round the head. You can't whack the old ways, can you?

When I think back now to that Crewe fan, and probably thousands of other unsung heroes like him out there, you cannot help but admire their tenacity, loyalty and optimism as they trudge for year on year round small grounds all over the country, drooling in the glory of a massive 5-1 away win at Doncaster or Darlington and then the chance of pitting their wits against an Arsenal and a Spurs and the excitement of drawing them in the cup and thinking; "This is it; this is our moment". And then the roof caves in, but that doesn't matter. Dust yourself down, pick yourself up and start all over again. Maybe that's even how Henry the Fifth beat the French at Agincourt against overwhelming odds. I dare say that on the day he had about a thousand archers with the same blind faith and optimism as that Crewe fan. They could all have turned and fled, gone on to easier and less dangerous battlefields, when they saw they were hopelessly outnumbered by the French about five to one. Instead they probably thought running away would be the easy thing to do. Besides, where's the fun in just winning easy and winning everything all the time? It would be much more of a thrill for them to come out on top and get involved in a real dogfight. And so, not only did Harry and his boys win, they even gave the French the famous "V" sign afterwards.

Every team dares to dream the impossible dream- and I'm not talking about Blackpool when they went up to the Premier. Can you imagine, for example, the sheer elation of following a lower league team for maybe 25 years, having won bugger all but the Daily Mirror's "Fair Play League" in all that time, and then one glorious season you strike gold. On the very last day of a very long season, you scrape a lucky 2-1 away win at Torquay and discover that all your wildest dreams have come true. As impossible as winning the lottery two weeks running, you find that five other results have all gone your way. And the result of this is that you've scraped into automatic third place and ended up winning promotion. You hark back to those long years of leaky roofs, rain down the back of your neck, salmonella poisoning and a 6-1 walloping at Scunthorpe, chased through the back streets of Barnsley after a last minute equaliser robbed them of the win, abandoned by the bus in Exeter and not even a point to show for it. All of that is forgotten, and forgiven, because your team, your reason for being, has been promoted. After you've been revived by the smelling salts, there's then the countdown to the following season and that long three month wait till August and some of the big boys that you'll be meeting. You'll be salivating in anticipation. You'll be thinking of some of these teams you'll actually be on the same field with, most of them not long out of the Premier League, bankrupt and popping down the leagues to keep you company for the next few seasons. It doesn't get any better than this, and you saying with glee as you punch the air: "Yes please, I'll take fifth off bottom now next season".

Those simple emotions for the fan of an ordinary lower league side, even for one glorious season, are worth more than three Premier League title wins to a Chelsea fan and the reason why is just so simple. Imagine you've climbed a mountain for the first time. It must be totally exhilarating. You get to the top and look down at the whole world below you and then you wonder how the hell you not only survived the journey up but how you actually did it. But no matter, you just did and you were so proud of yourself and your achievement. But if you went back the next year, and the year after that, and this time somebody made it really easy for you by giving you a ride up to the summit on the world's most expensive helicopter, would you still have those same feelings of elation? Of course you wouldn't. You'd have done it the easy way. And that, I think, is the difference between our Maurice following humble little Rochdale and Reggie with his Platinum Gold season ticket at Chelsea. Nothing personal, it's just a football thing.

You don't follow a team for 50 odd seasons without developing a sense of loyalty, love, devotion and passion similar to the above. You couldn't replicate those feelings by merely switching to an easier ride, so what would really be the point? And you cannot possibly know that feeling, buy it, or even begin to understand it until you have been through it, and go through the same whole life sentence with no parole.

As a fan of such standing, plus wearing your team colours, or even having a jacket with hundreds of badges on, there's no doubt you'll get some odd looks down the years even at places such as Peterborough, Barnsley, Plymouth, Brighton and Swansea, to name but a few. All these are sides have had their moments in the last few years. Not like your lot, eh? Isn't it comforting to know, though - a real sense of inner peace almost - that you've probably learnt more about football's experiences than those supporters of high-flier clubs will ever know. Keep saying and thinking that as you stand there and get the abuse hurled at you, too. Remember, too, that you learn a lot more about life, and real living, through adversity, failure, getting knocked down and getting back up again, than you ever will by being cosseted, comfortable and lazy. You'll never end up being the football equivalent of a 35 stone overweight slob, but you'll be a lean, mean and not very successful lower league machine.

Think about it the next time you are confronted by a nouveau riche, dedicated follower of fashion complete with a £1500 season ticket for The Bridge, Emirates or Old Trafford. When you laugh disdainfully at them, try not to make it too obvious. We wouldn't want them to think you were mad now, would we? The point I am striving to make here is that any daft bugger can put on a Chelsea shirt, blag his way into an expensive seat and hurl abuse at those less fortunate than themselves. It takes a real man to hold his head up high wearing a Torquay, Crewe or Exeter top. My mother once told me that there was nothing sadder than some poor bugger pretending to be rich when he didn't have two farthings to rub together. She had a way with words, my mother. Of course, it could have been a saying that she pinched from Confucius but I don't think it was. Any fan, male or female, will always be a fraud, win lose or draw if they don't have the courage of their convictions and the courage to follow their roots, and stick by them. And that applies in life, too.

What has caused this seeming division amongst fans, this difference if you like, between a modern fan and a real one? Is it a case of money or the age gap or what? If it were money then why aren't I one of them? I've got a few bob, big bungalow, no mortgage, second home, two cars, apartment abroad and an expensive to keep partner (hasn't everyone got one of these?). Is it the birth of the Premier league, the North/South divide, the soaring price of fish, or what?

I'd like to know. It's a safe bet to say that if you've followed a team who've won virtually bugger all since you were in nappies, and this can mean the 1930s for considerably older readers (I hope you reach the end of the book, by the way) then you are well and truly the genuine article. What's classed as one of the old school, a real fan who hasn't jumped ship, or deserted your post. In nautical terms, you're not sitting on the bridge at HMS Emirates drinking champers as your old battleship SS Huddersfield Town is bravely trying to keep its bows above water. Some of the other worthier vessels have had their repairs carried out and are back on the high seas. There's the SS Newcastle, Wolverhampton, Sunderland that I can see over there. Others are struggling with too much water in their bilges and need an overhaul before they are ready for the high seas again. There's the two Sheffield ships, plus SS Pompey, Derby and, way in the distance, almost below sea level you would think, those fine old vessels Luton and Grimsby. All capable once repaired, of blowing those big guns out of the water one day, provided that this time they keep their powder dry. The majority of the matelots on some of these old, less fashionable, warships are still keen on remaining on board in spite of poor rations. All of them, both young and old alike, are well versed and steeped in both the history and tradition of their vessel brought up by sensible forefathers who have instilled in them a sense of honour, loyalty, and commitment- even in rough seas. They see their ship, as rusty as it is, as one that should be held in the highest esteem by those other vessels, too. And that's only right, since the very history and tradition of a ship should always be judged on how many battles they've encountered. They form a very important part of their reason for being here unlike the many who seem to prevail on the more modern and expensive vessels. This lot would never go down with their ship. They'd merely hire a speedboat to take them to the next more affluent liner, preferably one guaranteed luxury European seasonal travel.

What makes fans what they are today is built firmly on solid foundations and unswerving beliefs that the old man from Crewe obviously had. How different and sad from the fans of those clubs who now dominate with contemptuous ease the current football scene and win it season after season. Those same arrogant fans seem to feel that anything of merit won even ten years ago is out of the ark, almost prehistoric, and remembered only by dinosaurs like me (there's that word again!).

These fans will scorn and deride the likes of Forest and Derby, two sides who achieved a football miracle from small provincial towns. Derby not only won the league against impossible odds in 1972, they actually did it again in 1975 playing on a ground that today would be the equivalent of a ploughed up field. Now I come to think of it, it was a ploughed up field then. Even mighty

Liverpool don't escape scot-free today from these modern upstarts. They too are ridiculed, because they haven't yet managed to win the Premier League, upon which all modern success is judged. Nottingham Forest, who not only won the league but also the European Cup twice, should be commemorated every ten years, not conveniently dismissed and forgotten about. Both they and Derby achieved, with limited resources, more than any top four side today will ever hope to emulate. They did it with virtually no real comparative financial clout and from a relatively small fan base. How many bought and paid for Premier League titles is that worth? And here's a football mathematics question, too. How many Premierships equal five European Cup/Championship Trophies? All answers on a postcard please to "Liverpool Football Club c/o Anfield, Liverpool".

Those fans who mock such achievements as being too far back to be important today are the sort who'd forget their own history, too, And yet, despite all this wealth and the fabulous stadiums they play in, both Chelsea and Arsenal cannot, even, with countless millions in the case of Chelsea, still win the biggest trophy of them all, the Champions League. And here's another bugbear from me. Didn't it sound much more grandiose when it used to be called "The European Cup"? It's just as grand as saying "The Football League". They'll never learn, will they?

The Champions League is, of course, a modern re-branded name that is almost as irritating as that classic rebuke you now hear at football grounds everywhere: "Who are ya?" That insult is right up there in my book with that other classic line: "Shall we sing a song for you?" Whenever I hear this, I'm always tempted to say "Yes, please, Bohemian Rhapsody by Queen". I cannot help laugh at perhaps the ironic thought of some haughty Forest fan somewhere deriding a Chelsea fan as they discuss the relevance of modern football. Obviously into the conversation, just after the mushroom soup, will spring the inevitable reference to the first of Chelsea's Premier League trophy wins, the first time they actually finished top of the heap since 1955. I wonder how that piece of good luck or sudden good fortune came about. I'm really at a loss to fathom out how they suddenly and mysteriously started winning all these trophies. The whole conversation might even slip to the Champions League. Inevitable really because the next logical step after winning the Premier League must be to try and win the Champions League. I know exactly what I'd be saying if I was a Forest fan too. "So how long do you reckon it will take you to win the Champions League twice then? Five seasons, ten, fifteen, never?" No doubt there will be the patronising response from the Chelsea fan that things were a lot different back then. Today, he'll tell you that you are competing against the elite and the mega rich of Europe, some of whom are just as rich as Chelsea.

Hang on, though, when Forest competed, everybody was richer than them. They not only had one hand tied behind their back, they had to compete against all of them from the back of the starting line with only their football as credentials. And their brand of football won the day against the lot of them - Hamburg, Bayern, Real Madrid. And they did it with the bare bones available.

You could have all the money in the world and not get anywhere near buying that kind of team spirit. Forest couldn't have afforded to buy Drogba's bootlaces, never mind pay his wages, but it was irrelevant. Chelsea would lose the argument and the comparison at all levels. Would that Forest team have beaten today's Chelsea? The answer is "Who knows and who cares". It's irrelevant now. However, if you look very carefully at the list of all the previous winners of the biggest trophy in European club competition, you will see the name of Nottingham Forest printed on it twice. I don't believe that Chelsea will ever come anywhere near that regardless of how much money they have to spend. And the even worse news for them is that level of spending pattern is now just not sustainable. There are signs both in and outside The Premier that the bubble is about to burst. Besides, all good things (as Forest and their fans so quickly found out) must come to an end. That's the difference between a fact and an opinion. You can buy the Premier League but you haven't got enough money to get anywhere near winning the European Champions League twice. How's that for bragging rights? By the way Aston Villa won the European Cup as well. And, of course, everyone knows that the first ever British winner of the trophy was a Scottish side, Celtic. How humiliating is that south of the border? That'll keep those Chelsea fans quiet next time they're knocking back the champers and Celtic, Villa and Forest fans start singing back at them: "Who are ya?" The irony of it all.

If you look in greater depth at the achievements of both Derby County and Nottingham Forest, you would still scratch your head now as to how they ever did it. It reminds me of that classic film "The Shawshank Redemption" when that poor bloke called Andy DuFreyne is wrongly convicted of murder and manages to tunnel his way out to freedom, taking him a full twenty years to do it and using only a tiny claw hammer. And then to top it all, he still managed to shaft the warden into blowing his own brains out. If you were to make a football movie today about what Forest and Derby did, that would be the equivalent storyline that you'd have to use, with Morgan Freeman obviously taking the part of Cloughie.

Both clubs would have both spent, by today's market comparisons, virtually nothing in the process. Derby County, in particular, had the ramshackle Baseball Ground that was a dump even when they were winning their two league titles. With just over a 30,000 capacity it should never have happened, but with two great managers in Clough and then Mackay, they went on to achieve Mission Impossible. Not even Tom Cruise would have got the part if they made a movie of it. All that, and they didn't even have a proper playing surface. There was no doubt that it did give Derby an advantage but they did have to play half their games away as well, and they were just as lethal on their travels. I used to see them regularly in London during their heyday and they were formidable to watch. They would have made just as much an impact, and maybe been as big as 1930s Arsenal, if Cloughie had stayed on. If you think that's a flight of fancy, then look at what he did later at Forest.

A lot of sides who also said that Derby's pitch was an advantage also had pitches that were equally as bad. For example, there were the golden sands of White Hart Lane. They could have kept donkeys on that pitch although Spurs fans will quickly tell you that for one or two seasons they did. Teams like Derby or Forest, even 35 years on, should be revered and applauded, not insulted. Even though both their days in the sunshine are now long behind them, I still regard both of them with a sense of wonder and admiration. If you were a real fan, you should too.

The Premier League now seems to have the same problem as they do in Scotland. For too many years there, Rangers and Celtic battled it out yearly amongst each other, while the rest of the pack - including us lot - were bored rigid by the inevitability of it all. The Scottish Premier League is finished and it's just a matter of time till the roof caves in. Here we have our very own equivalent of those two, Manchester United and Chelsea competing for the Premier. It will take some effort and money for anyone else to break their domination. Arsenal? I wouldn't put it past them to surprise everyone again. Even their youth team could hold its own in the Premier. Liverpool? Not for a while. Spurs? They are getting better but still a way off. And as for Manchester City, they have tons of money but they're a collection of expensive individuals and a long way from resembling a real team. The board there will probably run out of patience and money before they come anywhere near getting it half right. City appears to be a very expensive team of misfits and a look at their disillusioned and bored bench says it all in terms of morale and bonding. They are light years away, fortune or no fortune. Manchester United and Chelsea have cornered the market with their comparative mega bucks and pulling power, and for that they expect us all to be grateful. They both even attract the top fan base too. A gaggle of celebrities want to follow them, creating a real element of shallowness in their fan base. Always being one for the underdog, I admire the other end of the spectrum. Meatloaf, that chunky American Rocker, has now become a bona fide Hartlepool fanatic, simply because of the legend of the monkey. For those not familiar with this story I'll enlighten you. During the Napoleonic War a ship sank off the coast of Hartlepool, and a monkey washed up with the wreckage on the beach was mistaken as a French spy. Purely understandable as the people of Hartlepool had never seen a Frenchman before and so, I suppose, it was logical that it was hanged after a short trial. In their defence, Hartlepudlians will tell you it was a fair trial. The monkey was given every opportunity to defend itself but refused to say a word.

Admittedly even Man. United and Chelsea have the same hardcore fans who followed both sides when Derby, Ipswich, Burnley and Forest were winning the league. These fans, like the vast majority elsewhere, are equally annoyed at how their clubs seem to have been hijacked by a new wave of newcomers, all of whom you just know will scuttle quickly off elsewhere when the bubble bursts. If it happens, maybe we can all get our real game back.

My pet hate above everything else in football is how both these sides' supporters show blatant and arrogant disrespect for a team who I've admired since childhood. As incredible as it may seem, if you are a Liverpool fan coming up to the age of 60, then from the age of 12 onwards you'll have been brought up with a record of comparative success going all the way back to 1962 when they escaped the old Second Division. This is where I roughly came in as a supporter, and you can only imagine what it would have been like watching your own team for this amount of time knowing nothing but comparatively happy times. No one can emulate Liverpool's record, including Manchester United and Chelsea, both of whom have had spells in the Second Division, and years in the wilderness, since that date. Liverpool have held firm in the top league since August 1962. From Shankly through Paisley, and then on all the way down to Benitez and Kenny Dalglish, the fans on the Kop don't know how lucky they have had it down the years. I've followed Sunderland for roughly the same time span and all I've ever known is one lousy cup win in 1973, plus countless promotions followed by inevitable relegations. The only saving grace if you are a Sunderland fan is that at least West Bromwich in the last nine years have taken away our unwanted mantle of being one of the original yo-yo clubs.

Liverpool has won the lot and that is something that Chelsea, even with all their millions, still cannot say. And although the Premier league has still eluded Liverpool, then so what? Their fans haven't exactly been short changed. And if they think they have, then what about swapping your fortunes for ours for the next 30 seasons? That would really sicken you.

Just to rub even more salt into the wounds of every club in the Premier, never mind the top two, how long will it take each of them to win not even one, or two, but five Champions League Trophies? It would be easy to say they'd never do it, but I'll hazard a guess based on the law of averages past and present. I would say that it would take Chelsea possibly 50 years (and I'm being generous with them) but only if they carry on spending and the rest of Europe slows down. Man. United would be possibly 10-15 years as they only have two to catch up on Liverpool. Of course who's to say that before then, one, or both of them, might end up doing a "Portsmouth". Don't laugh at the impossibility of this happening. Look at what happened to Leeds. There's more chance of Ken Dodd still playing at the Sunderland Empire before any of them get anywhere near this colossal record. And who's to say that if by the time they both get to the magic number five, Liverpool themselves don't really sicken the pair of them further by winning it for the sixth time. They might even have upped the ante to eight by then. We would be then talking another hundred years on top of my forecast before the golden two drew level. Would football still be around by then or would the new modernists of the future have all invented some new fad by then? Floodlit Crown Green Bowls or something like that?

I suppose it's difficult, if not downright impossible, to quantify the difference between the two sets of fans I have described. Modern versus old, or maybe modern versus real might be a more appropriate comparison. Having established that a real fan would be generally older or a lot wiser than the modern variety then it would also follow that there is a pretty damning way of establishing just who is missing out in football generally. A real fan has his evidence based on just being there in the old days, and can make the necessary comparisons between good and bad, old and new, myth and reality, and still be here today to back up his judgement and, in some cases, experience and wisdom. A modern fan can only back his judgement on what he has been brought up with in the last few seasons, if he can bother to remember. He doesn't have all the pieces in the jigsaw. Who you would rather believe when they tell you what, who, when or where's best? Would it be someone who has seen both sides of the argument, or someone who's only just seen one? It was always that way, though. When I went to matches in my youth, I used to listen intently to those old fans that had been going to Roker Park back in the 1930s, some even back to the 1920s. I was fascinated by the names of Shackleton, Carter, Buchan, Halliday, Gurney and many others, and the endless debates and arguments about who was the better player or best player of all time. Even then, in the 1960s, the then modernists were dismissive of these silly old codgers. But what could they base their knowledge on? The older fans had seen players from both eras and could base their judgement on fact. The new 1960s variety could base their views only on opinion. If you were in a court, who would you believe in the dock? Would it be someone who could back up their side of the story with an opinion, or someone who had all the relevant facts? I rest my case, your honour.

I have always enjoyed great banter, or listening to someone older and wiser, who had experienced both sides of the argument, whether it was in life or football. That's how you really learn things. I've listened plenty down the years and all that knowledge gleaned and costing you nothing. I listened to all these tales, heard of great games from the past, great teams and players. Some you'd never even heard of and I'm busy reading up on them all the time, even as I write this. They are all long gone but still have a fascinating story to tell. I was told about some of them in my youth, their deeds and exploits. Back then, of course, I just didn't believe them. Flights of fancy I thought. Then, years later, with the advent of the internet (plus local libraries) I found it was all true. All part of our football heritage that we should never forget. There are some younger Newcastle fans out there who have never even heard of their own Hughie Gallagher, a fabulous and much more famous centre forward for them than perhaps Jackie Milburn, Malcolm Macdonald or even Alan Shearer. His only crime was he played in the forgotten era of the 1920s, pre-telly, pre-internet. They may have had library books available for the vast majority in the 1950s and 1960s to read up on this man, but a lot back then were all too busy grafting long shifts to have time for such luxuries. When Gallagher ended his own life in 1957, a lot of fans might have simply erased him from their memories, too. Anyone who doesn't think it's important to show any interest in the past should think again.

If you think that going back even to the 1960s must seem pointless to you, in much the same way that the 1920s was pointless for anyone back in the 1960s, then you'll miss out, through pure laziness and apathy, on all those great moments, great games, and fantastic atmospheres. That's when the league was important but the Cup was really King, along with coal - and I don't mean Ashley or Carlton. The 1960s was a time when England ruled the World and when all fans had a real respect for the opposition. Hype would then have just meant a barmy word used by even barmier people to dress mediocrity up as the genuine article. It was a time when over half the sides in the old First Division had a goalie good enough to play for England. When every ground was bursting at the seams each Saturday and it was get there early or serves you right when they shut the gates in your face. Then, weigh up that against what we have today. The modern fan shows a smug arrogance for the opposition as he wallows in his opulent surroundings, his comfort and security, covered by a blanket of complacency and backed up by a bottomless pit of money. A fan whose history of the game probably goes back no further than 1993 and after that, mate, he ain't really interested.

Next time you are out on your travels and you get a chance to see a Crewe game (they still play in the league every week in case you are interested) see if you can spot a really old feller, now late 80s and maybe still wearing a coat covered with many badges . If he's still alive and kicking, go and listen to what he has to say. You might learn something.

One of the most depressing aspects of getting older is that now when you approach people, invariably their first reaction is that you are either some nuisance or just trying to scrounge a cigarette off them. Down the years watching matches I've always made a point of trying to exchange a few words with away fans. In particular,to the two old Brighton fans gazing in wonder around The Stadium of Light, and who despaired of ever having a real home to call their own. When I told both of them that you never know what's round the corner, how prophetic was that remark? Brighton are nearly there. I hope you get your dream double of Championship football in that brand new 20,000 stadium. And, yes, I know you'll fill it. I'm not one to stereotype fans but I have noticed a common trend. The really younger element isn't one for talking or listening either. You do get the odd one but generally they are always in a rush. The words of that old Simon & Garfunkel song "Feeling Groovy" spring to mind: "Slow down you move too fast, you've got to make the morning last".

It's generally the older supporter who's always good for the conversation. At the 2004 semi final between Millwall and Sunderland at Old Trafford, I struck gold chatting in a cafe to a friendly bunch of Lions fans. Believe it or not, there are some out there in spite of the bad old days. As you also get older, then you don't really present any kind of threat to opposition supporters. They know you're harmless, or perhaps senile is the word they're looking for. In the middle of their group was an old boy that must have been in his seventies. The conversation turned to past games between the clubs at the Old Den. Then the old feller mentioned the 1937 FA Cup semi final between both sides and calmly announced "I was there that day". For me, it was another Empire Stadium moment circa 1923 with our old flatmate Arthur Ashe. All eyes were on him as he explained in detail his day out 67 years before. He was 12 at the time (I was already working out the maths straightaway to see if the story stacked up and it did). That would have made him a still young pup of 79 or 80. He and his mother had got the train up to Huddersfield for the match and were standing in a packed centre paddock, mixed in with both sets of fans alike. All he vaguely remembered is that all the kids were passed down to the front and he'd been one of them. That rang a bell with me and my youth. During the first half Sunderland had a throw in very near to where he and his mam were standing and he remembered one Sunderland player coming across to take it. He had his shirt collar turned up - many years before Eric Cantona invented the fashion - and all he could recall was this player being a really handsome bloke with jet black hair, piercing blue eyes and a broad smile. The reason for the broad smile was he'd spotted the young lad's mother who was smiling back at him. She was, apparently, a lovely looking woman and a real head turner everywhere she went. Straightaway I worked out the likely suspect. Collar turned up, jet black hair, piercing blue eyes? Was it Raich Carter? "That's the boy" he said. "That's the name I remember". He'd forgotten it all as the years ticked by. In 1937, Millwall lost 2-1 and Sunderland went on to win the cup. His mother apparently never stopped talking all the way back on the train about that brief, brief encounter. "He even winked at her as he took the throw in and she blushed" he added. Fancy anyone carrying those memories, not only of that game all those years ago, but those of his own mother. He waited a long, long time for his team's moment of revenge, and chance of cup final glory, and he got it that day at Old Trafford. I hope he even made it Wembley for the final even though Man. United won 3-0. The thought of how he'd have felt at Wembley at least brought some degree of consolation, but not that much.

And that left me wondering. I wonder if football will still evoke the same kind of fabulous memories for a 12 year old boy today who might be attending a match when he looks back on it 67 years from now. What will he remember, if anything, about the game, never mind one isolated incident occurring within it? It would have to be something really special to burn into his mind for all those years. What would be the story he would tell then round about 2077 to a young generation? Maybe it might be as follows "So I asked this number 5 called John, for his autograph. I forget his second name, but I think he played for Chelsea. I remember asking him twice after the match and he totally ignored me. He was playing against this other bloke who looked like that old cartoon character Shrek. I think his name was Mickey Rooney or something like that and when I asked him for his autograph as well, he told me to bugger off and set his minders on me". Happy days.

Look carefully at the current crop of players around today, hyped to the hilt, fame and all, a legend in their own lunchtimes, and the next lot coming through to replace them. None, I feel, will be able to evoke the iconic or legendary status of the likes of Dixie Dean, Charlie Buchan, Stanley Matthews, Tom Finney, Duncan Edwards and of course Bobby Moore. You can no doubt add a few dozen others to this list. Then, players built their reputations playing great football, season after season. Now, a player can come from nowhere, have a dozen good games, be given a £60,000 a week contract and be feted as the greatest player ever. It is almost as if the word "today" is the most important thing that actually matters today. It's instant food, instant celebrity, instant world football star, as far as the media is concerned. Even in the film world it is exactly the same. They can take the modern stars and dress them as celebrities in ritzy retro gear but not one of them will have the aura, charisma or iconic status as the likes of giants of the past like James Dean, Brando, McQueen, Cagney, Bogart or Clark Gable. They can try and imitate them, act like them and even dress like them. But really, it's laughable.

My past is littered with footballers who only added to the occasion of a match. Not so many coming through today, though. These memories and the stories I've built up and heard over a lifetime have probably been accumulated by maybe 24 hours in total spent just sitting back and absorbing it - call it a day in the life - and I'm all the richer for it.

I mentioned the Crewe fan and there have been other real characters of the modern game. One was a real throwback called John Westwood, librarian and Portsmouth fanatic who you must have seen on the telly. He resembles in real life a manic Isambard Kingdom Brunel with that Blue and white stove-pipe hat he wears. I first clapped eyes on him in a cup tie at Sunderland about 10 years back. It was another freezing cold afternoon but there he was ringing his bell and wearing a tiny waistcoat over a huge barrel bare chest. He was a pretty awesome sight up close and not a little bit frightening for small kids. Fans like him put the smile back on your face. Times are pretty hard for Pompey at the moment but he's still there, roaring them on. The match was instantly forgettable and the only endearing moment I remember of it now was seeing that jolly blue and white giant for the first time.

My dad once told me that when he and one of my other uncles, John, used to watch Sunderland in the mid 1950s, they regularly used to see players, home and opposition, sometimes walking to Roker Park on the way to the match. I suppose then most hometown players lived locally, and cars would still have been a luxury even for them. Most of the opposing teams used to stay at the nearby Roker Hotel on the sea front and only a five minute walk from the ground. On a nice day, players might have wanted to stretch their legs by merely walking to the ground. Even catching the tram to Roker Park would often see you sharing the carriage with some of the players. When Sunderland played Blackpool at Roker in the 1950s,on the tram was the great Stan Mortensen, having a chat with home fans too. That's how it used to be then. Football was the workingman's game so why shouldn't the stars of the show respond by giving them a little bit back? Could you imagine today sitting next to Wayne Rooney or Rio Ferdinand on the No.34 on the way to the match?

Even at away grounds, where the magic of going to them is still just as strong as in years gone by, you sometimes feel that you've just landed on Planet Hostile. Some grounds are very fan-friendly, others decidedly not so. Liverpool is but for some reason Everton isn't. Don't ask me why. Villa Park is a proper football ground, steeped in history, a great tradition with proper fans. The walk there once you've parked up has you thinking of all the greats of the past who played there, semi finals and all. For this reason I think that when they play the likes of former greats such as Newcastle, Sunderland, Sheffield Wednesday, Wolves et al there is always a sense of occasion, of theatre about the place, even if it involves you battling for three points to try and avoid the drop. Once a giant, always a giant, I think. The rest is just opinion.

There's a pub on the corner of Villa Park whose name escapes me. It's meant to be for home fans only, but it's fairly safe to go in if they know you're harmless. A couple of years back with Sunderland desperate for a win to stay up, again, I struck up an immediate conversation with a young off duty squaddie who was home on leave. His first home game in about 4 months he told me. He had his young son, about four, with him. He told us about his tour of duty, the dangers and horrors, and you quickly realised that football is totally insignificant by comparison. But not to him it wasn't. Not that day. As long as Villa won that would keep him going for another four months, he reckoned. In spite of the risks he was taking when he went back overseas, all that was forgotten and put to one side for that one afternoon. It made all of us listening feel really humble, and really honoured, to be sitting in his company. He'd also told us he'd lost one of his friends too, a big Wolves fan, and so before he went back, he was going to Molineux, just down the road, to pay his respects in the most fitting way he thought possible. A simple act of friendship and isn't this what football should really be all about, both on and off the field? We went our separate ways and it was only after the match, at twenty to five, with Sunderland snatching a fortunate 1-0 win, I remembered him and thought how he'd probably be cursing us for ruining his day. Villa couldn't even send him back on his tour of duty with a smile on his face.

Everybody has their own story to tell but unless you sit down and make the time to talk to them, you never know what kind of tale you'll hear, or what you'll miss out on. Football's only a simple game but it becomes a great one when sometimes you stumble across fans like that. It might be someone who just wants to get something off his chest and tell someone else who wants, or is prepared, to listen. Who knows? For that reason I just have to mention one funny story about Villa Park I heard from a friend of mine called Owen who was there in his teens in 1974/5 to see, again, Sunderland battling for promotion to the old First Division. Villa were promoted that year with Man. United (yes, Man. United) and Norwich. No play offs, just the top three promoted. Sunderland went to Villa that afternoon knowing that a win could push them into an automatic promotion spot. You know how this is going to end already, don't you? The gates were locked on 58,000, and on a red hot afternoon in more ways than one, Owen was crammed in the away end "sweating like a pig and that tightly packed you couldn't even scratch your nose". As a Villa move broke down, the ball moved quickly towards the away end. The crowd surged forward for a better view, and it was at this point that Owen was immediately lifted out of his shoes as the seething masses advanced about three or four yards. Then, as the move broke down, the crowd did a reverse shuffle back to its original spot. Here, incredibly, Owen found himself standing on his right shoe again, quickly followed by the left one. Unlike him, they had obviously stayed rooted to the spot on the terraces as he went for a short drag, and back again, with the mob. The only trouble he now had was that both shoes resembled a pair of flat, black leather kippers, trampled to oblivion by all those hemmed in fans. "Charlie Chaplin would have been proud of them" he laughed. Owen would have needed two square feet, two feet square, to get them back on again. He walked miserable and shoeless back to the coaches, Sunderland beaten 2-0, and their promotion dreams - as well as his shoes - flattened and in complete tatters. To complete his misery, the heavens opened as soon as he left the ground.

Football, as the old saying goes, is all about opinions. Dear old Jimmy Sirrel, a grand old sage and manager of Notts County, summed it up perfectly when he said simply that the score at full time was a fact, the league tables that Saturday night were a fact, and everything else was just an opinion. That's why you think your club is better than another one and why they, in turn, think that theirs is better than yours. Fact sometimes never comes into the equation and, besides, even if you happen to lose to that side, it doesn't change anything. They are still rubbish or fluked a 1-0 win, nine times out of ten you'd have beaten them. It's called being biased. Even if you've just lost 5-1 to them, you'll stick to the same beliefs or excuses.

There are even fans in the Premier League who think that some referees are biased towards the top four, and that they don't get a fair crack of the whip in terms of fairness on the field. I can't think where they get this idea from, can you? I've often thought too about this conspiracy theory going on with some referees who appear to wear celebrity goggles when they are in charge of a game involving a top four side against one of the strugglers. Do you think the same? That's a good topic of conversation next time you are jawing with a Villa, Pompey, Sheffield United or Derby fan. However, don't expect a civilised conversation with any fans from the top four sides. They'll tell you it's got nothing to do with poor referees. Only that "Your side are crap, mate. End of" Is it only the Premiership where this form of unfairness seems to prevail? Stoke

City, Blackburn and Wolves fans will tell you that when it comes to playing against bigger sides, they don't get a fair crack of the whip off some refs. And as for Blackpool, I've got to warn you, too. Once the honeymoon period is over, you'll be getting the same sort of treatment.

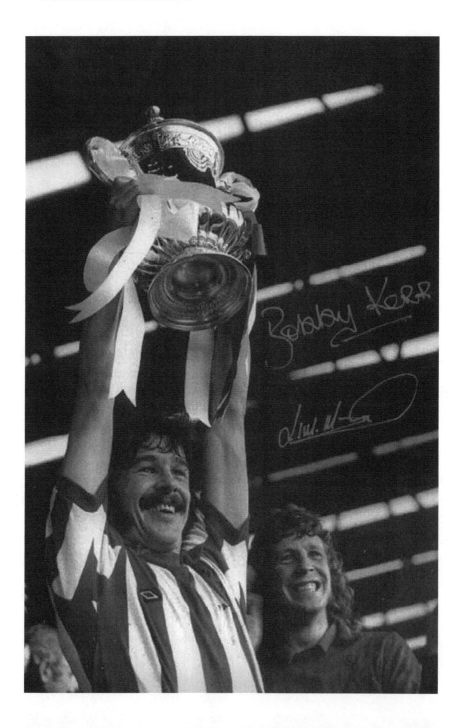

CHAPTER 10
WHATEVER HAPPENED TO THE FA CUP?

Is the FA Cup dying? If it isn't, then it's making a really good impression of it.

It seems to be more than ironic, coincidental, or perhaps just plain obvious, that since the introduction of the Premier League in 1993, both of our two cup competitions, the FA Cup and its much poorer Cousin, the League Cup (with all its various monikers its had in the last few seasons) have pretty much played second fiddle to this new monster. Maybe second fiddle is the wrong term to use. It's really more like fourth or fifth fiddle, so wide is the gap, a gap that appears to be widening season by season. So frail are the cup competitions becoming, that I'm just waiting for someone like Colonel Sanders and his KFC boys sponsoring one of them in the future. Can you imagine some poor team and its supporters waiting over 100 years to lift a trophy and then finding out that of all the finals they had to get to in their history, they've been saddled with winning the Kentucky Fried Chicken Cup 2015, complete with a free family bucket meal for every fowl they pick up on the pitch.

Both cups, in truth, have been totally devalued by the pressures, riches and hype of the Premier League. The demotion, though, of the once greatest cup competition in the world into nothing more than a second rate tin pot trophy does leave a nasty taste in the mouth. With the birth of the Premier, we have inadvertently created something akin to a Frankenstein celebrity monster, where every fan dreams of sitting at the top table and living in luxury beyond their wildest dreams, riches galore and the envy of the world. And that's exactly how it's turned out. The whole world now watches the Premier League three or four times a week and every team in it is known all round the world too, although some obviously more than others. It's wall to wall football saturation for the global masses. It's true that the FA Cup still holds some respect in other countries where it is still regarded as the father of all cup competitions. The rest of the world still sees it through rose-tinted glasses in much the same way that we did maybe 40 years ago. How on earth can a once a year competition compete with what's on offer today? Compare it if you will, traditional and quaint, with the glitz and hype that is the Premier and all its technology, global audience and army of sycophants serving it. If the FA Cup and Premier were both toys, it would be like comparing a spinning top to the latest PlayStation game. If you were a child what would you go for?

I once used to pride myself on being able to name every cup winner going back to when I can first remember watching the final on the telly, in my case 1961. Since the advent of the Premier League, I have struggled to remember who has won it from 1993 to the present date and I bet that this also applies to many other fans too. It just seems to be not quite so important than it once was. Everything seems to have taken a massive back seat to the Premier. I think that the basic, stark truth is that the monopoly or stranglehold of the game's greed since 1993 has now paid dividends. All the fun, glamour, romanticism and excitement of the FA Cup have now been stripped away completely.

Years and years back we used to have special names for different FA Cup finals. Who can ever be allowed to forget the classic 1953 final, when Stan Mortenson scored a hat-trick for Blackpool in a 4-3 win against Bolton Wanderers? That was known as "The Matthews Final" only because it sounded more romantic than calling it "The Mortensen Final". Poor old Stan had waited a long time for a bit of silverware, you know! Mind you, so had the other Stan – Mortensen - but his three goals would never have happened without the wizardry of Matthews.

I suppose it should have been an ominous sign of things to come when I vaguely remembered the 1960 final between Wolves and Blackburn being labelled "The Dustbin Final", the reason being that most people thought that it was absolute garbage, although obviously not if you were a happy Wolves fan and you won 3-0. I didn't watch it, although my dad later told me that he didn't bother either. He managed to get through to half time before falling asleep and in the second half went out to dig the garden. That told me how bad it was. He'd go to any lengths to avoid doing the garden, although obviously even he drew the line at sitting through the 1960 final.

How lucky, then, that my very first final the year after, was the game between Spurs and Leicester. It was not a great final by any stretch of the imagination, but it was regarded as immensely important at the time as Spurs were looking to become the first time in the 20th century to do the double. It was history in the making and although, again, I was too young to fully appreciate it, I was watching a team that broke records wherever they played, and sold out, too. Now winning the double is as common as going to Blackpool for the weekend or watching Sir Alex Ferguson blasting the ref for not adding on enough extra time.

Back then the cup was a lot more magical and seemed far more important than even winning the league. Don't ask why, it just was. Looking back now, it was probably because of that very word "magic". TV was still very much in its infancy and when the FA Cup was on there was some eight hours of wall to wall viewing connected with the final itself, including the whole game live. The whole country came to a halt for one day in May to take in this visual feast. Spurs won at a canter and thus achieved something that hadn't been done since Preston North End the century before. How cool was that for a budding historian?

The next year's final was even better. It was Spurs again, beating Burnley 3-1, and my nan was one of the few people in Easington Colliery to have a telly. It's funny, but thinking back I never remember seeing my grandfather that day. He'd have been either down the pit or down the local Workingmen's Club. Thirsty work being a miner.

There must have been over 20 people crammed into the front room watching that game. And the build up went on from early morning too, all in glorious black and white. We were all rooting for Burnley, the Northern team, but they didn't stand a chance. Spurs, and my boyhood hero Jimmy Greaves, just steamrollered them. That, to a young boy, was the real magic of the cup. But it wasn't just me that felt that way. All generations used to be gripped by the excitement every time the Cup Final rolled around. And thus it went on year after year, seemingly unabated.

I remember each year of the sixties and seventies clearly and never missed a final. I could even tell you where I was as well. All that was to change later but the question is why? In years gone by, there were only two channels, no Sky TV or numerous others. We put the flags out when BBC2 came along. There were no blueberries, blackberries, internet, iPods, iPads, peapods, mobile phones with latest scores, or tellies in cars keeping you bang up to date with it all. We did have the radio, though.

There were only two real ways of getting your team noticed. One was via the telly hoping that, once in a blue moon, they'd appear on the local news under the sports highlights (and then it was case of "don't blink or you'll miss them") or there was the even slimmer chance of seeing them on "Match Of The Day" which first appeared in 1964. And before that, there was basically nothing. The second, even more remote route, was for your team to get to Wembley and then the whole of the country would be guaranteed to watch them from first thing Saturday morning all the way through to Saturday night. It was Football Shangri-La but it was still only once a year. Your chances of your team doing it were slim. Maybe once every 25 years if you were patient enough. There was even a third way of getting noticed but this involved just reading about them in magazines or footy books. There was Charles Buchan's Football Monthly, but the trouble with this was a lot can happen to your team in a month. I once knew someone who had every one of these magazines in pristine condition, the full set covering over 15 years, and his wife threw the whole lot out when she was doing her spring cleaning. She said they were cluttering up the house. Those magazines would have been worth thousands today. No wonder he left her. Even with or without dear old Charlie and his monthly fix, it was not really the same. Football was very parochial then, and people didn't really travel great distances to watch their team the way they do today. Nobody in Blackburn cared about Newcastle, just the same as nobody in Newcastle cared about Stoke. And if you were a Millwall fan, you didn't care about anybody.

Today, you can get the saturated equivalent of the cup final every Saturday and Sunday, Monday nights, Wednesday nights and even Friday nights, too. It's the equivalent of being a football alcoholic without the drink. And you get a post mortem afterwards telling you in graphic detail how bad your defence was, and that if they had the ability of being wise after the event like the smug, smarmy idiots presenting the show, then they would have been able to prevent all three of the goals from happening. And all of it presented on a fabulous diagrammatic screen, with a twist of lemon and a cube of ice thrown in. It's very hard to say just when but I think that the rot set in for the cup final round about the mid 1980s. Up to then, I would say it was still possibly the highlight of the sporting calendar for everyone, regardless of who you supported either North or South. Certainly in the 60s and early 70s it was the football equivalent of a night at the Proms.

It's hard to even visualise now what you would patiently sit through back then, and I do wonder whether such a format would ever work today, either for the current generation or even those from earlier generations who saw it first time around. Slick it mostly certainly wasn't and cheesy it most definitely was. Would you, in all honesty, now sit there for hours on end and watch as teams were getting on the coaches and following them slowly, ever so slowly, to Wembley? Then, as the tension mounts there'd be the start of "It's A Knockout" which featured two lots of supporters, all high on happiness and making absolute arses of themselves (not a snarl of defiance amongst any of this jolly lot). It made "I'm A Celebrity, Get Me Out Of Here" look like TV entertainment. Then there'd be little clips of "how they got there" followed by more meandering interviews with mostly brain-dead footballers whose vocabulary consisted mainly of "you know" accompanying every other word (some things never change, do they?). Then it was cue the switch to the TV Panel, three idiots deemed to be experts. If this lot were experts then how come not one of them even hinted at a guess that Second Division sides Sunderland, Southampton and West Ham might possibly win the Cup? Not even given a remote chance by any of them and how we all laughed afterwards.

Then, just as you thought rigor mortis was setting in, it was "We're going back to the buses, Brian" (and shouts at the telly of "get on with it!") and then, wait for it: "Yes, here they come, they're here, the buses are here, they are definitely here, they are now here, they are arriving at Wembley. And I think, yes, the door is about to open", accompanied by more drivel and inane utterances from some bloke with a microphone: "And as I speak they are getting off" (Of course they are, you daft bugger; they wouldn't stop on there, would they? They've got a cup final to go to).

Then the hymns would start that went on and on, then the introductions to Lord Arthur, the 3rd Duke of Barnsley on his mother's side, the "shotty in" before the kick off and then finally they were off - to a cagey first 20 minute start. Is this how you remembered it too? Sometimes even then, after all that build up, that was better than the actual match. "Well, it was the nerves, you see. Nobody wanted to get this far and lose" especially so, if you were the favourites to win. And especially if the three Stooges back at the studio had tipped you to be the easiest winner ever of the cup. Talk about the kiss of death.

 People forget that for every classic they saw at Wembley there were three duds as well. And yet, in spite of all this, getting to Wembley and the cup final itself was still a sense of the occasion. Some people wore top hat and tails to watch the match, and that was just in front of the telly to get them in the mood. It was something to brag about if you were a supporter. Unless the worst scenario happened when you got there and the occasion proved too much for both you and your team. You just froze completely, and came home having been beaten. When that happened, how can you put the feeling into words? Imagine a lavish day out with all the family and that you had planned a really posh restaurant, no expense spared, somewhere really fabulous for a fancy meal. What happened next would be the Wembley equivalent of what just happened to your team freezing on the day. The whole lot of you would be violently sick all at once, just after you'd all had the pea soup and way before you'd even started on the main course. You'd all be chucked out en masse and be a laughing stock for weeks, months afterwards. That's how it would have felt, Sheer nerves, you see. Some coped better than others is what I'm trying to say.

I think that of all the finals watched, and some of them really took some watching, I've seen maybe only ten out of fifty - that's one in five, or 20% to you mathematicians - that I would describe as nail-biting, going way back from 1961 to date. Nail-biting? Some were positively toe-curling. But if it was your team that won the worst cup final ever, then I can guarantee it would have been like watching Real Madrid beating Eintracht 7-3 in the 1960 European Cup Final at Hampden Park. And if you've never seen the clips of that game, or even heard of it, then go to the bottom of the class. You've never truly watched football.

If you put to one side those rose-tinted glasses that you always have on when watching your side play, take a deep breath and just be honest with yourself. Winning a cup final the ugly way does not make it a classic and only history will tell you that years later. Or you can save the bother and the wait right now as I prove it to you by running quickly though each and every one, giving you my take, a potted verdict, on all of them. See how many you agree with. Hand on heart, I bet it's most of them. So here goes, 49 years, 50 cup finals in approximately six minutes, or maybe longer if you are a slow reader. Spurs are just kicking off in the white shirts and attacking the Leicester goal very early in the 1960s.

1961 Spurs 2 Leicester 0.
Dull; Spurs on their way to the double were always going to win. Plucky Leicester never at the races (they'd have been better off going there). Spurs adapted much quicker to black and white telly by playing in white shirts and black shorts. Poor Leicester looked positively grey by comparison.

1962 Spurs 3 Burnley 1.
Good game. At least Burnley made a fight of it. A classic early strike by Greavsie put Spurs in control. It was the breaking up of the famous double side and the beginning of the end for Burnley's last great side too. And little did we all know it then, it was the start of the elite sides coming to the fore in the First Division.

1963 Manchester United 3 Leicester City 1.
Good, bordering on excellent, with plucky Leicester, again, always on a hiding. United's first trophy since Munich although I didn't see the significance of

what this actually meant to some fans. I thought they were crying because someone had upset them or something. I never realised it. Denis Law was at his very best. Dad and me demolished a whole loaf of bread toasted on the fire watching this one. I think watching Leicester under the cosh for 90 minutes made us both feel peckish.

1964 West Ham 3 Preston North End 2.
This was an absolute classic. It kept you guessing right to the very end. West Ham blew bubbles while North End blew the Cup. Nobody put the kettle on for 90 minutes that day in our house. Mother was out shopping. Poor North End thought they were going to win it towards the end and I did too. We all know what thought does, don't we?

1965 Liverpool 2 Leeds United 1.
What an absolute damp squib, just like the weather. Extra time just about saved the game, but not for Leeds. Two sides frightened to make a mistake. If Leeds knew that Gerry Byrne played virtually the full game with a broken collar bone the score might have been different. Call me cynical, but they would have certainly exploited the situation. How ironic that they played a side down to ten and didn't even take advantage of it.

1966 Everton 3 Sheffield Wednesday 2.
Another absolute corker that was wonderful to watch. It was Wednesday's Cup at 2-0 up (see Preston, 1964) until some Cornishman called Mike Trebilcock did the business. Did that copper ever catch the Everton fan running on the pitch?

1967 Spurs 2 Chelsea 1.
Good, but Spurs were always more likely to win it. A London derby but wasn't it quiet? Mam quickly found the pin she heard drop in our house.

1968 West Bromwich Albion 1 Everton 0.
This was absolute rubbish, but not if you were an Albion fan; just one moment of excitement by dear old Jeff Astle. "We wuz robbed" said Everton. And they were. If you don't take your chances, then someone like Astle will show you how it's done.

1969 Manchester City 1 Leicester City 0.
See 1968. Okay but not great. Plucky Leicester, plus relegation too, as an added bonus for them. Neil Young took time off from his busy schedule, cancelling a rock concert to grab the only goal and win it for City.

1970 Leeds United 2 Chelsea 2.

Brutally good, Leeds chucked it away on a pitch that our local welfare team would have refused to play on. Today there would have been two sendings off but back then it was part, parcel and broken leg of the game with mistakes galore.

Replay Leeds United 1 Chelsea 2.

Ditto. Chelsea got their retaliation in first at Old Trafford. Not a pretty sight.

1971 Arsenal 2 Liverpool 1.

This was a classic match between two great sides. Gunners double year and the last of the Longhairs, Charlie George, inspired the way. It had you guessing all the way to the end.

1972 Arsenal 0 Leeds 1.

As forgettable as a Take That concert (I'm a Led Zep man, myself). Thousands switched off to go and watch the paint dry somewhere. Anywhere.

1973 Sunderland 1 Leeds United 0.

An easy win for Leeds said the experts.The whole country (bar Leeds and Newcastle) got behind Sunderland and their little general Bobby Kerr. When Stokoe ran on at the end there wasn't a dry eye in the house. Wembley's greatest ever save, too, by Montgomery. Sunderland would have been down to ten men in only the first minute if the match had been played today, following that Pitt tackle on Clarke. Looking back, who cares? Nearly every Sunderland fan who's ever written a book has covered the 1973 Cup final, so this is my bit on it. Enough said.

1974 Liverpool 3 Newcastle United 0.

Good but so one sided Liverpool could have declared early in the second half and gone home. A classic Long John Silver impersonation for 90 minutes by Malcolm Macdonald who promised to win the cup for Newcastle. He's still the same today on local radio.

1975 West Ham United 2 Fulham 0.

Fair to middling, but we all wanted Fulham and Bobby Moore to win. Fulham keeper Mellor made sure that wasn't going to happen. In the end, an easy day out for the Hammers and bargain buy Allan Taylor.

1976 Southampton 1 Man United 0.

An easy win for United said the experts. Good and exciting. This was a real slow-burner. After 1973, who said lightning doesn't strike twice? It did, and little Bobby Stokes did the rest.

1977 Man United 2 Liverpool 1
A tense affair which I thought Liverpool would win. United held their nerve and just about rolled over the finishing line. It was a great game for the neutrals. Undecided, I tossed a coin for it. When it said "heads" for Liverpool, I knew it would be United's day. I always was a hopeless gambler.

1978 Ipswich Town 1 Arsenal 0
Exciting and nervy throughout with underdogs Town's first and last cup win with Bobby Robson getting his hands on the trophy. It couldn't have happened to a nicer bloke or team.

1979 Arsenal 3 Man United 2
This was a classic topsy turvy match. I'd have bet money on United winning it at 2-2 but nice to see Arsenal calling on Sunderland (Alan) to help them win.

1980 West Ham United 1 Arsenal 0.
An easy win for Arsenal said the experts. The Happy Hammers do it again against all the odds. Speaking of odds I had a £2 bet on them at 5/1 to win that day. Back then, you could get drunk for a fortnight on that much. And you still can today at supermarket prices. A very rare Trevor Brooking winner with his nut, although I still say he was trying to dodge it. You'd have got 100/1 on the day for him scoring with a header.

1981 Spurs 1 Manchester City 1
A great game for the purists and a fair result, although I did fancy City to beat them in the replay - as long as Tommy Hutchinson knew which way he was kicking this time.

Replay Spurs 3 Manchester City 2
A classic and evenly poised until Ricky Villa scored a fantastic winner. What would it have cost Spurs today to buy both him and Ossy Ardiles in their prime?

1982 Spurs 1 QPR 1
A miss for me this one. The sign of a great cup final is one that never leaves your memory. This one must have been like a dodgy curry that passes right through you and leaves you with a burning sensation that you just want to forget.

Replay Spurs 1 QPR 0
See the above. Once Spurs went in front there was only going to be one winner. Spurs fans must have got the cigars out really early. On the fashion side of

things, I thought Rangers' natty black and red striped shirts were gorgeous. It was so very AC Milan, darlings.

1983 Man United 2 Brighton 2
A good game and Brighton should have won the cup. Who can ever forget Smith's moment of late glory and that astonishing miss? I was already up off the couch shouting "Goal!" Bet when Brighton move to their new stadium, none of the stands will be named after him. Brighton were beaten in the replay before a ball had been kicked.

Replay Man United 4 Brighton 0
Who said that high scoring games are never boring? This one was. I think I headed off to bed with my Horlicks and ginger biscuits not long after the final whistle. Brighton must have been demoralised from the off, and as soon as United went 1-0 up then that was it. Jimmy Melia left Brighton not long after. The crowd were with him all the way but he managed to lose them at the station.

1984 Everton 2 Watford 0
When you remember Elton John crying before the game rather than the game itself, then, really, what else is there to say? Everton won it on automatic pilot.

1985 Man United 1 Everton 0
The first sending off in the history of the cup final. This one was just stop, go, stop, go stop – bang - you're off! I think I missed the end of it; I'd dropped off to sleep. It was the start of the rot for all cup finals to come. Sod the occasion, the result is all that matters.

1986 Liverpool 3 Everton 1
A classic from start to finish with the crowd having a lot to do with it. Their noise spurred both teams on. Both sides wanted it from the opening whistle and weren't frightened to have a go. That's all fans ask. Liverpool won but there were no real losers on the day.

1987 Coventry City 3 Spurs 2
This was another epic. Nobody gave Coventry a chance, just like 1973, 1976 and 1980. Don't ask me how but I think after the first 20 minutes, City's name was on that Cup. Great to see ex-Hartlepool's Keith Houchen get the winner with a fabulous header. It was nearly as good as the one he once scored for Pools against Torquay. As an added bonus, there was even Nick Pickering, ex-Sunderland, too. Spurs were far too complacent that day and thought their name was already on the cup. It was, but unfortunately for them it was five years earlier.

1988 Liverpool 0 Wimbledon 1
Who says snarling and intimidation doesn't sometimes pay off? The Crazy Gang did a number on Liverpool in that tunnel and maybe it just worked. What might have been if John Aldridge had put that penalty away. That miss actually saved this final. If he'd scored, I think Liverpool would have gone on to win about 3-0. How long before the Dons get to these heady heights again? There were massive celebrations in that hot bed of football, Wimbledon, that night with both pubs still full well after 9 o'clock.

1989 Liverpool 3 Everton 2
I found this the saddest final of all I've watched since I was a young boy. Emotional post-Hillsborough and, really, I would have preferred it if both sides had claimed the cup for the city of Liverpool without a ball being kicked. On days like this, all rivalries go out of the window. It was a classic game that both sides must have been proud of. It should have finished 3-3 with both teams walking up the steps together.

1990 Man.Utd.3 Crystal Palace 3
It's amazing how rank bad defending and poor goalkeeping can make for a good game. It was only right that Man United didn't win it on the day. If United keeper Jim Leighton had picked up a winner's medal, he'd only have dropped it.

Replay Man. United 1 Crystal Palace 0
Both sides cut out the mistakes and every tackle counted. No quarter was asked nor given and both defences were as tight as a gnat's chuff. In short, it was pure dullsville. Give them the cup and let's all go home.

1991 Spurs 2 Nottingham Forest 1
Paul Gascoigne should have been sent off on that stretcher. An awful tackle and yet he gets all the sympathy. He's never changed from that day to this. The start, I think, of the hype coming into our game to over-glorify and nearly deify certain players. Forest would have won if the ref had done his job. Wonder if he managed to get Paul's autograph afterwards? If he didn't, he would certainly have got a piece of Cloughie's tongue instead.

1992 Liverpool 2 Sunderland 0
Sunderland's best opportunity to win this was in the first half. John Byrne missed a great chance to have scored in every round of the cup. At 0-0 at half time, I knew that we were going to lose. Not a patch on 1973 and I think even the Sunderland fans knew it.

1993 Arsenal 1 Sheffield Wednesday 1

These two must have been sick of the sight each other that season. They were that close it's a wonder they didn't get engaged. Best description of this was probably a stale stalemate. Wednesday fans now must only dream of such days as they languish in the First Division.

Replay Arsenal 2 Sheffield Wednesday 1

Seconds out; round two. No early submissions as both sides grappled to get a hold and an early grip on the match. Andy Linighan, another ex-Hartlepool lad, delivered the knock out blow which had Wednesday well and truly on the ropes.

1994 Man United 4 Chelsea 0

Shades of 1983 and Brighton all over again as Man United didn't break sweat and Chelsea quickly chased shadows. The game was all over bar the laughing at half time. Not the Chelsea we know today, but back then they didn't have the money. Just think what glorious future lies ahead again if they ever run out of dosh.

1995 Everton 1 Man United 0

This was one for purists and it was purely dire. I was just hoping someone, anyone would get the winner.

1996 Man United 1 Liverpool 0

Which idiot was responsible for the biggest ever own goal at Wembley before a ball was even kicked? Even more catastrophic than the seven goals Jamie Carragher has put through his own net? Didn't the Liverpool squad look absolutely gorgeous in their pre-match white suits? I wonder how they dared show their faces on the pitch after this but they did. I bet those eleven budding Walter Travoltas were still embarrassed when they took to the pitch, leaving United to go on to a functional win. As the great Eric Cantona said so succinctly after this one: "When the men in white suits look so ill at ease before a ball is even kicked then there is only one result - and that's without the help of the gulls that fly over the fishing boats".

1997 Chelsea 2 Middlesbrough 0

Poor old 'Boro. They waited over 100 odd years for a final and then when they get there, they've lost it after just 40 seconds. There was no way back after this and since then there's been no way back for 'Boro.

1998 Arsenal 2 Newcastle United 0

I think Arsenal Reserves could have probably won this one for them, so strong was their squad then. Newcastle never in it, and were as ineffective as their

1974 counterparts. So easy, it really did become very boring. It was a real anti-climax for the Geordie Nation - again.

1999 Man United 2 Arsenal 0
This was the start of Man United's supremacy as we ended the old century. Arsenal gave a good account of themselves and hung on for grim life but you always knew United were going to deliver the knockout blow

2000 Chelsea 1 Aston Villa 0
This was dull beyond belief. I don't think Villa really believed in themselves from the off, and neither did I when I got so brassed off with it I went out to do the shopping. Did I say it was dull? It was, unbelievably so.

2001 Liverpool 2 Arsenal 1 (at Cardiff Millennium stadium)
Remember the old saying "It ain't over till the fat lady sings"? How we laughed when cocky Arsenal fans thought they'd won the cup and then, before you knew what had happened, Liverpool scored two quickies. And just then, this huge female opera singer came waddling on with a loudspeaker.

2002 Arsenal 2 Chelsea 0
This was the start of the monotony in cup finals. All of a sudden the top four sides in the Premier started appearing over and over again. It was like watching the same old film you'd seen a dozen times, knowing how it was going to end. Easy win for Arsenal but Chelsea were about to dip in to a treasure chest and all was about to change with monotonous regularity.

2003 Arsenal 1 Southampton 0
What was I just saying above? This time it was Arsenal on their own and, with due respect to Southampton, they had as much chance as winning this as Millwall did the year after.

2004 Man United 3 Millwall 0
And now, ladies and gentlemen, the turn of Man United to get to a final. Millwall must have been pinching themselves just to get there. Man United's easiest win of the season but if you were a Millwall fan who cares? The Lions got a place in Europe so everyone was a winner.

2005 Arsenal 0 Man United 0 (Arsenal win 5-4 on penalties)
Man United and Arsenal in the same final. I bet footy fans everywhere couldn't contain their excitement. The first game to be won on penalties, but why not have made it a bit more interesting by maybe having a singing contest instead, or perhaps tossing a coin? Or even better, don't play the 120 minutes and go straight to penalties. What a lousy way to win or lose a final.

2006 Liverpool 3 West Ham United 3 (Liverpool win 3-1 on penalties)

West Ham must have thought they had this game won but then allowed Liverpool to come right back in to it. When it got to penalties it was anybody's guess. This was another awful way to settle a cup final. Wouldn't you think they'd practice penalty kicks before each final? Just a thought.

2007 Chelsea 1 Man United 0 (aet)

This time it's Chelsea and Man United meeting each other. I suppose it makes a pleasant change from Arsenal and Man United. This chore was completed with a late winner by Drogba. Anyone outside of London or Manchester must have thought "So what?"

2008 Portsmouth 1 Cardiff 0 Wembley

What's this, a cup final without one of the top four in it? How dare they, and how did this happen? Never mind, it did, and although it wasn't a very good one, what a refreshing change to see dear old Pompey lift the cup. What would they give for that today?

2009 Chelsea 2 Everton 1

Normal service resumed and, yes, this time it's Chelsea again, playing the blue half of Merseyside. What can you say about this? Everton lost.

2010 Chelsea 1 Portsmouth 0

For Everton, please substitute Portsmouth and read the above. I was hoping for a miracle here. Anything to break the bloody boredom of seeing someone else other than the top four win the cup. It didn't happen. Portsmouth missed the penalty - and the boat - which could have changed everything. We'll never know but I suppose I'll just have to learn to live with it.

And there I think is the reason why the FA Cup has lost its magic. When you consider that since 1991 - coming up for 20 years now - only twice has there been a final where one of the so called top four failed to win it. Sorry, Spurs and Manchester City. I know that you are now thinking that you can be considered to be top four material but actions speak louder than words, and until you've done it season after season, then I'm still talking Chelsea, Man. United, Arsenal and Liverpool. And I'm still taking one out of those four to win it over the next 20 seasons, too.

At least in the early years you'd get the odd shock with West Ham, Sunderland and Southampton, from the old Second Division, winning it but that is unlikely ever to happen again. A Second Division side might get there but they will probably do it by beating Premiership reserve sides on the way there, and what's glorious or magical about that? In the meantime, they'll be treated merely as upstarts and dismissed with contemptuous ease by the elite sides. And that, I think, has what has made the cup boring for all other fans outside maybe the top six in the Premier. Lets accept that occasionally Spurs or Villa or Everton might get to Wembley. They might have a chance of even winning it but only if one of the top four they meet have an off day. And as for the rest of them, then forget it.

At best, maybe once every 20 years, one of the other 14 Premier League sides might be given the honour of winning the cup but the other 24 Championship members? Their day has come and gone. Although maybe not altogether. By the law of averages, I predict a cup final looming for Doncaster Rovers in 2185. A sad, and unpalatable fact, that has made the majority of fans switch off altogether. You'll also note that apart from the minnows who still regard even getting to the third round as like winning the cup itself ("It's our Cup Final" they'll tell you), the rest treat the early stages as an irritant. Just look at the attendances and it tells you all you need to know. Even I don't even bother with third round games now because of three things;
a) Even my team don't take them seriously, generally fielding a weak side
b) The cost is prohibitive and
c) What's the bloody point? We'll get to round six and then end up meeting one of the top four who by then have stirred from their lethargy and think "Our turn this year". It's boring!

You will notice in the early years a combination of sides coming to the fore that you perhaps identified with, but now they've gone. Apart from Portsmouth and Wimbledon, where are Blackpool, West Bromwich, Birmingham, Coventry City, Preston North End, Ipswich and QPR? It's now nearly always down to the same old and depressing scenario. It's guaranteed that in pecking order we'll have Chelsea, Liverpool, Arsenal or Man United, queuing up in turn, waiting at the door, and seemingly arguing the toss with each other year after year. If it were really a formal occasion or function you might well imagine them saying to each other: "After you, really I insist, we won it last year".

Without even realising it, and they can't be bothered anyway even if they did realise, they have effectively killed stone dead the cup for the rest of us. They didn't mean to do it, of course, they just did. So complacent are they that they can't even take it seriously until the sixth round. Then, and only then, will they probably think that this will be a tidy piece of silverware to either add to or compensate for the Premier League and the Champions league.

Ditto if you include the League Cup as well. If it's possible, this competition is now becoming even more meaningless than the FA Cup. If you don't believe this, then when anyone outside the top four dares to win either of these trophies it's usually met with a disdainful "so what?" or the even more patronising" It's not worth winning". How very noble of them. Even more worrying, these views sometimes spill from the mouths of the media so is it any wonder supporters pick up on this attitude too? In other words, if we haven't won it, then it's not worth winning. Besides, Leicester and Middlesbrough have won it in recent years and look what's happened to them.

The FA Cup has been cheapened and devalued as a result of all this too and the telly itself has had a massive part to play in this. It centres around ratings which is why they hone in on the chance of any potential giant-killing act coming along. It's like clutching at straws just to try and get ratings up.

The abandonment of Wembley for Cardiff for a few seasons didn't help and if it were to be the case of a neutral venue, then why take it out of England? Cup finals were once played at Stamford Bridge or Crystal Palace before Wembley was built. What would have been wrong with Old Trafford or even Twickenham? When we eventually did get back to Wembley from Cardiff, we devalued it even further in the way of progress by having penalty shoot outs. Why not have a replay, let the fans in again for a fiver and give all the proceeds to charity? Is that radical enough for you lot?

And as if that isn't bad enough to devalue the thing, then another brainwave - sorry, mind storm-comes along. "Why don't we play the semi finals and the final there too, just to really devalue it even further and alienate the very people (the fans) who are most important? And because Wembley cost an absolute fortune to build we'll have a few more corporate seats, the ones we can fleece for real big bucks, and sod the ordinary fan. Also, out of a near 90,000 capacity we'll give the teams 20,000 tickets each." Believe it or not, some idiot actually pays another idiot big money for coming up with this piece of lunatic thinking.

I was always good at maths at school, so isn't it a tad selfish to cream off 50,000 - over 55% - for the hangers on, dignitaries, and the assorted FA rank and file members? Isn't that really taking the mickey? Add all that up, and is it any wonder that Joe Public has told you lot long ago where to stick your FA Cup. We can't even go back to basics, or tradition, or the way it used to be because some fruitcake with a clipboard will smugly tell you that "We've all moved on since then and so has the game. Now go away, the lot of you, and leave us in charge to screw it up even further".

Remember the excitement, too, of semi finals that used to be played like clockwork at both Villa Park and Hillsborough? The switch from Hillsborough was, of course, understandable but when White Hart Lane was introduced in 1988 for a semi final between Wimbledon and Luton, only 27,000 turned up, and maybe half of them were corporate, too. You knew the writing was on the wall then. It has just seemed to take ages for reality to set in. The game was well and truly up.

To add insult to injury, top sides have played reserves and even junior sides, against opposition they obviously thought they would see off. How we all chortled when it spectacularly and predictably back fired on them. It's still a big deal for those sides outside the Premier, and in some cases a real life saver, a matter of football life and death to be more precise. When non-league Exeter City drew at Old Trafford 0-0 and lost the replay the money they made from those two games was the springboard to propel them back into the league. Sometimes it's not even about the result for the plucky underdog, it's merely the occasion. It's not even right to call it giant killing anymore even if a Premier reserve side get toppled 4-1 at home by a lower league side. They both know it's not the same.

If it wasn't for underdogs taking huge support to away cup games, the match itself would be instantly forgettable. A couple of years back I went to a Sunderland v Barrow third round game at a half full Stadium of Light. The only reason I went was not really to see the match but more to pay homage to the 8,000 plus Barrow fans who'd made it across the Pennines on a snowy day, seen their team lose 3-0, then found out they were virtually trapped from getting back home due to a snow bound A66 being blocked. They made the game due to their magnificent support for a lost cause, and never gave up. That's the real magic of the cup, a magic now lost on many supporters today and, sadly, I am one of them.

Imagine, though, before general apathy set in what this fixture would have been like 40 years back. From round three onwards, cup fever gripped everyone once the draw was made. You would see some incredible crowds. A side bottom of the Third Division averaging 3,000 gates would land a home draw with Stoke or somebody and suddenly 15,000 would appear from nowhere. If one of the big boys came calling at your door, you'd ask yourself where the missing 20,000 fans had been hiding for the last twenty years. I used to see countless examples of games like this in my youth. Third Division Brentford once getting a lucky draw in the fifth round at Fourth Division Oxford United in front of a full house 14,000 at The Manor ground in 1964, and then an incredible 30,000 turning up for the replay. The same thing, and crowd, happened for a game against Burnley, and both times, the Bees let their fans down. Any young Brentford fan today would drool at the thought of a third of that number turning up. And how sad it is that he would never see his side play in front of even 20,000, even in a new stadium. The demand, the excitement and the captive audience just isn't there anymore.

And today now it seems they can't even get the actual draw for the cup right. It now resembles something you would see at the local bingo. You even expect someone to shout for a full house once Man United's name is drawn out of the bag. Why did they feel the need to abandon basic common sense and tradition for the sake of a "new look" approach for the cup? I'll give them a "new look". How about the entirely new concept of an empty stadium where once you'd be locked out an hour before the kick off? Is that contemporary enough for you? Is that more preferable to the old-fashioned look of a full house?

Even the cup draw leaves you totally exasperated as someone tries desperately to lift the excitement that just isn't there anymore. You hear them doing the draw and could weep: "And it's number 34, Oxford United who, of course, got to the last eight in 1964 versus number 21 Blackburn Rovers who were once winners of the cup way back in 1960." (No they weren't, you bloody idiot. It was Wolves!) Nobody listening to that would have a clue unless they were my age. But the reason why they are presenting it like this is to try and emulate what it was once like in those far away halcyon days. They are trying to recreate magic. They even show those "retro" images now on telly of genuine 1960s football legends inter-mixed with the modern lot. You even have David Beckham shaking hands with Bobby Moore and trying to make it look realistic. If it's meant to be realistic, shouldn't David try to make himself useful by trying to tie up Bobby's bootlaces for him?

It wasn't that long ago if you asked any fan old enough when they think the cup lost its spark for them, you'd get a variety of different answers. I have my own take, too. There's no rational explanation you'd get from anyone under 20. Basically they couldn't give a rat's backside anyway about the cup. To them it's not about a good run, it's just a good day out if they got to Wembley or possibly a good day out if they got to the semis (probably Wembley again) but apart from that they are not really interested. And if they live in London, as most Arsenal, Chelsea and Man. United fans do anyway, so much the better.

There's still the massive attraction of it all at lower league level but even the likes of Torquay, Macclesfield , Torquay et al must feel slightly disillusioned being drawn away to play Stoke, Fulham or Blackburn in front of maybe 8,000. 30 or so years back at least they'd be guaranteed 24,000. Everything - and I mean everything - is driven by money now and so sentiment, tradition and the old ways of doing it the right way are now pushed out the window. And that doesn't just apply to football either. Hype is the new guy in town everywhere now, and doesn't everybody just love being in its company. The magic of a good cup run now is measured not by glory but by how much money they can bring in. TV dictates when you play, and how you play, The introduction of extra time and penalties, and the abolition of replays makes it sexier for the fans. Forget classic cup ties you remember from many years going to a fifth round, fourth replay. That's gone, mate, it's boring. Who says so? "We do". My only surprise is that they haven't re-branded boxing to get away from that boring ten round spectacle. Why not just give each boxer a baseball bat, and just go for a quick and spectacular 30 second knock out?

The modern fan is missing out big time and it's down to the very principles of tradition and what it stands for. The modern fan knows everything about nothing and nothing about anything. They aren't really interested in anything other than what's happening now. Everything else is irrelevant and this is backed up too, it seems, by the media. They'd reinvent the game every day if they could get away with it. "If it isn't happening today, then it's just so yesterday" should be their motto. I and all the friends who went to football used to devour everything about the game so that we'd not only know practically everything about our team, but also the opposition; even their history. It's the politics of reverse envy today. Chelsea have a new breed of fan whose attitude, for some reason, towards a football institution called Liverpool FC is contemptuous beyond belief. What gives them the right to be like this? The answer is simple. Liverpool might have won cups during the last ten years but they've never managed to win the Premier League. Even Liverpool's own newly acquired non-Scouse speaking fans are disgruntled, adding more fuel to the fire.

And here, in a nutshell, hangs the real reason for the demise of the FA Cup and why it means nothing. Can you tell me, those of you who say that only the last ten years are relevant in football, hand on heart, who has actually won the last ten cup finals and who did they beat? No, I didn't think so. I can name them year on year from 1923 to 1981 and after that I am struggling. The reason being that the lure of the cup was slowly dying, being strangled, by the need to fiddle about and try to improve the competition and then seeing it being reduced to second fiddle until it became a meaningless side show. And then the very same people who were responsible for its demise had the cheek to turn round and ask "What can we do to make it great again?" I'd respond. "Why ask us? You're the ones who killed it stone dead. Besides, if you weren't bothered then why should we be bothered now?"

I even think that if the top four could find a way of opting out of the cup and be given a bye into round six, they'd probably go for that too. They're too busy being distracted elsewhere with things like the Champions League, a top four finish, winning the Premier and sorting out long term lucrative contracts.

An awful lot of fans of other clubs outside the top five or six will blame these clubs and their greed for the demise of the cup. Not really true. Whether they are greedy or not, they haven't exploited anyone. The powers that be have exploited them, thrusting obscene amounts at them in the way of massive bonuses for appearing on telly, where they finish in the league, how much they get for getting in the Champions League and how much they can get for winning that. Then there's the hype that accompanies all those lucky enough to be in this exclusive club (all four of them) and the near deification of really ordinary players into virtual gods. We didn't learn a thing from the World Cup, and we still haven't learnt. It's business as usual as players threaten to leave a club because they say that club aren't ambitious enough and then, hey presto. They then change their mind and decide to stay when they are offered a 100% pay rise. I'd get them out of my club like a flash. Even referees climb on board when they get involved with a top four side and their top four divas. It's first name terms with some of them. I've actually seen it, and if you were honest enough, and thought enough about the game and the state it's in, then you will admit to have seen it too.

And after all that, what have we got left? Oh, yes, the FA Cup. By showing it such scant regard, the disinterest in it has spread virtually everywhere. Even with this lack of interest, the elite still want to win it, even if it is second rate. And maybe that's another reason for its decline. When Man. United sloped off one year, with the full blessing of the powers that be to take time out for their World Domination Cup and conveniently ignored the FA Cup, what message were they setting? Still at least it gave the rest of the plebs a chance to win it. You can just imagine some of them doffing their caps, pulling at their forelocks and shouting "Thank'ee kindly, sir" in response.

This attitude seems to have spread like wildfire to others. How many times have you hit the roof when your side has fielded a practically reserve team in a cup game you fancied you'd win, and then promptly lost 1-0 to a team that you'd beat nine times out of ten? And then you'd get annoyed when you see who you would have got in the next round, also at home. That doesn't help either. You still console yourself thinking even if you did get through, you'd probably have gone out in the next round anyway by fielding yet another weak side.

Can any of the modern cup games compare with classics long ago? "Yes" to a few but "no" to so many more. There was a romanticism about the cup then that cannot be replicated today, under any conditions or any fancy rules and regulations. The same romanticism that some females try to recreate today reading classics like Wuthering Heights and then imagining finding the modern version of such a romance. You could, of course, by pretending, but it wouldn't be a patch on the original, would it?

Today we are occupied with other more pressing issues, numerous urgent and pressing distractions. The latest ring tone on your mobile, the endless messages, your BlackBerry or whatever else it is you keep in that shoulder bag you need to survive the stresses of the modern world. How did we ever cope before any of this lot? Quite easily actually. We had the time to stand (there's that word again) and listen and converse. Now, we are all so much smarter, live in a cynical, isolated and selfish age where people can change from one fad to another virtually overnight. All far too occupied tweeting, texting and holed up for 24 hours on facebook, or networking, to have the time or interest to take such a thing as an old fashioned real cup competition seriously.

Will we be talking in 40 years time of "The Michael Owen Final" or "The Cantona Final" as we did about Matthews in 1953 or The White Horse Final in 1923? Will we reminisce about the Chelsea/Villa Final in the same way as we did watching Bob Stokoe fly across the field at the final whistle in 1973, and the joy on the face of his "little general" captain Bobby Kerr, complete with his Porno Pete moustache and cheeky grin? Of course we won't.

Maybe the FA Cup hasn't even changed at all. You still get the odd exciting game with the odd packed house to add to it all. But that will be only rarely, and certainly not till things do liven up in the last eight. And it's only when round six rolls around that people can be bothered to stir their backsides to get excited, two steps off Wembley. That's probably the only time that the old urge will then hit you as you think that if your team got there then, maybe, just maybe, we'd end up with a real thriller just like 1953 all over again. And if we did, you'd remember that word "magic" and what it really meant all over again.

And it occurs to me now that the real reason the Cup has lost its charisma is that most fans, the young and, dare I say it, even the old, are no longer interested in it. It is as simple as that. And there's nothing further you can do and say to change it. The young man's excuse is that they have been suckled on Sky TV and wall to wall matches from all over the world. And the old man's because maybe we, too, have been bought off with the same proverbial 30 pieces of silver. Besides, we like our new toys, are living longer and we're considerably richer than all you young ones.

The FA Cup hasn't changed. Sadly, all of us have.

CHAPTER 11
"OVERPAID, LAZY FOOTBALLERS"

At the end of 1950, every club in the country, give or take a few quid in wages either way, operated roughly on the same wage structure. It didn't really matter who you played for. Manchester City, Blackpool, Bolton, Preston, Liverpool and all were all financially on the same level playing field. Players were just as ambitious then as now but the big difference was that moving from Blackpool to Liverpool would not have guaranteed you a huge pot of gold or overnight millionaire status. Admittedly it would still be a bit of a kick in the teeth for players at the time. Something clearly had to give. If you had been playing for Arsenal in front of 60,000 every other week and getting the same wage as a Preston player in front of 25,000 you'd be a bit miffed, especially if your efforts weren't even rewarded by the amount of bums on seats you pulled in (and by bums I don't mean the directors). You would also no doubt be asking: "Who's making all the money here because it certainly isn't us." It definitely wasn't going into players' pockets and there wasn't even the shallow excuse that it was being spent on stadium refurbishment at that time. Apart from the odd lick of paint every summer (and even then they used free labour with the apprentices) grounds basically remained unchanged for decades. Anybody who's stood in some of the cattle sheds masquerading as football grounds in the 1960s and 1970s will confirm that. Grounds even had their own affectionate nicknames by local fans. The Shed at Chelsea, the Chicken Run at West Ham and the Cow Shed at Leeds. Palatial and comfy they definitely weren't.

The end of the enforced wage structure in 1961 was to change all that of course but haven't we all reaped the whirlwind since? Season by season, decade by decade, players' wages started to climb and soon outstripped tenfold those of the working man, something that would have defied logic in 1960. It was only with the advent of the Premier League, though, that wages went though the ceiling, quickly followed by the roof and then the stratosphere as they still hurtle, unchecked, towards the outer galaxy.

Some disgruntled players had tried their luck abroad from the early 1950s to play in what then were the best paid leagues in the world. "Have boots will travel" became the cry for our own in-house mercenaries. Now it's the other way round as players descend here from all over the world. Every team in the country has them. Even Scottish football has had a massive influx all plying their trade. If you were being cynical - and I am - a lot of them could not give a damn or show an ounce of loyalty to whatever club they play for. If you need proof, look back at a programme from only two seasons ago and see the changes that have already occurred in the playing squads since then. They know very little and perhaps care less about a club's history or tradition. It's the money that counts, although winning silverware is important too, of course, providing they can achieve it at a club who will pay them even more money. But that isn't absolutely essential. And who can blame them given their circumstances? Many can set their families up for life after only one season in the Premier. For every Didier Drogba or Thierry Henry, there's about fifty others who would rather play in front of 18,000 at Bolton instead of 50,000 at Newcastle if the money's better. It's a fact, no matter how you feel about it.

I've lost count of the number of discontented Newcastle and Sunderland fans who have moaned about how "the likes of Wigan, Bolton, Blackburn and Fulham" can sign players that are beyond both their clubs" In fairness, Sunderland appear to have bucked the trend in this respect recently but is it sustainable, especially as their crowds have dipped by some 9,000 per game. They will ask "How can these clubs do it when they only play in front of half the crowds we get?" They miss the point completely. It's not about the fan base anymore. It helps, of course, that having big crowds does create a decent atmosphere, can inspire you and might even influence players to join you. But the danger of having big crowds is that they can also boo twice as loud when things go wrong, and demand too much of you. The only way fans will come into the equation in the future is if there is some massive collapse in future external funding and clubs will then need to rely on their fan base to pay the wages. I can see that day coming.

And it will be at that point, and only at that point, that fans might again be properly valued by their clubs. By then, though, it may be too late, with clubs needing to charge more to ever diminishing audiences to get back on their feet and service their hungry players, some of them with cast iron contracts to honour. And that's when the real problems will start. With crowds plummeting, wages rising and no money coming in from other external sources, clubs will need to increase admission prices further. In doing this crowds will fall even further and faster. And thus this suicidal trend will continue until both fans and clubs run out of money and it's then "Goodnight Vienna".

In the real football world of today, there are already some lower league clubs with limited resources whose mottos have always been "Cut your coat according to your cloth." Try telling that to some of the bigger clubs who have already hit administration problems, plus many Premier clubs, nearly all with huge debts ("all serviceable" according to modern accountants, of course). It's only serviceable, of course, if you stay up and manage to placate the brood of hungry playing staff. And to stay in the Premier you have to attract even more players on big wages. And to keep them, then you have to keep increasing their wages, and so the debt mounts. And the lunatic football ferris wheel keeps going round and round until somebody, somewhere, in the future puts their foot down and ends the madness by imposing a maximum wage on clubs. Even then, the top five or six will still find a way round any system, still pay way over the odds in transfer fees, pay top wages, and find some way of doing it legally with top-notch lawyers involved too. The apologists, the liberal elite, might well say that if we don't pay these wages, then these players will go somewhere else. Well, let them, and, besides, under a really strong revamped club charter where would they go to? Who could afford them? If we were all to hold firm, at least 15 other clubs in the Premier and 72 in the lower league pyramid might then have a realistic chance of remaining in business or even competing for the scraps-the odd spot in Europe or perhaps the crumbs of an FA Cup or League Cup win for their trouble. If you think all this is exaggeration then look at the state of the game in Scotland. It's a mirror image of how our game in England could turn out, or is already heading. In Scotland, there's apathy amongst fans, dropping attendances, a drying up of local talent and two powerful clubs cornering the market. Even Celtic and Rangers are bored with it all. The Scots realise all this and at Government level are investing heavily to stop the rot, and get the pot boiling again at grass roots level. How long before the penny drops here and we do the same?

It's the simmering resentment by genuine footy fans in this country, seeing Armageddon on the horizon, that has led to a festering anger building up, mainly at the obscene level in players' wages. A revolution is needed that could well lead to a return to a more sensible structured game, and an equally sensible structured wage. It could even lead, by marvellous irony, not only to sanity creeping back but also a return of missing fans. You cannot keep putting money into a bottomless pit.

Today, the vast majority of Premiership players, plus many others in lower league clubs, are potentially stuck with players they can't shift on fat contracts. Any of them who feel that that they are under stress, and feel that they deserve their money, should join the rest of us in the real world. There are many more players throughout the whole league structure who do earn much more modest salaries but even their wages would still be the equivalent of someone working in senior management with a responsible stressful job, staff of about 500, a 60 hour week with ulcers, pending heart attack plus gold watch on the near horizon. Even going down to Championship level, they have a fair intake of ex-Premier refugees who still retain most, if not all, of their bloated former wages, tied down to contractual agreements after their team has been relegated from the Promised Land. Or even worse, they are given a pay rise in order to stop them straying off to some other club. Call it a form of blackmail if you were cynical about the situation.

When you journey back through the history of the game, there is no doubting that in its infancy, players were really shafted for decades and got an appalling deal .You have to read your history - just as I told you at the beginning - to get into context where we are today, too, and where we could possibly end up tomorrow. It wasn't that long ago players were, relatively speaking, still living on the same financial planet as the rest of us. As little as 45 years ago, great players like Jimmy Greaves, Alan Gilzean, Bobby Moore and even Kevin Keegan (when he first started to make his mark) were on roughly £40-£60 a week. When they were subject to a possible annual pay rise, the manager would probably offer them an extra fiver a week and they'd come out of his office singing and dancing. When Bobby Moore was a young professional at West Ham, his then girlfriend, a secretary, actually earned more than he did. Some players would thank their lucky stars to be in the profession they were in and willingly say "yes" to any slight weekly increase. A fiver increase was big bucks and their wage was maybe three or four times a week more than the average man in the street would earn. A great deal back in the 1960s but not exactly a king's ransom. Many lower league footballers used to have to supplement their income with either seasonal or part-time work to survive and eke out a decent standard of living for their families. There were no agents around then, and why should there be? They would have been chased by player and club alike. Why should a professional footballer, a grown man, need a babysitter or minder to get the best deal for him? The idea would have been unheard of, a bit effeminate even to let someone negotiate on his behalf. Besides, wasn't that what his wife or dad was for?

Today a footballer in the top league earns probably 200 times a week more than the average working man. There are even players in the Championship pulling in £15,000 a week and there's one you might have read about in the tabloids still on his former Premiership bung of £45,000. No wonder his club can't move him on. If you're an ordinary Joe in an ordinary job on £300 a week - and in our neck of the woods £300 is a good wage - it will take you 3 years to earn that weekly amount You'd probably be glad to hear that fact, too, because at least it would mean that you were guaranteed three years steady work. Is it any wonder most fans do not have any real affinity with today's footballers and quite a few are turning their backs in droves on the game they once loved? This is the real issue clubs need to address.

Going back to the 1920s and 1930s - and before you start moaning those days of austerity might well return if the game remains unabated and unchecked today - anyone playing football at any level then would have considered themselves lucky. It meant that they had escaped from the mines, shipyards, steelworks, factories, mills or pot kilns up and down the country. It really was a working man's game. Working men watching other more gifted working men playing football and who made sure those spectators got their moneys worth. Grounds were full and it was local pride in the real sense of the word. The wage cap then meant also that there would have been very little difference between someone in the top division and someone in the bottom, maybe a differential sliding scale of £10, £8, £6 and £4. If you were a really ambitious Third Division club you could even try to poach players off the top teams too. That's also why the likes of Blackpool, Bolton and Blackburn could hang on to their best players for years when their more illustrious Lancashire neighbours came sniffing around. If you were a Blackburn or a Stoke lad why leave for Wolves or Arsenal when your local side could offer you the same wedge?

This system, a form of virtual cheap slave labour, was to remain permanent for the next 30 or so years and ensured parity among all teams in the top flight. It certainly made the game more exciting too, as anyone could have a chance at reaching the top. In spite of all this, the game always threw up the superstars of the day. These would appear in any era. Great, gifted individuals who just stood head and shoulders above the rest, inspired not by how much their club could pay them, but by a need to prove their brilliance in front of massive crowds, week in and week out, and be the best. Their rewards, long after their playing days were over, would not be measured in financial gain but in immortality, as fans from future generations (but not enough of them!) revered their names and wished they could have seen them play. Some fans were lucky enough to catch the tail end of real football legends' careers and passed on the stories to their children. i know; I was one of them. I learnt of great players from my dad and passed them on to my two lads. Some players, long gone, live on over sixty years after their career ended. I wonder if in 60 years the current crop will be held in such esteem.

When the system changed and was finally smashed with the abolition of the set wage structure then in place for seemingly forever, it heralded massive change. It led to the first £100 a week footballer, Johnny Haynes of Fulham. It was the dawn of the 1960s and the dawn of a new era for football. It also signalled the death knell of all those cosy clubs who could compete with their more powerful neighbour season after season. Everything was to change and not for the better. Critics argued that this would mean that England could now hang on to their best players who would no longer be tempted abroad by rich foreign clubs, mainly Italian. Others saw a more ominous sign of things to come as bigger clubs could now throw off the imposed financial shackles and sweep the high seas of the league in search of the best catches. And they did.

Most English players didn't want to play abroad anyway. A lot must have missed out on the financial opportunity of a lifetime for a life in dear old Blighty. The money was nothing flash but at least you didn't have to leave home and your family and friends. Besides, what did places like Naples, Rome and Madrid have that we didn't have here in dear old Burnley, Nottingham, or Blackburn? You couldn't even get a decent cuppa there, either. Many people accepted that the abolition of this imposed wage led to football developing fast into the great spectacle it has become today. Some would argue that it led to the creation of an overfed and bloated monster. Many believe that the pendulum has now swung too far the other way. The top level footballer in this country has gone from being little more than a serf to landed gentry in 50 short years. Many observers today who have seen both ends of this development happening over a fifty years span ask "What went wrong?"

No doubt many fans have at some time bumped into old players they once watched play. In 1994, at a local community event, I met Wilf Mannion, Middlesbrough & England legend, who lit up the 1940s and 1950s. Everyone who was there that day, young and especially old, wanted to talk to him. It was surreal to see sons with their dads, neither of whom would have been even been born when Wilf finished his career, jostling to get near this frail but still charismatic old man, beaming all over his face at the attention he was getting. He even had his minder with him, not some ape-like creature as you'd expect, but a boyhood friend roughly the same age as Wilf who still went with him everywhere. Wilf told us all exactly how it used to be back then, warts and all. About the time he was playing against Scotland for England at Hampden Park. He was given the princely sum of £5 expenses and out of this he had to make his own way from Middlesbrough to Carlisle and then up to Glasgow by train - second class of course - and from there to Hampden. He then played and won in front of a 120,000 crowd and made his way back home again. All receipts had to be kept too by him to verify that he wasn't trying to fiddle the FA. I dare say that if there was any change left out of the fiver, then that would have to be handed back. And if by some miracle you overspent or didn't have the receipts to prove it, then tough. It came out of your own pocket. How much would he have been worth in today's transfer market, we all asked? Not sure, he replied, but if he'd have been given a pound every time he'd been asked that question he'd have been a millionaire by now. He still lived in Middlesbrough and in very much the same lifestyle he enjoyed as a player - and a real superstar too - 50 years previously. Not bitter, not envious, just very grateful to have had the talent to play, and get paid for something he loved doing. Now contrast that man and his humble attitude with a lot of today's players and how they would have completed a similar journey today. Luxury coach or plane there and back, chauffeur driven from the airport, five star hotel (Wilf had to make do with a café and sandwich) then afterwards through a VIP lounge to a waiting taxi if they didn't fancy talking to the media for whatever reason. You can just imagine it in the lounge, can't you? "Hang on to that receipt for the all day breakfast, Wayne and Rio, and make sure you have them ready first thing Monday morning for inspection".

Also there that day was a fellow team mate of Wilf's, George Hardwick, also ex-England. George was a real handsome bloke in his youth (known as "Gorgeous George" amongst some of Boro's fans) and he still looked pretty dapper in his twilight years with that roguish glint still in his eyes. He, too, had wonderful memories playing for both Middlesbrough and England. During his playing career he would have been up against some giants of the game. And the best he ever played against? "Stanley Matthews; he had the lot". George went on to manage Sunderland in the mid 1960s and had fond memories of them also. Even then the game was already changing dramatically with player power, virtually unheard of in the subservient past, creeping very slowly into the game. It started to cause all kinds of problems, both on and off the pitch, and I gather that he was glad to get out of it at the finish. Sunderland cruelly sacked him when, by their standards, they were going pretty well under his reign. Both these two grand old men are sadly no longer with us, but compare their stories to their modern counterparts and who do you have real affinity with?

Back in both their heydays, and even in the 60s too, you'd see players walking to the ground, or even on the bus. I remember in 1972 listening to two young Brentford fans who were talking about getting the bus to Griffin Park for the previous home game. There in the front seat was John O'Mara, a big Irish bruiser of a centre forward, who played for the Bees. Not a famous name but at the time he was to two young fans who even got to sit right behind him and chat with him. That was the norm back then. John moved on to Blackburn where he didn't pull up any trees (even though he was big enough to).

I once saw Wilf Rostron of Sunderland pull up in a battered old mini in the Roker car park round about 1978. There was more rust than there was car, and the exhaust was defying gravity to stay hanging on. That didn't seem to bother Wilf. With his footy boots slung casually over his shoulder in a carrier bag, he sauntered into the player's entrance. No need for any steward to keep an eye on that car. They'd have had to pay you to steal it. Today you'll see a Mercedes or a Bentley in any Premiership car park and that'll just be the reserve players. When I was watching QPR at Loftus Road in the old First Division in the seventies, with 15 minutes to kick off, a Rangers fan told his mate that he'd just been talking to Stan Bowles, the QPR forward, in the betting shop round the corner; "He can't be playing today" he said. He was. Stan had obviously nipped out for a quick bet on the 3.30 at Doncaster before strolling back over the road, getting changed and still banging in two for Rangers. Characters seem to be in short supply, too, these days.

The era that Wilf Mannion, George Hardwick, and even Wilf Rostron and Stan Bowles played in, is so far removed from today's game that you ask yourself how and why it happened so quickly. I was told by a good friend about a young local Second Division player playing league football only five years ago. He'd just turned 18 year old and was still learning his trade as a very promising professional with a great future ahead of him. He was on £700 a week with less than 40 league games under his belt (a novice you would have thought). He was, however, fed up starting on the bench most weeks. Maybe he was ambitious but obviously he wanted to run before he could walk. Not only was he demanding first team football, he even felt he was worth a pay rise as well. Not surprisingly at the more sensible end of the league structure he was quickly moved on. Today, five years, on he's now playing non-league football .Where would he have been now if he had a wise old hand to put him straight and tell him to bide his time? Failing the words getting through to him, a clip round the ear and telling him to grow up might have registered home. Even now, £700 is a great weekly wage for anybody especially up here in the North East. My two sons would fight each other for it but for an 18 year old in 2005? Stop the world, I want to get off.

Footballers today who are not even moderate and at the back of the queue when it comes to either a decent IQ or humility (even having one of them would make them a better person) can live in a million pound house paid for with less than a year's wages. No mortgage, no responsibility. They'll have a £200,000 car, plus three more in the drive, and think nothing about blowing £10,000 a week, or if you live in London a good night out. They'll even have their own bodyguard, minder, agent and also either be married to a Miss World look alike, living with a Miss World look alike or having a queue of potential wannabees who'll do anything to be the next in line for the throne of Miss World look alike. When Peter Crouch was asked what he would have been if he wasn't a footballer and replied "virgin" he wasn't kidding. If the hunchback of Notre Dame was real and played for Bolton Wanderers today he'd have a queue of women going twice round the Reebok all wanting to move in with him.

How did it ever get to this? To make matters worse, some players already on £50,000 a week who are then offered a further four year contract extension, angrily demand – and usually get - a £20,000 a week increase to tempt them to stay. And then three or four months down the line some idiot in charge of another club will offer them even more, and of course he's off. A result, even though he's just kissed the badge. How much money does one sane person actually need and can spend in a week? Could you survive comfortably on say £5,000 a week? Of course you could and you'd still stash £4,000 away for that rainy day. It would still need to be a monsoon lasting about five years to get through it all as well.

Football now is the new politics of the madhouse. If you ran a business like this, you would be certified and put in a straitjacket before sacking yourself for gross stupidity. It isn't a player's fault that they accept or demand such sums. After all if they are offered it and more they are going to grab it. That's why clubs should all get their collective heads together and don't offer it in the first place. Put a cap on wages so that every team - every team and every time, too - sticks together like a band of football brothers and put the signs up: "Maximum wage here £12,000 a week (still a fortune). If not acceptable please bugger off and try elsewhere". If all other clubs put that same sign up (worded differently of course) then sanity might prevail and return to our game. They can always go abroad. And if anyone else tells me that old excuse: "They've only got a short career in the game" I'll strangle them. If you were on a minimum wage of £12,000 a week and had a short career in the game, for just six years then by my reckoning you'll have made £3m. One of my sons has worked hard all his life, in and out of contract work, and would have to work 120 years- that'll make him 155 when he retires - to accumulate that kind of dosh. Some footballers are making £3m every 15 weeks. I realise that I'm maybe being old and out of touch with these things but my sanity and reality aren't yet in danger. It's too late in the short term to do anything now, but for the long term good of the game someone, somewhere, has to make a stand and say enough is enough. Or as they say in France to describe an egg: "Un oeuf est un oeuf". There has to be a wage cap or the game will simply die. No ifs, ands or buts. Compare football to the state of the country at the moment, and the drastic steps put in place needed to stop us going under. Then compare that to, say Portsmouth FC. It just isn't sustainable, Sky money or no Sky money.

Years back my dad explained the basic law of economics to me. Luckily, I was able to fill in the gaps (all the high brow stuff covering bankruptcy, corporate mismanagement, share collapse, fraud, insider trading and financial incompetence) by looking it all up in my Encyclopaedia Britannica. It's a very simple concept. If you spend more than you earn then you are in trouble. But if you spend a lot more than you earn then you are in big, big trouble. Do you have a mysterious benefactor at home who pays all your bills for you and also buys all your expensive Christmas presents? (and I don't mean your mother and father, silly boy) Me neither. So just imagine the scenario, your worst nightmare, if the benefactors at the big club you support suddenly ask for their money back immediately, or even worse than that. Instead you go bankrupt. Those clubs out there now that are sensible enough to have a cap on wages and only spend what they bring in will be able to survive and ride out the storm. Those who are foolish and spend maybe 90 % of their total income on players wages in the equally foolish belief that those same players will keep bringing home the bacon for them in the way of tin pots are deluding themselves. Not only will those players turn tail and flee when things go wrong, they'll also come after you, too, demanding that you cough up their £80,000 a week wage for the next five years on the contract that they signed with you. Ask Leeds and Portsmouth to explain how it works to you. Simply put, when you are in a hole, stop digging.

If you are one of those clubs whose foundations are built on sand, hundreds of millions in debt but with a squad of Galacticos to die for, then be very afraid. When the hammer does fall, and it will, which other sucker out there is going to pick up the tab for the £800 million deficit before he even takes you out to dinner? You'd be one expensive hot date that he'd avoid like the plague. Cut your losses now. You might not win the trophies every year if you do have to drastically tighten your belts, and it will probably be a gastric one with all that excess fat you'll have to shift, but at least you'll still have a team to support. And even better it will be full of hungry players, rather than the bloated ones you had before and still have now. You might even discover a cheap Mannion or Greaves out there. The clock's ticking. Can you hear it?

To achieve the above, let's just think back to 1961 when that Jimmy Hill started the ball rolling. In hindsight, what they all should have said then was that they were imposing a maximum wage capped at £400 a week (still an absolute fortune then) subject to a cost of living rise every year. By my reckoning that would be somewhere in the region of about £9,000 today maximum, give or take a Hollywood contract or Pizza Hut advert. Anyway, Jimmy and others didn't do that, although he did stick his chin out to push a deal through. So rather than blame him, let's blame the clubs. Today they are still flooding the already over-bloated market trying to keep up with the Jones's. Let's face it, if you were a young buck walking about with a hundred grand in your pocket every week you, too, would have the air of an invincible superman who can buy anything or anyone. Is it any wonder then that because this level of money and fame puts them in this position, ordinary people outside this surreal bubble living on Planet Mundane feel the need to gatecrash the party, too? They'll do anything to be invited. How do you tell a 22 year old to look after himself and put something away for the day when it all goes pear-shaped? Some go through this money like water and have nothing to show for it. Even breaking a leg is a nice little earner. While he's off recuperating with a four month leg injury he's already made more money doing nothing than you ever will by getting up and going to work for the next 40 years, seven days a week. That's enough to last you and me two lifetimes, and go out supping seven nights a week. It's not their fault that clubs are throwing money at them. The old chestnut that it's all relative and that it's always been this way doesn't stack up really, does it? Nice work if you can get it and a nice broken leg if you can get one of them, too.

The tipping point for the game is fast approaching and it will mean not so much a financial crash (clubs will carry on paying regardless) but more a social one. There is already a backlash happening, a trend with people deserting higher league football and going back to watch it at grass roots level. When Manchester United season ticket sales are falling and a non-league club called FC United of Manchester ("the people's team") can pull in crowds of 4,000 (Accrington Stanley and Macclesfield would kill for those gates) then you know it's time to start a radical re-think. And before you start sniggering this is all pie in the sky, then how do you suppose the original Manchester United started out as true Corinthians and pioneers of the game? Who is to say that the revolution and backlash hasn't already started? I know a lot who are giving up watching top level football and if ticket prices go up anymore, I'll be one of them.

The game cannot go on at this pace otherwise it will implode. There are already signs of erosion happening, and I visualise more fans growing away from the game, disillusioned people who find the cost of everyday living a struggle without the cost of a football match ticket. If we lose half the next generation of fans in this way, there will be even less from the generation after. And then where will future fan bases emanate from? We are ignoring the creeping signs of this indifference. Where will this leave us in ten years if professional footballers grasp more and more, in a country where people have been told to tighten their belts for the next few years? Where does that equate with fairness and the desire to go to a football match? I am one of the lucky ones with a concessionary season ticket. If my club asked for another £100 a season from me to meet wage demands then that would be the parting of the ways. Arrivederci after 50 years and I wouldn't even look back. Anyway I'll do what even more and more are doing now. I'll watch them on the pirate TV in "The Flying Ferret" just round the corner along with the rest of the army of free-loading armchair critics.

Two things are likely to happen. Firstly, the game will disintegrate fairly quickly, go under just like the Titanic (those on board didn't see the iceberg till the last minute, what's our excuse?). Maybe it will be just like the fall of the Roman, Egyptian, Greek and Mongol Empires. All got too cocky for their own good when they thought they could go on for ever spending money like there was no tomorrow, promising Utopia to the seething masses, and trying desperately to keep one step ahead of the angry mob. Or, secondly, sanity will prevail, football will listen to the voice of reason and pull back from the brink. It will take a lot of courage and a lot of bottle to do this. And it will all need to be done at Club level. Call players' bluffs and put the word out elsewhere. It would only take a few mercenaries to get about 10 or 20 league club doors slammed in their faces for it to start registering with the rest of the mob. I even heard on the radio recently an ex-professional player say that Club X had shown complete disrespect to player Y because, after five years loyal service, they weren't going to offer him an increase and that he deserved one. That player must be on at least £40,000 a week and probably a lot more. Even the media are tied in to this fantasia land mentality. Did none of them on the air have the guts to tell him how lucky he was, instead of fawning round his every word? They talked in great detail of loyalty, however. There are people out there taking pay cuts in order to hang on to their £300 a week jobs. That's loyalty. And as for disrespect, give over.

Those supporters taken for a ride will soon clear off to pastures new and watch local Blue Square Premier football or whatever they'll be calling it next season. Don't say it won't happen, when some are already there. It's inevitable and already underway. Every time someone reads in a paper of a player with massive gambling debts blowing twenty grand on the turn of a card, you are watching football's slow decline. It's very interesting and just like a history lesson from long ago. It will be football's very own global warming, with players becoming the last of a dying breed, multi, mega rich dinosaurs who didn't even see it coming, completely unaware that their own extinction date draws near. I've seen fans sweat more at the match than they do.

I keep banging on about this point but if we see sense, then it's going to take real club unity, lots of guts, a lot of bluff and mainly commonsense by the powers that be. And therein is the problem again. Those in authority, a whole army of chinless bureaucrats on fat salaries, will want to protect their own backs and so will quite willingly go along with this madness. Just like those flunkies when Nero set alight to Rome. I can see by maybe in 2050 or 2060, some young guns setting out all over again, just like they did in the 1880s. They will reinvent the game by taking it back to basics. You don't believe that the greatest sporting spectacle on earth could just wither and fade away and that it has a divine right to last forever? Anything that wants to endure and survive must be based on clearly thought out ideas and the strongest of foundations. From an economic point of view, it must also have a strong financial base. When whole countries can just collapse through inefficiency, laziness, complacency and stubbornness, then what chance does football have if it ignores the above?

And here's a bit more history for you and a warning, too. If you ever visit Rome, you'll see the greatest stadium ever built. There was nothing in the world to compete with it for nearly 2000 years. In terms of scale, size and majesty nothing in the civilised world matched the Coliseum until the Twentieth Century. In its heyday 50,000 crowds came flocking in to see today's equivalent of our current football Gods. Not a nice analogy, I know, but then it was the culture of the time. It was the people's game then. The Romans had their culture and way of life and that worked for them just as we have ours today. No difference. Theirs was brutal and vicious but it was also real life, and only what society of that time demanded. The more the games continued, the more mobs turned up. The cost of holding these spectacles was enormous and virtually crippled Rome's economy. Eventually, even the Ancient Romans had their fill of this especially when Christianity took root and told them it was morally and socially wrong to attend and honour such an event. Is there any difference, from a cultural, social and economic point of view, between then and what's happening now? By the way, they also used to let them in for free at the Coliseum, and if you were lucky you would get a free bread roll thrown in, too. Of course, if you were really unlucky, you even became part of the entertainment in the arena. A last minute substitute, so to speak.

Today the modern equivalent, without the bloodbath obviously, costs a man and two kids well over a hundred quid to sit in a half empty stadium and watch two Premier League teams scratch out a 0-0 draw with complete indifference to what the crowd think. It isn't sustainable to continue like this, season after season. Something will have to give. Have you seen all the empty seats lately? The drift has begun from the Premier League, as fans are watching games in the comfort of their own homes on satellite TV, pubs, clubs, any place that's free - just like the Coliseum.

And so, fans look downwards towards the lower leagues at a more affordable level. They are trickling slowly but surely towards the final exit, turning their backs on these pampered prima donnas and giving them all a huge "V" sign or maybe even the thumbs down, just like the Emperors used to do in that Coliseum again. There will come a time when all the media and all the hype and all the over bloated excuses from the experts and the media will all just fall on deaf ears. I'll prove it to you now. Look no further when they try to get you to recognise the aura, majesty and magic of super stars such as David Beckham. He's a nice enough lad and likeable, but that's all. They portray him as having iconic status, as he flew to the USA, made a big noise, got a few more tattoos, flew back again via Italy, achieved little, and was then feted for it. You really know that the game is well and truly up when something like this happens. What exactly did he achieve that led to this world acclaim? Think carefully before you answer. He did succeed in adding to a huge bank balance with a bit of PR work and also help his wife earn a few quid selling her designer wear, and fair play to the pair of them. Even then, you'd think she'd at least smile a bit after making all that dough, wouldn't you?

And then, lest we forget, our glorious modern gladiators. More writing was on the wall when we had the European Championships in Germany. Our boys were surrounded by the sickening sight of wives and girlfriends. They had, of course, gone there to spur our boys on as well as take quality time out for shopping and photo opportunities. I can remember when the word "WAG" actually meant someone who was a comical sort of bloke who made you laugh. Maybe that's why these modern WAGs have ended up with the same name. You couldn't help but laugh when the whole lot turned it in to a circus as they outperformed their men folk with their shopping and clubbing antics. Somehow, I don't think Sir Alf and Bobby Moore would have tolerated such a shambles. Then again, England in 1966 set out with a game plan to actually win the World Cup, not set out to glorify themselves in self-induced publicity stunts. And as for South Africa and that World Cup, don't get me started. Don't tell me you fell for all the hype and were shocked when we bombed out against Germany? My only amazement was that we actually got through the group stages.

Today, we not only go along with these types of debacles, we actually encourage them as well. We even heard some journalists say that the European Championships had been a morale booster for the lads, and we should repeat the experience in South Africa. We didn't, but would it honestly have made any difference if we did? Maybe even I might have agreed to get the girls on board in South Africa if England actually reached the final in Germany, or won it. But maybe that's the other problem. We've spent years putting up with glorious failure that we daren't even say "no" to the squad of players anymore. They in turn daren't even say "no" to their WAGs. Instead we crow over a meaningless, hollow 5-1 away victory in Germany, yet can't get near to those same Germans when it matters. Except for 1966, of course, when a WAG-free England put paid to them.

As a fully paid up member of the Grumpy Old Gits Club, and season after season you'll find yourself drawing ever nearer to becoming a member too, you can ever so slowly see the rot setting in to our game. Footballers in the past may have been many things but they were never allowed to become petulant divas or drama queens as they appear to be today. Two or three month bans were prevalent for anybody stepping out of line in the past, even in the 1920s where the FA thought it only right to teach these £7 a week footballers who was boss. The John Terry fiasco (I couldn't give a monkeys either what happened) had all the press jumping on the bandwagon for a salacious story just like out of the old Titbits magazine (the clue was in the name, folks). Watergate I can understand but Terrygate, followed presumably by Rooneygate, Ferdinandgate and Crouchgate? Give it a rest. They'll all be demanding that gates are named after them as part of their contract deals next, you watch. And the lunacy is that someone will agree just to appease them. These same footballers are followed by an army of sycophants who, when they do step out of line, protect their guilt by covering them with alibis galore. They can get away with anything by virtue of a witness saying he didn't do it. And if you expect retribution from the FA or whoever then forget it. These are part of the self-preservation society I've mentioned earlier, all drinking from the same trough, and won't rock any boats. They too are on a nice little earner and don't want any of these high profile celebrities on their backs, do they?

And so their actions also spill down to the rest of the football pile, too, as those paupers from lower league and non-league clubs, right down to school boy level, try and emulate those above. They might not have the same financial clout but the old saying "monkey see, monkey do" arises in some cases. Some of the lower league players, though, those with a shred of decency left, do tend to try and redress the balance when they might come up against these upstarts in cup competitions and, boy, don't we all laugh when they do. And watching on more despondently than ever, as the drama unfolds, is an audience growing ever more totally disinterested, in fact, in some cases, acting more and more like the mob back in Rome's glory days. They'll carry on in the same vein, till the roof eventually does cave in. And just like that old Coliseum, it will then become a ruined monument to glory days long gone.

The end result to our beautiful game will be just as painfully inevitable. I hear the words from that old classic "Road to nowhere" by Talking Heads. Perhaps where our game is going now, "Down, Down" might be more appropriate if you happen to be a Quo fan. I get even more disillusioned watching England games because then you get to see a whole gathering of them - a plethora of divas, if you like. And to cap it all, you watch Sky and the budding game in Third World countries. You see them also trying to emulate us and you feel like yelling to them "If you are going to copy, then do yourselves a massive favour and base it on an earlier model". Presumably the new version of their up and coming modern game will include the essential art of diving, cheating, conning, gamesmanship and influencing refs to send off a fellow pro or book opponents by rushing towards the poor hapless sap en masse. And don't forget the shirt pulling now so prevalent in our game. Be careful what you wish for, you feel like telling them.

Will the whole world have the same attitude to the game in, say, the next 30 years? How will it change as footballers from African nations overtake and dominate those from the soft West? I can already see signs of radical change in the Premier League but what affect will this have on the traditional English game as it is today? Will we look back nostalgically in 20 years and remember its heyday? What will it say in ten years and how will FIFA, UEFA, the FA, the Premier League, the Football League and Uncle Tom Cobley and all try to stick their oar in, as they always seem to do, to hinder it at every turn? As talent subsides and mediocrity kicks in, with the almost inevitable "play it safe and try not to lose rather than win it" philosophy, you wonder where it will all end.

And by then future fans of Tottenham Hotspur, Fulham, or even dear old Accrington Stanley (if they are still around) will care even less for the traditions of their past glories. After all, anything over 10 years old will be like something from the dark ages. There'll be no point at all all, and by then no point in carrying on. There will be one saving grace, though. They'll not have heard of any of the current crop who caused its demise.

Football is merely an imitation of life with its ups and downs, good and bad, elation and sorrow. There are the inevitable links to history too. Even the ancient Romans who ruled the European and World stage for hundreds of years and won trophies galore with great managers, eventually lost the plot and were flushed away. They believed their own hype far too much and, of course, the inevitable happened. They also went bust which quickened the whole demise. So even if you have a manager as great as Julius Caesar at the helm and you think that everything is hunky dory, then beware the football equivalent of the Ides of March. If you don't, you'll be relegated from existence, not just the Premier League.

CHAPTER 12
FOOTBALL'S FUTURE - A BLAST FROM THE PAST

In the early days of football, some 20 years before the end of the 19th century and even way before the invention of something as simple as goal nets, teams must have screamed long and loud at disallowed goals every week that weren't given simply because referees didn't see them. Luckily, a fisherman in 1891, probably watching a match at Grimsby or Hull, might just have had a brainwave that unfortunately somebody else would beat him to. Along came the invention of goal nets, less the fish that were removed from them, which changed all the doubts and made the game a lot simpler for refs everywhere. Can you imagine the furore if some bigwig at the time decided that nets weren't necessary, that this piece of technology would be the ruination of the game and it would be far better to rely on human error and leave things as they are. Carry on with the weekly "Was it or wasn't it in?" Make it a bit more exciting for the spectators and all that. It would, after all, balance itself out over the course of the season. Ridiculous twaddle you'd say but no more ridiculous than today where nearly every sport - except football - has taken advantage of the latest technology to help determine whether a decision is right or wrong, and bringing in a massive degree of fairness to the sport.

Football today is light years away from then of course. The rewards are far greater and the difference between success and failure can be financially massive and also very marginal. Fortunes can be the difference between just one bad result and one bad decision by one bad referee on one bad afternoon for your team. And it could be a decision that could effectively ruin your season, plus your Saturday night out. Yes, referees are a lot fitter but in spite of that, the game is much, much faster. Teams from the 1970s would be on their knees after about 60 minutes at the pace of the modern game today. A referee would have to be able to do a twelve second 100 metres sprint to keep up with some of today's speed merchants. There's also the added stress for referees in knowing that the whole world could be watching them amidst this real pressure cooker atmosphere. Maybe, some referees could be quite easily forgiven for "not seeing" a decision and passing the buck to an assistant. Easier to ignore it rather than give it, just in case. If he does give it, and it's the wrong decision, then he's hung up to dry, and all that in just a split second. And if that isn't enough there's the added dilemma of some teams in The Premier who have finally twigged on to some officials who they see as "celebrity refs", who favour the top four when key decisions are made. I wonder where they got that idea from; how can they possibly think that?

Tennis, golf, cricket, rugby league and rugby union, even crown green bowling, have all embraced new technology and rightly so. But not, it would seem, dear old football. Not the biggest, most watched, richest, most influential game on the planet. It's as if those at the top running the game are saying that they know better than anything and anyone. So the provision of 100% proof of accuracy and fair play continues to remain on hold as the lions led by donkeys wait with bated breath.

"We'll think about it" say the FA and UEFA and FIFA even when two of the most blatant pieces of injustice have happened right before their very eyes. The most important of them prevented firstly Ireland perhaps progressing into the World Cup stages in Africa in that infamous "Hand of Henry" incident that saw them lose to France. I wonder what would have happened had the roles been reversed and Robbie Keane had done the same thing to the French at the same crucial stage in the game. Do you think Messrs Platini and Blatter would then have said there was little that could be done and ushered Ireland through shame facedly? No, me neither. It was little old Ireland and they didn't matter. They were dismissed from the banquet without an ounce of remorse.

The second was also an even bigger piece of injustice. England against Germany in South Africa and a shot that was so far over the line, everybody in the stadium saw it. Everybody, that is, except the two people who mattered most. Can you imagine how both that referee and his assistant must have felt when they saw the telly at half time? I'll give them one thing. They must have guts - or two brass necks - to come back out for the second half. That "goal" would have put England level at 2-2 and who's to say then what would have happened? "Germany would still have won" say the experts. Based on what theory? What might have happened to a young German team if it was 2-2? They could have collapsed and England wouldn't have needed to chase the game in the early part of the second half. Speculation and history now, but at least if we did lose, then wouldn't it have at least been justice to lose fairly? I wonder if UEFA are still thinking about it when these cock ups keep on occurring (and they will) well into the future. And how long before the FA decide that something has to happen as fans scream for it. But what do we know? We're just the daft buggers who have to put up with it and watch it every week. We're even getting such massive errors in the Premier league on a weekly basis that it's now regarded as almost acceptable. Why?

How many times have you left a match seething that you've been robbed? Take your pick from "that ball was a yard over the line, he dived and slid five yards into the penalty area, three blatant handballs and he missed every one". We've all been there and we'll continue to keep going there, and see our team usually lose about nine or ten points a season through human error. Fine if there's nothing we can do about it, but fans now are demanding that there is something that can be done about it. We have the technology, even if means adding another three, four or even ten minutes on to a game while the experts look at the telly (I want that job!).

And when that day comes, won't it be a relief to all of us? Personally I don't care when the referee blows his full time whistle, just as long as he blows it without me questioning his parenthood. I'd feel better, along with 38,000 others, and I bet the ref would certainly feel better and a tad relieved too, if he knew that he was 100 per cent right every time. Would you rather slope off bang on 5 o'clock at the final whistle and see your team lose 3-1 or would you rather see fairness carried out and maybe see your team reverse that score line into a 4-2 win and not get out of the ground till 5.30? What's the rush? There's only X Factor on the box and I bet there's bugger all for tea when you get in. I'm not exaggerating here (not about your tea, anyway). I've seen games where this kind of swing could have actually happened and I've winced at the injustice of it all even as a neutral. I remember being down South a few years back and going to a night match at Dean Court. There's only so much you can do in Bournemouth on a wet Wednesday night and so Dean Court seemed an attractive proposition. They lost 2-1 and I remember thinking "They've been shafted by that ref". I'm not kidding. They could, should and would have won 4-1 except for one small obstacle. Try as they might, the ref was waiting for them at every opportunity to ambush and knock them back. Even the pies were criminal that night.

The last thing that I want to hear on the radio is that jolly jester of the airwaves coming out with the inevitable smart-arsed remark and his tried and trusted- and tired- football classic comment "Oh, its swings and roundabouts; it will all balance itself out over the season". Oh, that's alright then isn't it? Firstly, no, it's not swings and roundabouts. It's football and secondly, I can't contain my wrath long enough to see us balance things out. Even if that happens, then all it means is we'd be robbing some other poor team about a month down the line by cheating them the way we've just been cheated. That nasty taste in your mouth is nothing to do with sour grapes. If my team win or lose, I want us to do it fairly. Winning by cheating is not winning in my book and if you think it is, then the game's had it. And I've heard a few others say that too. As for being lucky in a match, that's an entirely different matter and one you can easily live with. Luck is just plain fate.

I know a lot of fans who've fallen out of love with football, totally disillusioned by many things, including terrible refereeing, and not bothered to go back. It's a combination of things adding up to this deserting of the cause. Sometimes it's easier to just sit and watch the match at a bar somewhere. But mainly it's a protest against the astronomical wages being paid to footballers who, in many cases, do little to justify them. You cannot motivate a 20 year old millionaire to either "get his finger out" or fight for the shirt. He doesn't need to do either. Win, lose or draw his money's in the bank. And if he's shunted out of the door, he's laughing even more with his severed contract. Fans don't seem to realise that the more money is paid in wages to a player doesn't mean that he will battle ten times harder. It just makes it ten times easier for him to switch off. That's an opinion from someone who sees Premier League teams play like world beaters one week and then clowns the next. From beating Aston Villa 1-0 one week with a battling display and then a week later wave the white flag of surrender and go down 5-1 at Newcastle. There are only so many players who really battle in the Premier League and even they are castigated for their rough house tactics. If you want to see footballers fight in the purest sense of the word, and fight to the last drop, then go and watch non-league or lower league football. Some of them probably aren't paid a hundredth of their rich cousins up the league but in terms of blood, sweat and tears they'll shed the lot and leave them standing every time.

There is no worse feeling than coming out of the ground at full time, losing 1-0, having two perfectly good goals disallowed, a man sent off for trying to tackle and missing the opponent and the ball by a yard, three blatant penalties not given, and then the piece de resistance. Their bloke who got the winner shouldn't even have been on the pitch. He should have been red carded earlier for use of the elbows. You're cold, miserable, soaking wet and, to top it all, you've wasted two quid by spilling your Bovril at the start of the match before sipping a drop. Then some bright spark says to you as you slope off into the dark: "I thought they deserved everything they got". No matter which team he was on about he was wrong. Speaking of spilling stuff, I once poured the entire contents of a scalding hot mince pie that I was cautiously nibbling on, down the back of some bloke's neck, on a freezing cold night at Roker Park. Sunderland scored very early and my arm was pushed from behind by some excited lad. Before I knew it I was left with one hollow pie and no meat. The poor bloke in front got the lot right down the back of his shirt and was screaming in agony and joy at the same time. As the night wore on, and Sunderland clocked up a 6-1 win over West Bromwich, he told me that the mince had started to freeze and gave him a quite pleasant tingling sensation. We still got relegated. You just don't get that sort of banter in the seats, do you?

Anyway, accepting the fact that no technology in the world will ever sort out where that ref got the extra three minutes of added on time, during which you conceded the equaliser in the 97th minute, there has to be a better way as you trudge off home in the rain having witnessed yet another travesty of justice. It's at moments like this, usually when you realise also that one of your shoes is also leaking, that you start the debate of more up to date technology. 130 years from the birth of the game to today is a long time, and even if you look at the 1920s and the radical change in the offside law, then it's easy to suggest that modern thinking by those that know best, the ones who turn up every week, is not keeping up with modern technology.

When somebody watching your game on the other side of the world in Australia at four o'clock in the morning can tell you quicker than the referee forty yards away that you've just been denied a blatant goal, then that's when you say enough's enough. You have images of long gone Herbert Chapman spinning in his grave saying: "Have those idiots still not sorted things out yet? They've had long enough". What's needed is the football equivalent of a revolution by fans, a mass boycott of games which will show those at the top "We're not taking this any more. Put it right now or we won't be back". In the meantime, the donkeys running the show will appease you by saying that they'd need a committee meeting and a public enquiry before they decided on adjourning the decision till a later date. And before you say that's far fetched, then players threatened strikes years ago for better working conditions. So why shouldn't fans now do the same for better viewing conditions? Don't accept that it can't be done. After all, if you can send men to the moon and back in the 1960s, and rescue 33 miners half a mile underground when they've been down there 69 days and given up as a lost cause, then anything's possible.

We all know the arguments that will be lined up and hurled against us about bringing in video technology to dispute every decision. They'll tell you the game could take an extra twenty minutes to finish. The answer to that old fob off is simple. We don't want to dispute every decision, just the key ones.

Penalty decisions, offsides leading to a goal, ball in or not, red card or not. The key ones that will rule out human error and could lead to less tension and sometimes violence amongst fans. And what if the game lasts another ten to twenty minutes? Some fans always leave twenty minutes before the end and others always stay to the bitter end. What's the rush to get home when you definitely know that every major decision called by the ref and his assistants and/or the video was called right. Even though it meant that you actually lost rather than nicked a draw. Yes, I could live with that. And here's the bonus. We'd save a fortune in wages on all those gormless experts whose opinions we'd no longer need. ("Yes, we know it was offside, yes we know it was a penalty, now go away!") It might even lead to the added bonus of getting rid of most of the dead wood in all spheres of the football hierarchy, plus a selection of experts, too. What a result, and what a glorious day for fans and football if that happened. We could even watch the highlights of the culling of these wasters on "Match of The Day"

They've already got stringent rules in the workplace to prevent unnecessary accidents happening there, so why not extend this to the football workplace to prevent further unnecessary "accidents" i.e. incidents that wrongly change a match score so that dodgy results can be eliminated, avoiding stress and potential punch-ups amongst fans. Everyone's a winner. I am sure that football fans from Macclesfield to Millwall, Plymouth to Preston would all feel the same way. Everything's eventual anyway, so just bite the bullet and do it now. There are hidden drawbacks to any new way forward and one I've touched on above. As unpalatable as it may seem, fans will need to take the rough with the smooth. You'll go to one game where you would have clogged out a 1-0 win that could, in fairness, end up becoming a 2-1 defeat. But the key words here are "in fairness". Video evidence might well reveal that their first disallowed goal was a clear penalty and their second one that was chalked off would be quickly chalked back on again as it was clearly over the line. Job done and how can you argue with that? You wouldn't want to win by default would you, especially when the whole world, including that bloke in Australia, would see it as a false victory?

It's time for some real honesty in the game at all levels and in society as a whole, and if that also gets rid of cheating then that's a double bonus. I never much cared for cheats .They are the ones who pinch other people's ideas and gain an advantage because they were too lazy, or couldn't be bothered or come up with their own thoughts to do a job properly. All that would be eliminated. Technology would also put an end to that old chestnut "swings and roundabouts" too. We'd never have to hear that old saying ever again and it could be eliminated to where it belongs - the playground. You can put it in the bin with steel toe caps and bamboo shin pads, along hopefully with most of the FA, Premier League and perhaps even loveable Jimmy Greaves's old catch phrase "It's a funny old game". Not anymore it wouldn't be, Jimmy. It would become deadly serious, sensible and would change to a fair old game. And wouldn't that be more fun for everyone? People would still be laughing or crying with just that little bit of fairness and justice brought in.

Think what could have happened to the game 50 years ago, and even the impact it might have had on the game today, with the sort of technology we so blithely ignore now. How those defining moments then might have caused a massive change in the history of the game today. You've got to have a pretty vivid imagination to try and work this one out, but just think "Back to the Future 2" and the parallel universe that was created by Marty McFly as a result of changes made in the past (What do you mean, you've never seen the film? Shame on you).

Here are just three personal memories - you must have dozens of your own - that might have drastically changed the concept of the game today not just for the country but also an individual team:

1) Wembley July, 1966. Geoff Hurst's shot crashes off the crossbar and England go 3-2 up. But wait a minute, the Germans have gone over to the referee and they are looking at the playbacks. They still can't make their minds up but the Russian linesman definitely knows. He's not sure either but do you really think he'll disallow it? Goal! So what was all the fuss about all those years later? And besides, there's one definitive camera angle taken near where that linesman was standing that quite clearly shows the ball being well over the line at normal speed. If you don't believe me, try and get hold of an old film called "Goal" made not long after the 1966 Final and watch that ball crash down clearly over the line and see the reaction of little Alan Ball. He never cheated in his life. It was in. And would that Russian linesman lie against the Germans 20 years after World War 2?

2) Elland Road, May 1968. Leeds United v West Bromwich Albion. A vital game which Leeds lose 2-1, but at 1-0 down Leeds are well on top and an equaliser looks inevitable. Albion break and their front man is at least ten yards offside. I don't believe it, the referee has given it. No, he's quite correctly looked at the monitor and after much protesting by Leeds he's disallowed it. Leeds stay 1-0 down, and shortly afterwards go on to equalise. A winner soon follows and it's three vital points for them. Leeds go on to win the league in 1968 and Manchester City finish second. City are so demoralised that some players end up leaving to get away from the massive disappointment of it all. The following

season, City still manage to get to the FA Cup Final but miss out by losing 1-0 to Leicester. There's no Neil Young to score the winner. He's just joined Crosby, Stills and Nash. Leicester already relegated, don't know whether to laugh or cry, and so do both as they go down singing and dancing with tears in their eyes. This means that Manchester City do not win the Cup Winners Cup in 1970 and are no longer a major force at the beginning of the 70s.

3) World Cup 1986. Diego Maradona's "Hand of God" goal (years later to be adopted by Thierry Henry) puts Argentina 1-0 up. The biggest robbery since Ronnie Biggs and his mates nicked millions from that mail train. But the referee doesn't give it. Not only is it disallowed, Maradona gets himself booked and, minutes later, gets sent off for trying the same thing again. Will he never learn? No first goal scored by this petite, permed punk means that there's no second either, and England go on to win but lose out in the final. Even I can't stretch my imagination that far by suggesting that England would have won the World Cup, can I? Let's keep it real. Possibilities are one thing but fairy stories are an entirely different matter. Maybe they'd have been better off going out to Argentina earlier, to avoid the later disappointment. On second thoughts, Diego, we'll allow that goal.

Think of all the ones you can remember and, with a really vivid imagination, see how that one defining moment can have changed your team's history. Just think, Grimsby fans, if that goal had gone in and you hadn't been relegated from the Second Division so many years back, where would you have been today? You get where I'm coming from, don't you?

There are loads of others to add to the above that I can recollect, some not so important on the scale of things, but they would have been to you if your team were on the wrong end of any of them. Remember the Spurs goal two feet over the line against Manchester United at Old Trafford or the Bolton goal some years ago clearly over the line that was missed against Everton? That latter goal, had it been given, would actually have sent Everton down and kept Bolton up come the end of that Premier League season. How does that possibly equate to the magical "swings and roundabouts"? One team breathes a huge sigh of relief and carries on in the top league and the other curses their luck as they head for the relegation trap door and exotic trips to Scunthorpe, Port Vale and Shrewsbury? Even at a local level I can think of maybe twenty games where similar instances all went unnoticed. Technology would have cleared up nearly all of them.

I laugh at people who say that if we take away the human error from the game it would also take away all the uncertainty, fun and drama out of the game. Well, yes, of course it would, but it would also put a lot more certainty back into the result. Where's the fun, anyway, when you've just been robbed? A team that has also worked hard at training all week can see all that hard work undone just by one minute of incompetence on a Saturday. And where's the remote fun in that? Better also a real life drama based on real life correct decisions, instead of a surreal nightmare unfolding before your very eyes. That's how riots start, you know. The list of these howlers goes on and on, and the only absolute certainty is that you'll still be reading about them in ten years time unless of course someone sees sense. What is the point of having all this useful technology and the benefits it can bring if someone decrees that it not only cannot be used, but also decree that they cannot come up with a valid reason not to use it. Would it slow the game down? Yes. Would it lead to all fans going home at least knowing that win, lose or draw the result was absolutely fair. Yes, you can bet on that, too. My own view is that radical changes will come anyway. They'll reach the stage of such embarrassment, they'll have to. It'll happen one day. It will probably be when Germany beat England in the World Cup Final, with Germany's winning goal bouncing two yards short of crossing the line and some French linesman, looking strangely like a younger version of Michel Platini, gleefully screaming "It was over by a mile!" as he danced wildly to the centre circle embracing the German players.

UEFA and the rest of the asses will continue to pass the buck and tickle round the edges, allowing us in their supreme majesty, to try at local level any subtle little changes. So that means Eastbourne versus Hayes and Yeading being used as guinea pigs, then. They aren't going to budge on goal line technology yet. So instead, after further delay, we'll get maybe a radical solution of two goal line judges behind the goal to help the referee out. The same method that was used in the 1880s before goal nets were introduced and judges then could determine whether the ball had crossed the line or not. We've certainly come a long way in 130 years haven't we, Mr. Blatter?

In spite of them, the game will change. There are now so many arguments and counter arguments for and against technology that the easiest way to remedy most of these slanging matches is to reach a civilised level of compromise. And so, when you introduce compromise, then you are bringing in change anyway via the back door or whatever else you want to call it. That's how the game evolved in the past, a bit of give and take, to the one we know today. And that's why the game in the future will similarly evolve. We're all just passing through and it's time we got off the fence and called it like it is. You can't keep your head buried in the sand forever resisting progress. If the game we profess to love today is to survive and flourish in the future then it must happen. Otherwise, those "stick in the muds" on and off the field may as well pack in now and go home.

Let's have some changes on the field, too. We all despair at players who keep asking for more, more, more without ever wondering where this comes from. They will bleed their clubs dry without a second thought and then move on elsewhere and do the same thing. Clubs and managers must stand up to them. Off the field are those who pander to the needs of those on it, pretending that all is well when clearly it is not. If players are cheats, greedy or lazy, then get shot of them and let them go and ruin someone else's club. Technology will root them out and then it really will be a case of "The whole world is watching". Mine are just the thoughts and concerns of an ordinary fan but I know that there's an army out there who feel exactly the same way. I know because I've talked to some of them.

So much is wrong with the game today as those at the bottom get ever more desperate to even survive and those at the top have money to burn. But people who burn things invariably go up in smoke. It seems grossly unfair that teams are going out of business for debts totalling little more than a Premiership's player's weekly wage. It smacks of complete injustice no matter which way you dress it up. Monies could easily be reinvested on a top down level so that all teams throughout the whole league structure could flourish. Cap Premiership wages so that every £5,000 saved off salaries be used to keep afloat those clubs whose very players might one day provide a future star to the elite sides. It would be a bit like a league nursery structure and a fair deal for all. Besides, if you place a cap on Premiership wages where else can they go to? Certainly not anywhere else in Europe and with nowhere to run and nowhere to hide, they'd have to accept the inevitable, the poor dears.

It is absurd and immoral that clubs are allowed to rack up debts of £80m or £90m unchecked before someone steps in (usually the tax man) to ask questions. If I ran a whelk stall at Scarborough the same way I'd be sacked in a day, so why do clubs get away with it? What's more galling is that the ones at a club who cause all this financial chaos are the very ones who are ultimately rewarded when their gaffe is exposed. A bit like the bankers who win the jackpot for getting themselves into a profitable situation after heavy losses which they incurred in the first place The way the system works now is that those who caused the chaos at a club, plus the players themselves, have to be initially recompensed and bailed out before poor Joe Public gets any of his money back. That is wrong, so change it. Would it really hurt if they were told they'd not get £8 million wages, only £3million, and that the balance was going to be used to keep maybe fifty businesses afloat? That sort of bankruptcy clause could easily be fitted into any future contract and, if it was fitted, surely no one would begrudge this type of sacrifice. Although would it really be classed as a sacrifice if a player was told that, instead of a £3million payout, he was only going to get £1.5 million? It's not exactly hardship, is it? And if they didn't like it, then it was in the contract and the same deal would be struck wherever they went. Besides, did anyone at this sorry club ever have the guts to say "Actually the reason why it's all gone pear shaped is because we've got six mercenaries like you on the books and every one of them is bleeding us dry too".

Someone somewhere needs to put in place a rigid and financial list of regulations that all 92 clubs must adapt to. You could even call it something really old-fashioned and very uncool like "The Commonsense Code." Rules could be so strict, watertight even, and one of them could even simply specify that you can spend no more than 50% of your total income on players' wages and that even with the provision of external monies (and that mightn't be around for ever) it should still be 50%. The rest goes on all those real grafters behind the scenes who end up losing their home and their £13,000 a year wage due to recklessness caused further up the food chain. Anything after that would automatically be ploughed back into the grass roots of the game so that we might then have an army of hungry kids coming through in the future who would all be re-taught about the basics of financial and economic management. Their first lesson would be that you can't get eight pints of milk to fit into a jug holding four pints. And after those rules and regulations, every player, you are well and truly embedded into the real world with the rest of us. There'd be nowhere to go if every other club was saddled with the same restrictions.

The point to all this is simple. You wouldn't run a business so recklessly, so why should a football club be any different? Players wouldn't become paupers overnight. They'd quickly readjust to living on twenty grand a week. It'll be a struggle at first for them but once they bought just the three cars, instead of the fourteen on their driveway, they'd quickly adjust. They might even have to save a few bob by sacking their agents and getting some real fatherly advice from their old man. Just like I once did. It won't cost them a penny and if they moaned they'd have the swift reassurance of a foot up their over-rated backside, and a wise word in their ear. Now, that would be a revolution.

A wage structure league by league and eventual wage capping is as inevitable as night following day. Forget that old crock about wages have always gone up year by year. Before 1961, it was the pauper's game. Nothing lasts forever and the current scenario cannot continue. Even more so when the whole country is locked into a whole new different type of ball game and is going to have to knuckle under to it for the next few years. It'll just be like the 1930s all over again and we'll all get a chance to live in it. What goes up must come down. If we don't get to grips with the disease that's eating away at our game from both above (at far too over-ambitious boardroom level) and below (the players with their ludicrous demands in some cases) then the game's a goner anyway. It's inevitable that it will only go one way.

It's not difficult to work out what's happening and you don't need to bring in an army of economists to tell you. They've all been made redundant anyway. It's what's known in the trade as a busted flush, something that is not sustainable. A common working man's phrase that will tell it like it is: "You can't spend what you haven't got. If you haven't got it, don't borrow it". Plus some real words of wisdom from my nan who once told me "Pay as you go, and if you can't pay, then don't go". I never went anywhere for nine years after that advice, but she was right. You see what I mean, don't you? I can envisage a load of teams going broke in the future trying to chase the dream. Portsmouth, Southampton, Leeds, Palace, Leicester have all been on the brink. Some dreams are proving that expensive that they aren't worth dreaming about. Far cheaper to just count sheep instead of following them.

The excessive external demands on the game are throttling it everywhere. TV coverage of matches now has reached saturation point. Most fans don't even feel the need to go to matches anymore and who can blame them? When you can now spend your match money on 60 cans of lager and then realise you would still have needed another tenner to get into even the cheapest seat at a Premier League match, then you aren't going to bust a gut to go, are you? And if the match is on the telly or down the pub, then guess what? We now have the era of the super modern Couch Potato Non-Season Ticket Holder seven nights a week. To hell with actually going to a live football match when you can see it in a pub next to the ground where your team are playing. One of those empty 9,000 seats will previously have belonged to you. As long as you don't start complaining when they can't improve their depleted squad and drop near the bottom of the league because of it. It's your fault, they'll all tell you, so get along to support them. But hang on, you can't. There's a recession on. I don't know what it's like where you live but it's pretty grim in the North East at the moment and especially round where I live. In Easington we have the most deprived area in the whole country. How's that for being top of the league with the world's most unwanted title? I think there's a long way to go before we even see any signs of a recovery. Money's tight and some people have only got thirty quid a week to live on by the time they've paid all their bills. They're not going to blow that on football when they have other priorities such as eating, are they?

Clubs offer cheap discounted seats but they don't equate with the amount of disposable income that's available. Football admission prices have soared in the last twenty years and wages haven't kept pace with them. Remember when I mentioned how cheap it was to get into Chelsea in the 1960s compared to how much I was earning weekly? Clubs need to re-examine that pro-rata split between wages and match entrance. How can it be right for a working man to be expected to fork out 20% in some cases of his net weekly wage to get into a football ground? It is lunacy and that is a fact.

Maybe some clubs are missing a trick and should conduct some real market research in their area on how much people are prepared to fork out to watch football at all levels. I think they'd get a shock at some of the replies. What that would suggest is that some clubs are always going to have half empty stadiums as they remain hopelessly out of touch with local economic circumstances. I know of season ticket holders at Sunderland who would not begrudge anyone who is genuinely struggling financially paying as little as £5 to get in. It could so easily be means tested but, if this were done, then they'd easily pull in another 8,000 or more. Clubs with a vision will do this one day. If we were to see players being wage capped, there could be a saving on wages of some £10 million a year at just one club and that could be used to offset a marked reduction in seat prices. Imagine ten wage capped Premiership wages releasing savings of at least £300,000 a week and that would give an incredible £15.6 million a year. And that would be from one club alone. Those same ten players would still have a minimum and more realistic £30,000 plus a week to "live on"(and the rest) plus their sponsorship deals. Can you begin to imagine the impact on football overall if just one team then passed even half those savings in one season on to the fans? You could, in some cases, easily halve the admission prices. You'd then have a combined club spirit second to none, a genuine collaboration between club, board, player and fan. And then let's see how many supporters would rather watch their team play in the pub. At those discounted prices, they could easily afford to go to the match every week and there wouldn't be an empty seat in sight. This already exists now anyway at bottom tier level.

A lack of English players coming through into the top level is of real concern but what if the other half of those savings was reinvested into youth academies even in schools nationally to attract even more youngsters into the game? There would be no shortage of clubs available to snap up any talent and offer each of them genuine hope, a basic standard of education as they learned their trade, as well as a decent standard wage. Forget the £30,000 a week to start off with, lads. Those days would be long gone at your tender age, but I'm sure you can be tempted to try and reach the top with the lure of only a grand a week. There'd be plenty of jobs too for the most talented of these lads. At the last count, there were 92 clubs. I am sure most of them, looking up at the top earners, would welcome a return to sanity.

Without such radical change then never again will we ever see any England team win a World Cup or European Championship. Football isn't just about change. It's about hard choices too. Carry on with the current rules, the blinkered set up, blind intransigence and ostrich mentality, and you can have a million experts on the box spouting on whether "this time" we can get somewhere whenever the World Cup comes along. The answer will always be "No". If you want proof look at how both the German and Spanish leagues suffered a few years ago when it was fashionable - and highly profitable - for foreigners doing to their leagues what they are currently doing to ours. Both have since gone on to win the World Cup with radical change. We'll need to do exactly the same, not just drone on about it.

Twenty years ago, the state of grounds in this country was nothing short of scandalous. It's sad of course that the great old grounds of the past are now no more. Some clubs, with one eye on where the game was heading, moved lock, stock and barrel into fabulous new homes. Others renovated their old ground until it bore no resemblance to its previous look. A bit like those colliery houses with outside netties and tin baths in the yard that were part of my youth.

Whilst most fans do value tradition, there comes a point when you have to move on. Southampton had to move from The Dell. A full house of 15,000 there might have made for a cracking atmosphere - and it did - but you can't hope to buy champagne and caviar when you're only bringing in fish and chip money. The same for their neighbours, Pompey, who need to move to rebuild. Even Everton and Liverpool might have to bury the hatchet and opt for one stadium holding 70,000. It's sensible and the days of two clubs in the same city having two entirely new stadiums, especially when they are next door to each other, I think are gone. It's all about economics, common sense and the practicality of the thing. Spurs too must feel that they are being left behind when they look at the Emirates but their day will come in a new home.

When all these new grounds are built, I'd like to think that fans were somehow involved in the design aspects, but somehow I doubt it. Clubs would save a fortune on consultancy fees too, but, no doubt, they'll bring these corporate experts in to tell them what they want to hear, as opposed to bringing in the real experts - the fans - who'd tell them what they should really do. Perhaps what you might need here is the best of both worlds when designing new stadia. The "devil may care, blood and guts" approach of the old guard merged with the sedate, safe and bland approach of the new, featuring a risk assessed health and safety approach embracing the new era we all live in. This would include no shouting, no flags, no standing, no hippies, and no scalding hot mince pies down the back of people's necks on the concourse. I'm not being far fetched here. Years ago, if a light bulb went out at work, you'd change the bulb. Now they'd send the whole office off somewhere on a "coping with darkness" seminar. It's the same with football. Even the council, police, TV and the weatherman have a say in it all and that won't change in the future. Won't we all feel all the better and safer for it?

These super duper stadiums of the future may have heated seats, heated pitches and heated stewards (especially if you stand up and wave a flag) but if there's one inch of snow outside the ground then guess what? Match off. Dangerous walking conditions might see someone fall over and hurt themselves and sue for compensation. Let's put an end to this madness now. Just stick a few signs up telling us all that if you walk on snow and ice, chances are you might slip. So be careful you don't fall over and have an accident. Just call them accidents and you'd eliminate the compensation aspect. Job done and paperwork sorted.

And here's a funny thing when you talk about football's future. The game was always, and always will be, better in the past than it will ever be in the present or the future. That's based purely and simply on the fact that every new generation coming along will eventually look back nostalgically at things they can no longer have, or are now gone from their lives forever. The past represented our youth and virility, all that was good, exciting and innocent about us. The present is where we currently are with our memories of that time. The future represents the uncertainty we all find ourselves in and how we would like the game to go forward, all based on our past experiences and good memories that we will always carry with us. Just like in the words of Neil Sedaka's "Hungry Years".

If you have ever read autobiographies or old footy books going back 30, 40 or even 50 years, the one constant in all of them is that they'll all harp back to the game's golden days of a bygone era. I read a book by Bill Shankly in 1976 that spelt out in detail how the then modern Liverpool - and what a great side they were in the 1970s - was founded and built on the same principles, beliefs, strengths and experiences that he'd been brought up with himself learning his trade at Preston, Carlisle, Huddersfield, Grimsby and Workington. Even from his own family. That never changes. You learn from your experiences and build on them for the future. There'll always be constant change but you never forget your roots. Bill Shankly also once said that if you stand still in football then you go backwards. Well, aren't we now in danger of doing the same thing?

And in case we forget, if you were 50 years old in 1900, you'd yearn for the more genteel days of the 1880's. A 50 year old in the 1930s would pine for the good old days of the 1900s. When I was 20 I used to listen to old men on the terraces reminisce about the last really great Sunderland side of the 1930s. And thus it goes on. I now remember fondly my days in the 60s and 70s. Anyone twenty year old listening to me now will think I sound exactly the same as those old men sounded to me not so long ago. The game will always be better in the past because apart from today, that's where we've always lived.

I do wonder if, thirty years from now, those youngsters and my then grown up grandchildren, will pine so nostalgically for today's game. They might, if some semblance of sanity prevails and we get to grips with the hype that's so patently ruining it. In the future, how can you get nostalgic and teary eyed over an Italian once managing England "back in the day" who was paid £120,000 a week to manage a side who'd probably get turned over by a hungrier, well organised Peterborough United? I hope that there is the same element of nostalgia then as there is now. It's important for the game's future that there is. If I am a bit sceptical I'll tell you why. How can anyone get nostalgic over something or someone that now lives in a parallel universe to us? The game is changing but not for the better. Where is the bond between those players and you? Are we losing those links that used to tie us all together, and losing the things that we all used to have in common? It wasn't like that years ago and the situation is likely to remain unchecked as the gap widens even further.

When I'm not devouring football books or autobiographies, I'm still quite keen on my music. Even there, we live in a world where image is absolutely everything. As a classic example, for anyone to make it in the modern, manufactured music industry today you have to look great, but not sound great. And boy, don't we have loads of examples out there today. Will we look back on them in years to come with nostalgia? I don't think we will. It is impossible to look back on anything nostalgically where there's no substance in the product. And, besides, you listen to great music, you don't look at it. So sadly, if today your music's great but your look isn't, then you'll struggle. There are thousands of great musicians out there who'll never be heard simply because they'll never be seen. They don't fit. Remember what I was telling you about the experts and their take on modern football? Well, now they're doing exactly the same to our music too! It's unfair of course but then again so is life. That's why so many disenchanted genuine teens today, with a love of real music, are turning away from today's bland stuff. They're leaving all of it to Cheryl Cole and the rest of them. They're going back to the roots of it all and coming up with a new way forward, based on a combination of the old. They don't want the current dull, safe and ever so predictable stuff. That mainstream garbage they are force fed on is the sort of thing teens need to be rebelling against anyway. It's what I rebelled against, too, in my youth. They are shunning the modern style, fitting the modern image where if you fit into one of the modern boxes, then you're in, kid. I genuinely think it's this same view, link, attitude, call it what you will, that's also creeping into football. Footballers today have forgotten who they are, and what their purpose is. Their role has gone way beyond entertainer. They have now somehow been re-branded by themselves, and others, into over-inflated and in some cases over-rated superstars with very little depth or talent. It is now all about image with "brand this" and "brand that", Hollywood glitz with agents and hangers on, male and female. And do you know something? It's all bull and its beginning to get on people's nerves and alienate them. It's all a bit like the tale of "The Emperor's New Clothes". It only takes one brave person, one fed up, disillusioned punter to stick his head above the parapet and say defiantly "He's got nowt on!"

Not everything that is old is bad, and should therefore be automatically confined to the dustbin of history. And definitely, not everything that is new is good. You just need to have some basic knowledge and common sense, and vision, to tell the difference, sift out all the great stuff that can be used and ditch the rest. Do that and stand by your principles. The game has to change and to adapt, not only to the needs of the fan, but to the needs of basic commonsense too. Every generation learns to adapt, reinvent and improve. It's only human nature, after all. Just as people's tastes and demands change, so too does the frenzied need to feed that change. Either do it or get left behind, where you too, will become a dinosaur.

Just like life, football evolves and learns from its mistakes. I still have all my old desires and dreams still intact. Many of those great players that I grew up watching are no longer with us. But we should never forget them, remember and, above all, learn from them. Gone, too, are the truly great managers of my youth: Shankly, Catterick, Busby, Nicholson, Clough, Paisley, Stein, Mercer. And, especially not forgetting dear Bob Stokoe, who gave me my greatest ever moment as a Sunderland fan.

And as you look and remember your own past, and wonder what lies ahead that will affect all of us, I am reminded of a great line from a cheesy old film that I can't even recall the title of now. About a simple man looking back on his simple life and the changes he has seen in it, and comparing them to nothing more than a simple game.

Suddenly you are running along, the next you are no more.